THE JOY OF GRANDMA'S COOKING

A Treasury
of Recipes
and Stories
from the Heart

CLARICE CARLSON ORR

ISBN 1-886225-45-1

Cover design and illustrations by Angie Johnson Art Productions

Library of Congress Cataloging-in-Publication Data

Orr, Clarice Carlson.
    The joy of grandma's cooking : a treasury of recipes and stories
from the heart / Clarice Carlson Orr.
       p. cm.
    ISBN 1-886225-46-1 (alk. paper)
    1. Cookery. 2. Cookery Anecdotes. 3. Family Anecdotes.
I. Title.
TX714.0774 1999
641.5--dc21

99-40213
CIP

We would like to acknowledge the following for permission to reprint the subsequent material.

The recipes Celestine Crusts, Kuechlie, Knee Patches and the Editor's Note are from the *Nebraska Centennial First Ladies' Cookbook* compiled by Maxine Morrison, edited by Catherine J. Hillegass, and published by Cliff's Notes, 1966. They were reprinted with permission by Catherine J. MacDonald and Maxine Morrison.

"For Everything There is a Season..." from *Patches*, 1975; "Coffee: The Great American Tradition" from *Gleanings*, 1982; and "People Still Neighbor" from *Prairie Panorama*, 1988; all by Chrys Daniel were reprinted by permission of the author.

Several bits of information denoting the introductory dates of food were excerpted from the Cuisine of the Century series by Knight Ridder Newspapers published in the *Lincoln Journal Star* in spring and summer 1999.

Dageforde Publishing, Inc.
122 South 29th Street, Lincoln, Nebraska 68510
Ph: (402) 475-1123; FAX: (402) 475-1176
email: info@dageforde.com
Visit our website: www.dageforde.com

Printed in the United States of America
10 9 8 7 6 5 4 3 2 1

DEDICATION

The Joy of Grandma's Cooking *is
lovingly dedicated with much
gratitude to all my Dear Ones,
my children and their spouses—
Becky and Nick,
Cyndi and Doug,
Cheryle and Lou,
John and Marilyn,
and my grandchildren—
John and Tanya, Mark, Matt,
Carrie, Phil, Emilie, Claire,
Michael, Patrick, and Alex.
May they know the blessings
of the cultural heritage
of all their grandparents.*

CONTENTS

FOREWORD

In 1963, Chrys Daniel needed a dining room table, so she began a column, "The Farm Wife's Sampler," for the Madison (SD) Daily Leader. She got the table and even replaced it, but "South Dakota's Erma Bombeck" is still delighting, uplifting, and in-spiriting her audiences with that column (other columns have graced farm magazines) as well as luncheon and banquet talks.

Chrys is my friend, mentor, and role model, but she's more. Recently, she gifted me with the years of letters I had sent her…literally, my life in a box. In a 1972 letter I had written, "Mom is so happy that I have you since I've never had a sister." We have said we should adopt each other since neither of us had a sister, but Mom's blessing makes it official. Chrys Uthe Daniel and Clarice Carlson Orr are "adopted sisters."

Postage was six cents when two young women struck up a kinship that has spanned more than 45 years of growing. Clarice Carlson Orr and I met when we accompanied our husbands to a business dinner.

Both young stay-at-home Moms with four children each, we found much to connect us in a unique friendship reinforced with "coffee pot letters." When the children napped or played, we would sit at our kitchen tables with a pot of coffee and write our hearts out. At the other end, after the mailman came, the recipient would make a pot of coffee and sit down for a "visit."

Through these letters that grew from a couple of pages to packets of writing, clippings too good to keep to ourselves, and snapshots, has come a love of writing for both. We have been able to nurture and encourage one another.

Clarice combined this love of writing and her passion for her grandchildren in her first book, *The Joy of Grandparenting: Grandparents*

Make a Difference. Her warm, witty, and practical writing has followers all over the country.

Now, she has added still another dimension in her writing as she called on friends and family to share their stories about favorite family recipes—especially those of their grandmothers.

"Comfort Food" is an apt description of a homemaker's cooking. Women express their emotions through their cooking and baking. They fix fancy foods for gala occasions, hearty foods for busy workers, and put their hearts into hot dishes and baked goods to express sympathy when words are not enough. "Here, I made this for you" is an offering on the altar of life.

Witty, serious, clever, simple are the stories behind the foods featured in this collection. Memories abound as persons from many backgrounds share their traditions. Much, much more than a guide to cooking, Clarice's latest endeavor, *The Joy of Grandma's Cooking: A Treasury of Recipes and Stories From The Heart*, provides delightful entertainment as we travel down memory lane together.

Chrys Daniel
Long-time Newspaper Columnist

PREFACE

While visiting with friends after Christmas Eve services, the main topic of conversation was about what we were going to be doing the next few days. More specifically, what we were going to be eating. Everyone was going to be with family. Some large family groups needed halls or church basements for their potluck dinners. If a family member had to work on Christmas Eve or Christmas Day, somehow time was arranged to be a part of a meal—perhaps the day after Christmas or the following Saturday night or Sunday. Widows and singles with nowhere else to go formed a new family for the day and shared their special dishes.

As I talked with friends, I was intrigued by the stories that went along with the family celebrations.

- "My kids insist that we have turkey and I have to make two kinds of dressing."
- "It wouldn't be Christmas without Uncle Bill's Butterscotch Buttons."
- "Aunt Lois always brings cranberry salad in that beautiful lead glass bowl."
- "Clarence insists we have pickled herring, even though he's the only one who likes it."
- "You can be sure Aunt Betty will tell that old story about Bill and the Prune Cake again."
- "I remember the time I ate too much of Cousin Martha's mince pie."

It struck me how food, family, and memories go together. I've always taken it for granted that in my family—both the family I grew up in and the family my husband and I raised—food has always been at the center of any family event. But it amazes and amuses me that my Baby Boomer children and their spouses often request the same menu—roast beef, mashed potatoes and gravy, green bean casserole, and a lime Jell-O cream cheese salad the grandkids call "green stuff." And when we get together we have to play Trivial Pursuit, the gals against the guys.

Cooking and baking stories have always had a hold on me. Then when I heard folks rave about their grandmother's cooking, or they told me, as they stifled giggles, about hiding their dumpling failures, I realized that people want to share their stories. Most people like to be reminded of their simpler, growing-up years. The memories of foods, even plain, humble foods like cornmeal mush and custard, evoke pleasant emotions for most of us.

Seeing the need to help save the birthright of our food culture, I prepared and handed out a flyer announcing that I was gathering material for a book that combined recipes with a story. People were thrilled about documenting their memories. Some asked for additional flyers to share with relatives or friends. Folks whom I have never met sent recipes by e-mail and snail mail.

The variety of recipes submitted surprised me. There are more sour cream raisin pies than the legendary apple pies. There are more recipes for pfefferneusse than for sugar cookies (and each "pfefferneusse" has a different spelling). I learned that folks who work outside the home are making time to cook and bake traditional recipes of their grandmothers in their contemporary kitchens. Many are adapting their grandmother's recipes to their healthier lifestyles while some are savoring the rich, calorie- and cholesterol-laden foods for family reunions.

I was amazed at the varied mixtures our grandmothers and mothers accomplished with their scant staples and few spices. They utilized their farm products—milk, cream, butter, eggs, lard, garden vegetables—to the max. And when a hog or cow was butchered, every part of the animal was used, except the squeal. If they had raisins, cocoa, coconut, syrup, and brown sugar on hand, that was literally the frosting on the cake.

TV commercials and magazine ads play on our memories to consider their pies, cookies, stuffing, and sandwiches are "just like Grandma used to make," although I'm sure Grandma never heard of carrageenan, sodium stearoyl lactylate and yellow 5 food coloring—those ingredients found in most commercial "home-made" products.

Now however, many of Grandma's recipes have been altered to include new commercially prepared foods. We use frozen whipped topping instead of cream that has to be whipped. Cake mixes and pre-made frostings combine with other ingredients to create fantastic concoctions in only a few minutes time. Frozen bread dough relieves us of the kneading and raising time.

I often think how fortunate we are to have an abundance of good, safe food in our markets. I am grateful for convenience foods, packets and cans of sauces and flavorings that create bountiful, luxury cuisine that meets our changing food culture. Sadly, I think my mother may have lived longer if more low-fat, salt-free, and sugar-free foods had been available in her time.

The intent of this book is not only to provide unique, old and new recipes but to remind us of the good, unpretentious, soul-satisfying foods we remember eating at home or family gatherings.

May you gain an appreciation for the creativity our mothers and grandmothers had in utilizing the few ingredients that were available to them.

I hope this treasury of recipes and stories encourages you to search through your grandma's cookbooks, make connections with past generations, and pass on the "receipts" for old-fashioned cookin' as well as the stories told at the family dinner table.

The Joy of Grandma's Cooking serves up a heaping portion of "delicious and delectable" (Mom's favorite phrase) recipes blended with a treasury of charming, funny, and sweet stories from the loving, caring hearts of family, friends and acquaintances accented with dashes of food for thought.

TACK SÅ MYCKET

As we left Grandma Rosenquist's Saturday afternoon kaffekalas (coffee party), we were always prompted to say "thank you so much"—*tack så mycket* (tahk sa micka) or *tusen tack*—"thousand thanks."

This collection of recipes and stories is my tusen tack to my mother, Edna Rosenquist Carlson, and grandmother, Anna Christina Rosenquist, for the simple, good food and wisdom they dished out at the table. I am also indebted to the Swedish foremothers I never knew.

I'm grateful to more than 150 wonderful folks including many Carlson and Rosenquist cousins who entrusted me with their recipes and stories and blessed their own mothers and grandmothers—their Grandma, Grammie, Gram, Grama, Grannie, Gammaw, or MeeMaw—to make this Treasury of Recipes and Stories from the Heart. I'm also thankful for my Disciple Bible Study group: Eunice Cade, Lori Davis, Judy Frederick, Annette Hall, Marge Jessee, Diane Scott, Jan VanGerpen, and Twila Wilson; my prayer partners who were generous with their encouragement. Also, I'm indebted to my SAGE Writing friends who critiqued my writings and shared gentle advice.

A huge thank you to my publisher and friend, Linda Dageforde, whose expertise blended my words into a book and cooked up another dream-come-true for me. A heart-felt thank you to Angie Johnson who caught my vision and added the frosting to the cake with her delightful art work.

Tusen tack, a thousand thanks to Susan Macy and Jackie Robertson, as well as my mentor and "adopted sister," Chrys Daniel, who are always there to comfort my anxieties and share my joys.

YOU ARE INVITED...

Introduction

My maternal Grandma Rosenquist was hard of hearing and didn't speak much English. She couldn't hear my little voice and I couldn't understand her Swedish lilt. But food surrounds my memories of her, and although we didn't talk much, the breads, jams, fruit sauces, and cookies that she made spoke volumes of her message of loving care.

I remember sitting at her dining room table when we stopped at her house after our "Saturday trading." The round table was set with amber Depression-glass dishes on a white damask tablecloth. A small sauce dish at each place held half of a gleaming home-canned peach and in the center of the table beside the ample sugar bowl, big cream pitcher, and spoon dish was a big plate of s-shaped, melt-in-your mouth spritz cookies.

However, what I loved most of all was Grandma's sweet, molasses rye bread laced with store-bought butter. Our homemade butter wasn't as good as the store-bought; in the spring the cows nibbled too many wild onions in the pasture. Making butter in the Daisey churn at home was my job and then Momma spanked the whey out of the butter with a paddle and patted it into a small, round, 2# crock. I have that butter paddle and, to this day, it's silky smooth and slightly buttery.

Without Grandma's written instructions, I've tried different recipes for rye bread, but usually have been disappointed. This year I combined a couple of recipes and I think I found the secret: use brown sugar and molasses, half white flour and half rye, add a dash of dried orange peel and a smidgin of crushed anise seed.

Now, I lather on real butter and dunk it in coffee "diluted" with cream, almost like Grandma let me have when I was a little girl—Grandma fixed Postum not coffee. The homesteader's clock on my dining room shelf is a twin to the one above Grandpa's captain's chair and it keeps me company with its peaceful chimes. Although the lull of the voices of my immigrant grandparents is missing, I can re-remember that warm, cozy, safe, loved feeling.

We lived on a farm in South Dakota and, on Saturdays, Mom drove my little brother Keith and me, the seven miles to Mitchell in our 1931 Chevy. It was the Dirty 'Thirties when there was little income. My mother exchanged eggs for groceries at Bauer's store and sold the cream at the Equity Creamery.

The men in the family milked the cows twice a day every day. A pail of whole milk was saved for family use, then the cream was separated from the milk with the DeLaval separator, and the cream saved in a three-gallon can. Washing the separator bowl, strainer, and disks was a job I detested. Gathering eggs, brushing them clean, and packing them in a twelve-dozen egg crate was not so bad.

My dad's asthma required a hired man, until my brothers were older. A procession of hired men lived with us many years, making seven mouths to feed at every meal. A couple of years,

the teacher, Miss Oster, also stayed at our house. Years later, Mom told me that the sale of the eggs bought the groceries and the hired man got the cream check along with his board and room.

Like most folks in the country, we had an icebox and the iceman stopped when he saw the card placed behind the mailbox flag. Sometimes Mom bought a block of ice in town and hauled it home on the bumper of the car. It often was my chore to empty the ice pan (which was always overflowing) under the ice box. Not until the REA poles came marching down our road after World War II did we have electricity, hence, a refrigerator, electric stove, toaster, electric fan, and other conveniences.

In spite of all the hard work on the farm, my mother liked to cook. On Saturday mornings, she cooked and baked so we could have special Sunday dinners. While she was in the kitchen, I had the task of dusting the furniture, running the carpet sweeper, and straightening the week's clutter. Then, in the afternoon, my reward was to go along to town…and stop at Grandma's before we came home.

After they moved to town, Mom kept on cooking and baking, sometimes sharing a loaf of fresh bread with Dr. and Mrs. Skogmo who lived across the street. Her weekly letters often included a new recipe she'd gotten from a neighbor or one of the ladies at church. And she'd tell me what she served at Ladies' Aide or the Social Hour Club.

When we took our four growing children to South Dakota to visit, there was always a pantry full of cookies, bars, pies, and cakes to top off the generous helpings of roast beef, mashed potatoes, and gravy. Mom often said,

"I like to have your children come—they aren't finicky—they will eat anything."

Mom repeated those words long before Mary Pipher described the different generational attitudes toward food in *Another Country* (1999). Pipher says the older generation associates food with security as they urge their children and grandchildren "to eat, and eat more." Their food offering implies the message, "I love you and want to show my love."

The next generation grew up with plenty of food and now worry about their weight and health. Boomers and Generation Xs have learned about obesity from Uncle Don's struggle with diabetes. They know that high cholesterol precipitated Grandpa's five-way-bypass surgery. Mid-lifers and youngers are making the connections of genes, food, exercise, and stress in their own lives and are intentional in having a vigorous and vibrant lifestyle.

While healthy foods, aerobics, and strength training are highly valued, there's another understanding of living too fast, too deliberate, and yet too erratically. We are realizing that we must take time to smell the roses. Something in us insists that we strive for a simpler life, whether it is going back or moving forward.

When I was a girl, Laura Ingalls Wilder's *Little House on the Prairie* books charmed my little notions of the simplicity, purity, and integrity of pioneer life. Now as a grown-up, having heard of the drudgery and struggles of my own Swedish immigrant grandparents, I know that wasn't the whole story. Recently however, Laura Ingalls Wilder's words, as collected by Stephen Hines in *Saving Graces* (1999), affirm a simple truth that I want to pass on to my children, grandchildren, and great-grandchildren. My favorite childhood author wrote:

"Let's not make such a habit of hurry and work that when we leave this world, we will feel impelled to hurry through the spaces of the universe using our wings for feather dusters to clean away the star dust."

Yes, we also need to feed our souls. We need to connect with our spiritual side—the challenge that TV talk show host Oprah issues each day. I believe we need to be aware of who we are—who God created us to be—and how we can live purposefully and abundantly.

To find our authentic selves and some of life's simple pleasures, I like the advice of Vicki Morgan, in *Woman's Day*:

"Track down a recipe for one of the favorite foods your grandmother used to prepare and make it yourself."

I have cooked up new titles for the categories of food that are reminiscent of Grandma's cooking.

Grandkids' Favorites—sugar cookies, gingersnaps, bars, and brownies still bring joy and rapture to children, grandchildren, and folks of all ages. No other foods are so closely tied to Grandma with loving thoughts. The recipes may seem the same, but Grandma's special touch makes the difference.

Comfort Foods are those homey dishes served at family suppers. These foods made us feel better when we had a cold, a bad report card, or broke an arm falling out of the elm tree. Rice pudding, cinnamon rolls, custard, potato soup, and apple sauce raised our spirits and made everything okay.

"Receipts" from Hard Times and Pioneer Days utilized the basics—flour, cornmeal, sugar, salt, baking powder, eggs, milk, butter, and lard—and stretched meager groceries to fill empty stomachs with mush, lefse, kolaches, dumplings, and noodles. Knee Patches, Schtritzell, Kuechlie, Fattigman, and Fry Bread were the same kind of doughnut made by different ethnic groups.

Breakfast and Coffee Time includes an old-time ranch pancake and an up-to-date Grandpa's Mickey Mouse pancakes. Egg casseroles, baked oatmeal, coffee cakes, and yummy muffins always warm our mornings.

The Staff of Life has instructions for Grandma's wholesome rye and wheat breads (the right amount of flour "feels" right). Airy biscuits, flaky dinner rolls, and crusty spoon bread fill us up and nurture us to the core.

Sunday Dinner includes roast beef, chicken, barbecue, ham loaf, and Swedish meatballs. On the farm, we usually had our "best" meal on Sundays when relatives were "company" or old neighbors came back to visit.

Salads and Covered Dishes carried to potluck suppers, picnics, and church socials include salads—Jell-O, chicken, tuna, and potato—scalloped corn, and macaroni casseroles (only now we call it pasta). My mother's wish was to furnish a dish that folks would clean up. She was offended if her pan wasn't empty when it was time to go home.

All-American Pies make any snack or full-course meal complete. Pies are distinctive to American cuisine whether it is apple, pumpkin, butterscotch, or rhubarb custard. Aunt 'Manda's lard pie crust won her the title of Pie Queen of Hanson County in 1942.

Desserts for Club and Ladies Aide are rich, buttery, and often chocolatey cakes along with sometimes light, foamy, whipped cream delicacies that were served to "the girls with the grandmother faces." Today's grandmothers often take out the calories and reduce the effort and time with ready-made mixes and frozen whipped toppings.

Holiday Treats stir our memories with the aroma of Old World breads, cranberries, spicy pumpkin, date pudding, and mince pie. Pfeffernuesse, steamed puddings, and ostkaka may not be everyday fare, but some of the younger generation insist on making their grandmother's recipes at holiday times.

Munchies and Backyard Bonuses were not in Grandma's cookbook. We have invented dips for chips and crackers to eat while we're waiting for Thanksgiving dinner or real food. And I think men devised grills to fix steak and trout to their tastes but also to recreate the campfire feeling in the backyard.

This 'n' That covers all the extras. Candy, ice cream, and cocoa are in this section, along with lemon cheese and watermelon pickles. Here too, you will find Grandma's recipe to relieve constipation.

Fun Stuff includes old and new potions and concoctions that delight grandchildren of all ages—bubbles, play dough, spaghetti painting, dog biscuits, and dough balls for fishing bait.

PLEASE NOTE that most of these recipes have been "kitchen-tested" many, many times by the mothers, grandmothers, and grandchildren who submitted them; however, I have not personally tried each one. My editors and I have made all attempts to reproduce the recipes as they were submitted.

GRANDKIDS' FAVORITES

There are two lasting bequests we can hope to give to our children. One is roots and the other, wings.

Grandmas Like Good Eaters

"I like to have your kids come—they're such good eaters," is one of the highest compliments grandmothers pay their offspring. All grandmothers like to see their children heartily partake of the fare they provide when visiting.

No child is too chubby for Grandma—"He'll outgrow it," they say. Thin, wiry children are a challenge.

Cooking and lavishing food on their families is Grandma's way of saying, "I love you. I'm glad you came." The richer and the fancier food, the more she means it. And when one has gone all-out to prepare such a lavish spread of love, it is heartwarming to see it heartily received.

The success of a visit to Grandma's is summed up when she can tell her friends of the visit and how she enjoyed having the children there because, "they're such good eaters, you know."

From *Gleanings*, by Chrys Daniel
Wentworth, South Dakota, 1981

I am not sure if it is possible to talk about grandmothers
without discussing food. Grown men wax eloquent
on Grandmother's baked beans or homemade noodles.
Over time, Grandmother's cooking becomes
a metaphor for Grandmother's love.
Meals at Grandmother's house are communion.

—Mary Pipher
from *Another Country*

My Father, the Original Candy Man

My father was a sweet, gentle man who loved children and especially his 13 grandchildren. He carried packages of candy LifeSavers in his pocket and, after church, all the children flocked around him to get their Life Saver "fix" for the day. My children remember being proud, when we visited their church, that he was THEIR grandpa!

Pa also was the neighborhood repair man and champion salvager. Kids on South Minnesota Street in Mitchell, South Dakota, knew that he would put air in their bike tires or repair a broken doll bed. When Pa came to visit us, he always brought his tool kit along and found time to put up a shelf, replace a washer on a leaky faucet, or find a new seat for a tricycle.

Pa would stop anything he was doing for a neighbor who needed help. We often stopped to help someone with a flat tire—no matter how late it might make us for church. Before the time when all the farmers had pickups, Pa had a four-wheeled trailer to transport all the necessary loads. He hauled pigs and chickens to market, grain to be ground into livestock feed, and Aunt Minnie's household goods when she moved.

I remember one time, a neighbor had borrowed this wonderful vehicle and, in turn, loaned it to someone else…someone that Pa didn't know. This generosity was a source of frustration for my mother. She pointed out that he had to buy the replacement tires that others wore out. Pa always said, "Whatever you do for someone else will come back to you when you need help." Pa was right. Years later, when he was suffering from emphysema, his neighbors organized a corn picking bee for him. Folks came from near and far with their tractors and big corn picker machines and finished the work in only a day.

Although all his grandchildren were old enough to know him, his life was cut short by a heart attack shortly before his 70th birthday. I like to think that even now he knows what each and every one of us is up to—and that he's "busting his buttons" relating the achievements of his grandchildren and 27 great-grandchildren to the other angels!

Grandpa's Famous Root Beer Floats

My Grandpa Carlson did not really cook—that was Grandma's job. But each time we came to Mitchell, Grandpa entertained and fed us at the same time with his famous root beer floats. The recipe is nothing new—Grandpa, John, Cheryle, Becky, and Cyndi get in the car and head for A&W Drive-In. Grandpa buys a gallon of ice cold A&W root beer in a glass gallon jug. Next, on to Zesto for soft serve vanilla ice cream. The finale…home to create root beer floats and memories as only Grandpa could make them. Grandpa is gone now, as are most of the A&W drive-ins and Zesto ice cream stores. So, Grandpa's recipe cannot be duplicated except in the hearts and minds of his grandchildren.

Cyndi Orr Parrott
My Daughter
Omaha, Nebraska

My father's name was Clarence Carlson but everyone called him Kelly. My niece, Kelley, who was named for her Grandpa Carlson, is the daughter of my brother Keith. Kelley also sent her memory of my father's famous root beer floats—without any preplanning on my part. Grandpa Carlson won all their hearts with A&W and Zesto!

Grandpa Kelly's A&W Root Beer Floats

I remember driving in the car from St. Louis to Mitchell, South Dakota to visit Grandma and Grandpa Carlson. Every time, as soon as we would get there, Grandpa took the kids in his car to A&W. We bought a gallon of root beer and took it back home. We went straight to their basement—under the stairs—and we made awesome root beer floats. Then we'd sit back and enjoy!

Kelley Carlson Baruzzini
My Niece
St. Louis, Missouri

Vanilla ice cream　　　　A&W root beer
Frosty mugs

Put 2 scoops of ice cream in a frosty mug. Add root beer to the top of the mug. Carefully lick off the foam and slurp up the delicious concoction through a straw. Enjoy!

Scorpa (Swedish Rusks)

Being one of the youngest of Grandpa August and Grandma Ida Carlson's grandchildren, I did not get to spend a lot of time at their home or get to know them very well. However, I remember visiting them in Mitchell when they lived on East Fourth. It was a stucco house with a big open outside entry or porch. I remember playing on that porch. We could sit on the wide ledges of the stucco-wall sides. I remember Grandma Carlson giving us either a sugar cookie, or what she called a scorpa, which was like a hamburger bun, cut in half, buttered and sprinkled with sugar and cinnamon. It had been put on a cookie sheet and baked in a slow oven until it was toasted.

I have made these many times for my family of six when they were growing up. They're good dipped in coffee, tea, or hot chocolate for a snack.

Helen Kunze
A Carlson Cousin
Huron, South Dakota

Clarice: Some of my Swedish recipes spell scorpa as skorpor. The recipes for rusks have variations of a sweet rich dough, sometimes made without yeast, that may include crushed cardamom seeds and ground almonds. The cinnamon/sugar/butter combination sprinkled on top was a frequent addition. Jackie Robertson provides her mother's recipe for rusks using prebaked commercial tea rolls in the Holiday Treats section.

From the time I was very young, I remember my mother reading letters from my Grandma Carlson. Grandma wrote long, newsy accounts of babies, deaths, illnesses, and church activities. The common thread that ran through all of her letters was food. She would recount every detail of what was served at both everyday and special meals. Of course, there were editorial comments about the taste, texture, temperature, and reaction to every dish that you could imagine. I'm happy to say that my mother has carried on the tradition of food reporting.

My mother gave me a copy of Grandma's Bethany Cookbook when I was married 25 years ago. Now, the book is tattered with grease and cookie dough stains throughout. It was created in a different time, when ladies were "Mrs. Clarence Carlson," never Edna Carlson. I love the recipes and the memories they represent. Grandma Carlson's Spicy Apple Bars are in that cookbook.

Cyndi Orr Parrott
My Daughter
Omaha, Nebraska

Kelly's Spicy Apple Bars

2/3 cup margarine	1 cup sugar
2 eggs, beaten	1 cup sifted flour
1 teaspoon baking powder	1 cup rolled oats
1 1/2 cups diced pared apples	1/2 teaspoon soda
1 teaspoon cinnamon	1/2 teaspoon nutmeg
1/4 teaspoon cloves	1/2 cup chopped walnuts

Cream sugar and margarine, add eggs one at a time, beating well after each addition. Sift all dry ingredients together, except oats. Add to first mixture with apples and nuts and oats. Spread in 11 X 13 inch pan [brownie or jelly roll pan] and bake at 350º for 20-25 minutes. Frost with powdered sugar frosting and cut in squares or rectangles.

Clarice: My Bethany Cookbook looks much like Cyndi's. I, too, treasure the grease and dough stains. In their later years, Mom often made this recipe for my dad. The church ladies knew Mom was on the "lunch committee" when they saw Kelly's Spicy Apple Bars on the serving counter.

Grandma's Sugar Cookies (Sockerkakor)

1 cup butter
1 cup sour cream
2 eggs
6 1/2 cups flour
1 1/2 teaspoon vanilla

2 cups sugar
1 teaspoon baking soda
2 teaspoons baking powder
1/2 teaspoon salt
1/2 teaspoon almond extract
(optional)

Cream butter and sugar. Add soda to sour cream. Add sour cream mixture to creamed mixture. Beat in eggs. Add flavorings. Sift together flour, baking powder, and salt. Add to first mixture and mix well. Chill dough. Roll out dough to 1/4 inch thickness. Cut into desired shapes and sprinkle with sugar. Bake at 375° about 10 minutes.

My grandparents and their three children emigrated to the U.S. in 1910 coming to Wausa, Nebraska, which was a community settled by the Swedes. Whenever I visited them on the farm or in town, Grandma was always busy cooking and baking. She was also eager that we all had plenty to eat! A part of the eating time was reminiscing about their lives in Sweden…and how much they missed the water and the trees. On my first trip to Sweden, I realized that the lakes and the woods were such a part of their growing up.

Carol Reed
Lincoln, Nebraska

Best Ever Butter Cookies

2 1/2 cups all-purpose flour
1 cup butter, softened
1 teaspoon baking powder
1 tablespoon vanilla

1 cup sugar
1 egg
2 tablespoons orange juice

Frosting:
4 cups powdered sugar   1/2 cup butter, softened
3 to 4 tablespoons milk   2 teaspoons vanilla
Decorations such as food coloring and colored sugars

In a large mixer bowl, combine all cookie ingredients. Beat at low speed, scraping bowl often, until well mixed. Refrigerate 2 to 3 hours until firm. Roll out dough, 1/3 at a time on well-floured surface to 1/2 inch thickness. Cut with cookie cutters. Place one inch apart on cookie sheets. Sprinkle colored sugars on some of the cookies or bake and decorate later. Bake in preheated 400° oven 6 to 10 minutes or until edges are lightly browned. Cool completely. In small mixer bowl, combine all frosting ingredients. Beat at low speed, scraping bowl often, until fluffy. Frost and decorate cookies.

A holiday tradition I have done with my 3 grandchildren is to bake rolled out cookies. My oldest grandson is now 22 and this last year he still wanted to come and bake the cookies with his 9-year-old cousin. Next year, we will have a great-grandbaby to join us. The tradition lives on.

Ione Hieter
Lincoln, Nebraska

When I visited Gramma Hull, I always made a beeline for the cookie jar full of round sugar cookies. I was never disappointed.

Several years after both she and my mother died, I was going through my mother's recipe box. I found a piece of white stationery folded over into quarters. Written in my mother's perfect penmanship it said, "Gramma's Sugar Cookies."

In my mind's eye I visualized my mother and grandmother sitting at Gramma's round oak table. In my head I heard my mother say, "I would like to have your sugar cookie recipe." The piece of stationery was handy and my Gramma would have recited the ingredients from memory: "1 1/2 cups sugar…1/4 teaspoon nutmeg, and not too much flour."

For years, I experimented with the recipe. Cookbook recipes gave varying amounts of flour for what sounded close to Gramma's cookies. I eventually decided 4 1/2 cups gave me a consistency that would roll out, bake nicely, and resembled the cookies I remember.

However—I have no idea how much is "too much" or what happens if I don't follow her advice.

Jo Ann Blackledge
North Platte, Nebraska

Gramma's Sugar Cookies

1 1/2 cups sugar	1 cup butter
1 teaspoon vanilla	3 teaspoons baking powder
1 cup sour cream	3 eggs
1/2 teaspoon soda	1/4 teaspoon nutmeg
Flour—not too much	

Sugar Cookies

3 cups flour	2 teaspoons baking powder
1 scant teaspoon soda	

Cut into this 1 cup margarine

In another bowl, beat 2 eggs thoroughly. Add 1 cup sugar, 4 tablespoons milk, and 1 teaspoon vanilla. Beat this well, then pour into dry ingredients and mix well. Then chill a couple of hours or overnight. Roll out and shape any size you prefer and bake 350° for 8-10 minutes.

You can bake all at once or dough will keep in the refrigerator a couple of days or longer. They keep real good after baking, too.

Amanda Gocke
Utica, Nebraska

14 ♥

Selma Nelson's Ginger Cookies

Cream together:
    3/4 cup butter
    3/4 cup sugar
Add and mix together:
    1 egg
    4 tablespoons molasses
    2 1/4 cups flour
    2 teaspoons baking soda
    1 teaspoon each of ginger, cinnamon, cloves,
        allspice
    1/2 teaspoon salt

Roll into balls and roll balls in granulated sugar. Bake on greased cookie sheet for 10-12 minutes at 350°.

Food brings memories of cozy, warm family gatherings, heartfelt traditions, and the prevalence of a mother's concern and love! So many recipes come to mind, but I've chosen to share one that was passed down from my husband's Swedish grandmother through two more generations to our grandsons.

Grammie Nelson came to this country, speaking no English, at the tender age of 16. I'll never forget the way she called us "Suscie and Ricka." The smells of baking bread, braided pastries, crescent rolls, and sticky buns on Saturday—Baking Day—produced an aroma we fondly recall.

Grammie always kept a tin of gingersnaps in the pantry and, after our visits, she'd give us a box of them to take home. Selma's gingersnaps became a family favorite and we passed the recipe down to our three children. My daughter-in-law, and co-author of *Grand-loving: Making Memories with Your Grandchildren*, Julie Carlson now makes them with our grandsons.

The cutest thing happened last Christmas. When our grandson, Nicholas, was visiting he asked, "What's your favorite cookie, Oma?" I answered a predictable, "Gingersnaps!" Nick disappeared to return twenty minutes later with a stack of cutout circles hand colored in brown crayon—his gift of "lasting gingersnaps for Oma!"

Sue Johnson
Writing Friend
Fairport, New York

Clarice: Sue and I became friends through our mutual interest in writing about grandchildren. We have not met face to face, but have talked on the phone and been in touch by e-mail. She and her daughter-in-law, Julie Carlson, have gathered hundreds of ideas for their book Grandloving: Making Memories with Your Grandchildren. *Call 716-223-4309 or find their website at www.grandloving.com to learn more about their book.*

15

As I read Mom's recipes, there are no oven temperatures given. I guess most of the stoves and oven had no thermometers. Mom always "felt" the oven with her hand to see what the "temperature" was, and I assume most people did bake that way. I remember lots of burned food. What an "art" it was to add wood and bake right.

Joan Martin
A Rosenquist Cousin
Concord, California

My nephew Richard, a city kid, loved to stay at our house on the farm when he was young. He loved the freedom of the country and all the activities that went on there. He especially loved "Gammaw's" cookin'.

The time was during the late '30s and early '40s when the Depression Days were lingering around and Mom was still cooking on a wood-burning stove. One day, Mom decided to make Richard's favorite jelly-filled sugar cookies, so she told Richard that if he would go get a load of wood for her, she would make his favorite cookies. His reply: "Gammaw, I didn't know you could make cookies out of wood!"

Barbara Patronsky
Lincoln, Nebraska

Aunt Lillie's Easy Sugar Cookies

1 cup sugar
1 egg
1/2 teaspoon each of cream of tartar and soda
1/2 cup each lard and butter
2 cups flour

Roll into balls, flatten, and bake.

Clarice: I didn't know there were so many different sugar cookie recipes! However, for Aunt Lillie's recipe, you don't have to get out your rolling pin and cut out the thin rolled dough. You roll the dough into balls and flatten before baking. I like to dip the bottom of a small glass—like the ones that cheese spreads come in—in white or colored sugar to flatten the cookie balls.

Jelly-Filled Sugar Cookies

1 1/4 cups flour
1/4 teaspoon baking powder
3/4 cup sugar
1 egg
1 teaspoon flavoring (vanilla or lemon)
1/4 teaspoon salt
1/2 cup soft shortening
(half butter)
1 tablespoon milk or cream

Mix together thoroughly the shortening, sugar, and egg. Stir in milk and favoring. Sift together and stir in flour, baking powder, and salt. Chill dough. Roll chilled dough very thin (1/16") and cut with biscuit cutter. Place on lightly greased cookie sheet. Place a dollop of your favorite jelly in the center of each cookie. Roll and cut the same number of cookies as on the cookie sheet. Cut a hole in the center of each cookie with a thimble and place over the top of each cookie on sheet; this makes a sandwich cookie. Bake about 7 minutes, or until golden brown, at 425°. Makes about 2 1/2 dozen 2 1/2 inch cookies.

Clarice: Barb's soft drawl reminds us always that she moved from "TENnessee" to Lincoln when she married Rick. It's been my pleasure to enjoy her Southern cooking—like the Grits Casserole. She also knows how to fix fish and game. A Canada goose that she prepared was the "main event" at a Golden Girls New Year's Eve supper.

16

Banana Cookies

Cream 1 cup sugar and 1 cup margarine

1/2 cup sour cream (or condensed undiluted milk or low-fat sour cream or plain yogurt)

1 teaspoon soda

Combine soda and sour cream and add to creamed sugar and margarine. Add 2 eggs and 3 mashed (very ripe) bananas. It is optional to add 1/2 cup chopped nuts or chocolate chips.

Stir in 3 cups of flour and 1 teaspoon baking powder sifted together.

Drop by heaping teaspoonsful on greased cookie sheet. Bake at 350° until set—about 12 minutes. Do not overbake. Makes about 5 dozen soft cookies. Freeze well.

Clarice: I hope Rosemary, this Cookie Grandma, makes a double batch of these cookies so all the children, their spouses, and the 22 grandchildren get a taste. That takes a lot of cookies! However, you are not alone, Rosemary. I know a grandmother in Nebraska who has 60-some grandchildren.

Filled Cookies

1/2 cup sugar	1/2 cup lard
1/2 cup milk	3 1/2 cups flour
2 teaspoons soda	vanilla

Mix all ingredients together. Place dough on floured board and roll thin. Cut cookie rounds from rolled dough. Put a spoonful of filling on one cookie round; cover with another round sealing the edges with the tines of a fork. Bake in 375° oven for 10 to 15 minutes.

Filling: 1 cup ground raisins, ground dates, 1/2 cup water, and 1 tablespoon of flour. Boil together until thick.

Joan Martin
A Rosenquist Cousin
Concord, California

This banana cookie recipe was used by my mother and older sister when I was growing up on a farm in the 1930s. It was our favorite and remains a favorite of our own 8 children and now our 22 grandchildren. All of my daughters and daughters-in-law make them. I'm known as the Cookie Grandma and I always have a batch of banana cookies baked when I know my family are coming.

Rosemary Reinsch
Lincoln, Nebraska

Now, I occasionally bake cookies, but my family seems to be dieting a lot anymore and having cookies around is just too much of a temptation. However, this brownie recipe of Aunt Jeanne's is always good. She never failed to bring a big pan of brownies to our sons, Paul and David, when she came to visit several times a year.

Once she flew to Lincoln from Kansas City to help me out when the kids were small and Glen was in the hospital having sinus surgery. The kids were hoping she'd bring brownies, but I told them she couldn't do that since she was flying instead of driving. You can imagine their delight when she stepped off the plane with a big box of fresh brownies. Both boys are in their mid-thirties now and they still love these brownies!

Joyce Tyrrel
My "Heart Transplant" Friend
Lincoln, Nebraska

Aunt Jeanne's Brownies

2 cups sugar	1/3 cup shortening
1 3/4 cups flour	1/2 cup cocoa
5 eggs	1 1/2 teaspoons vanilla
1 teaspoon salt	

Put all in a bowl and blend. You may add chopped nuts. Bake at 375° for 15 to 25 minutes.

Frosting:

1/2 stick margarine	3 heaping tablespoons cocoa
About 1 pound powdered sugar	
Enough cold coffee for desired consistency.	

Clarice: It's been ten years since Joyce got a new heart. Joyce shared some of the journal thoughts she recorded while she was waiting for her heart. One day she was baking cookies when she realized that her cookie recipe card was stained and tattered. She wondered, she told me, if she should copy the recipe onto a new card—or would she live long enough to use that recipe again. That thought gave me much consideration for the appreciation of life. Joyce is still doing very well and continues to work at the University of Nebraska-Lincoln.

Crisp Molasses Cookies

Heat to boiling:

1 cup shortening
1 cup Brer Rabbit molasses
1 teaspoon ginger
1/2 teaspoon salt

1 cup sugar
1 tablespoon vinegar
1 teaspoon cinnamon

Remove from stove and cool.

Add:

2 eggs, well-beaten
1 teaspoon soda dissolved in 1 tablespoon hot water
6 cups of flour

Turn out on a floured board and roll very thin. Cut out and bake on greased baking sheets in a moderately hot oven (350° or so) about 15 minutes. Makes 6 dozen crisp cookies.

Joan Martin
A Rosenquist Cousin
Concord, California

Aunt Minnie's Ginger Cookies

Cream together 3/4 cup shortening and 1 cup sugar,

Add :

1 beaten egg
2 cups flour
1 teaspoon cinnamon
1 teaspoon ginger

4 tablespoons molasses
2 teaspoons soda
1/2 teaspoon cloves

Mix all together. Roll in one inch balls. Then, roll in white granulated sugar and flatten with a fork. Bake at 350°. If you like the cookies chewy, take them out of the oven while the cookies are still soft. Others prefer cookies that are more dry and crisp.

Clarice: Joan found this collection of cookie recipes in her mother's recipe box. Her mother, Lillie Rasmussen, was my mother's younger sister. The Rasmussens moved to Montana in 1934 in the midst of the Depression, leaving behind the South Dakota Drought. I imagine that Aunt Lillie treasured the recipes "from home" as their family shaped a new life in the West.

We have wonderful memories of Grandma's cooking and baking. I remember a molasses cookie she made when I was little. She rolled them out and baked them. We didn't have any fancy cookie cutters then, so our cookies were always round. We dipped them in milk when we ate them. Our children still talk about her cinnamon rolls and pies. She never came to our house without bringing some baked goodies she had made. This Ginger Cookie recipe was in her recipe box.

Alyce Knutson
A Carlson Cousin
Lakewood, Colorado

19

I have some of Mother's recipe cards and this one for Ice Box Oatmeal Cookies is one of the most used. It looks almost as worn as her Bible. She made great cookies and rolls, and always had a treat for anyone who stopped by.

Ken Hanson
A Carlson Cousin
Custer, South Dakota

Minnie Hanson's Ice Box Oatmeal Cookies

1/2 cup butter	1/2 cup lard
1 cup white sugar	1 cup brown sugar
2 eggs	1 1/2 cups flour
1 teaspoon soda	1 teaspoon salt
3 cups quick oatmeal	1/2 cup chopped nuts
1/2 cup coconut	

Cream butter, lard and sugar. Add eggs and beat. Stir in flour, soda, salt, and oatmeal. Mix thoroughly. Divide dough in half. Add nuts to one half and coconut to other half. Shape into balls. Chill overnight. Bake at 375° about 8 to 10 minutes. Makes about 130 cookies.

Clarice: I was surprised and pleased to see that both my cousins, Alyce and Ken, who are brother and sister, submitted the same Oatmeal Ice Box Cookie recipe of their mother, my Aunt Minnie. However, their versions are slightly different. Ken specifies lard and butter, while Alyce only requires shortening. Alyce suggests the addition of raisins as well as coconut and nuts. Alyce shapes the cookies into a roll and then slices them after refrigerating, while Ken shapes the dough into balls. I find it interesting that, as adults, siblings develop their own preferences!

This is a great recipe that we discovered. It has become a staple at our house...if not for the baked cookies, then for the dough!

Claire Reisinger
My Granddaughter
Seward, Nebraska

Oatmeal Da-Dahs

1 cup shortening	1/2 cup sugar
1/2 cup brown sugar	2 eggs unbeaten
1 teaspoon hot water	1 teaspoon vanilla
1 1/2 cup flour	1 teaspoon salt
1 teaspoon soda	2 cups oatmeal

1 package of chocolate chips (At least! Add to your taste.)

Cream together shortening and sugars. Add water and vanilla. Sift flour, salt, and soda and add. Mix in oatmeal and chocolate chips. Mix well. Place by teaspoonsful 2 inches apart on ungreased cookie sheet. Bake at 375° for approximately 8 minutes or until golden brown.

Frosted Cremes

3/4 cup oil	1 1/2 cup of sugar
1/4 cup lard	
1 cup of raisins (cooked and cooled)	
1 1/4 cup of liquid from cooked raisins	
(if not enough, add water)	
1 teaspoon soda (dissolve soda in hot liquid)	
2 eggs	2 1/2 cups flour
1/2 teaspoon cinnamon	1/2 teaspoon salt
1/4 teaspoon baking powder	

Step 1. Mix oil and lard together.

Step 2. Add beaten eggs and sugar and mix well.

Step 3. Add spices to the flour and add flour mixture alternately with the liquid from the raisins to the batter.

Step 4. Add raisins.

Bake in 350° oven in jelly roll pan. Bake for 25 minutes and check to see if done.

Frosting: Melt 2 sticks of oleo over low heat and add 1/4 teaspoon vanilla. Add 3 to 4 cups powdered sugar. Add milk a little at a time until spreading consistency. Toast a small amount of coconut in the oven. Watch closely. Put coconut on top of frosting before the frosting gets too firm.

My Mother always had these bars on hand in case someone might just happen to drop in. Sometimes she froze some so she could always be prepared!

Wayne Berkland
Lincoln, Nebraska

Peanut Butter Star Cookies

1/2 cup shortening	1/2 cup peanut butter
1/2 cup brown sugar	1/2 cup sugar
1 egg	2 tablespoons milk
1 teaspoon vanilla	1 3/4 cup flour, sifted
1 teaspoon soda	1/2 teaspoon salt
Chocolate star candies	

Cream first four ingredients together. Stir egg, milk, and vanilla in alternately with the dry ingredients. Make into balls using rounded teaspoons of dough. Bake 8 minutes at 375°. Remove from oven, place chocolate star or chocolate kiss in center of each cookie. Return to oven and bake 3 minutes longer.

This recipe is a holiday favorite. I have to be on guard or our family will eat them the minute they come out of the oven.

Claire Reisinger
My Granddaughter
Seward, Nebraska

Clarice: Granddaughter Claire started baking cookies for a 4-H project when she was about ten years old. Now, she continues to bake cookies for her brothers and her friends— when she isn't playing softball, her favorite activity.

21

Clarice: Miller & Paine Crumb Cookies are legendary in Lincoln. Miller & Paine was a fine department store that had a wonderful bakery and tearoom in their downtown facility. Although the store was purchased by Dillards several years ago, their cinnamon rolls and crumb cookies continue. Donna Klopp answered the request of a Lincoln Journal Star *reader and I am including it here, since I know it is in close contention with many grandmothers' cookie recipes.*

Miller & Paine Crumb Cookies

1 1/2 cups sugar
1 cup shortening
3 eggs
1/4 cup milk
1 cup Brer Rabbit dark molasses
2 cups raisins
    (soak in hot water until softened and drain)
1 pound cookie or cake crumbs
5 cups flour
2 teaspoons soda
2 teaspoons baking powder
1 teaspoon cinnamon
1 teaspoon ground cloves
1 teaspoon salt

Mix together; drop on cookie sheet. Bake 12 to 15 minutes at 350º.

Donna Klopp
Lincoln Journal Star Contributor
Eagle, Nebraska

I'm not sure where Mom got this recipe, but we had it for Easter and Christmas every year.

Sylvia Iwanski Chalupsky
Burwell, Nebraska

Mom's Blarney Stones

2 cups sugar	4 eggs
1 cup boiling water	2 cups flour
3 teaspoons baking powder	Pinch of salt
1 teaspoon vanilla	
Powdered sugar	Butter
Ground peanuts	

Cream sugar and egg yolks. Alternately add water and dry ingredients which have been sifted together. Add vanilla and fold in beaten egg whites. Pour batter into 9 X 12 pan. Bake in 350º oven about 35 minutes. When cool, cut into 2-inch squares.

Make a stiff frosting of powdered sugar, a lump of butter, and a little hot water. Frost a blarney stone on all four sides and roll in freshly ground peanuts. Let them set about an hour and then put in a pan and cover well.

4-H Peanut Butter Criss-Cross Cookie

1 cup shortening
1 cup brown sugar
1 cup peanut butter
3 cups flour
Dash salt

1 cup white sugar
2 eggs
1 teaspoon vanilla
2 teaspoons soda

Cream sugar and shortening. Add eggs and peanut butter to the creamy mix. Add flour that has the soda and salt mixed in, to make a soft dough. Roll into balls the size of walnuts. Press a fork tine on top in a criss-cross design. Bake at 350° for 10-12 minutes.

Clarice: Ellen's story brings back lots of memories of our three daughters getting things ready for the 4-H Fair. They learned much and earned many ribbons for their efforts. Although they were awarded purple ribbons for demonstrating how to make cookies and cakes, their baked cookies did not earn any purple ribbons!

Bill, the 4-H Cookies, and the Wrongful Spanking

It was about 1941 or 1942 when I was taking 4-H cooking. I was 13 years old and needed to make my 4-H Peanut Butter Cookies for the Fair and they had to be special.

On the day of baking, I had some cookies baked when brother Bill smells cookies and comes in to help himself. I give him the bad-looking ones, as the perfect ones are being saved to take to the Fair. Bill leaves, so to keep him out, I hook the screen door to the porch. It isn't too long when Bill is at the door wanting in for more cookies and I won't let him in. So he kicks at the screen and breaks the cross bar on the door. And, oh-boy, here comes Dad around the corner of the house. He asks, "Who broke the screen door?" Bill tells him it was Ellen who locked the door. About then, Dad picks up the broken lathe and spanks ME! I always felt that I got the spanking that Bill should have had. After all, I was 13 years old and he was only eight!

Ellen Goerl
Grand Island, Nebraska

Fruitcake cookies have been a favorite in my family since the early 1950s when my sister-in-law first introduced them to us. Their flavor is wonderful and the candied fruit and black walnut meats give them a chewy consistency. There are several advantages to this cookie. First, they make a large number of cookies that improve with age rather than becoming stale in a day or two. Second, the rolls of cookie dough don't have to be baked all at once; additional rolls may be baked as desired to provide fresh cookies throughout the holiday season. Finally, the ease of cutting each cookie from a roll makes them a joy to make. Fruitcake cookies are tops in my family.

Sarah Viola Gregory Cox
Raphine, VA

Fruitcake Cookies

1 cup brown sugar, packed	1/4 cup sugar
1/2 pound margarine	1/2 pound butter
3 eggs	1 teaspoon vanilla
4 1/2 cups sifted flour	

(Use 1/2 cup flour to mix with fruit and nuts.)

1 teaspoon cinnamon	1 teaspoon soda
1 teaspoon baking powder	1/2 pound raisins
2 cups black walnuts	1/2 pound dates
1/2 pound candied cherries	
3 slices red candied pineapple	
3 slices green candied pineapple	

Place raisins in a pan and cover with water; bring to a boil; cool, drain, and blot with paper towel. Chop walnuts, dates, and candied fruit. Mix raisins, dates, walnuts, and candied fruit with 1/2 cup of the flour. Set aside.

Cream butter, margarine, and sugars until light and fluffy. Add eggs and vanilla; add remaining 4 cups of flour in about 6-8 additions and mix well after each addition. Add raisin-nuts-fruit mixture and mix all together by hand.

Shape dough into rolls that are about 1 1/2 inches in diameter and about 12 inches in length and wrap in wax paper; refrigerate rolls over night. Each roll should make about one dozen cookies, and there should be 10 to 12 rolls making 10 to 12 dozen.

When ready to bake, remove wax paper and slice rolls of dough into 3/4 inch slices and place on ungreased cookie sheet. Bake in oven preheated to 350° for 10 to 12 minutes or until lightly browned. Bake as many, or as few, rolls of sliced dough as desired. Store baked cookies in a sealed tin or plastic container in a cool room—not a refrigerator. Flavor improves with age.

Calendula Cookies

Pick petals from 2 or 3 fresh calendula blossoms. Put them in a strainer and pour boiling water over them to clean them and make sure there aren't any critters left on them.

1/2 cup sugar	1/2 cup butter
2 1/2 teaspoons baking powder	
2 eggs beaten	2 cups flour
1/4 teaspoon salt	1/2 teaspoon vanilla

Cream sugar and butter and add beaten eggs, vanilla. Add flower petals and dry ingredients. Mix well to distribute the petals throughout the dough. Drop by tablespoons on greased cookie sheet. Garnish with a gumdrop or blueberry in the center of each cookie before baking. Bake at 350° for 10 minutes or until lightly browned but not hard.

With this unusual cookie recipe, I won a blue ribbon at the county fair in the "any other type of cookie" category. The cookies bake up to be a bright yellow cookie and when you add a gumdrop or a blueberry on top, they are beautiful. Of course it helps to have calendula flowers growing in your yard or garden.

Connie Mertz
Omaha, Nebraska

Dream Bars

Mixture No. 1

1 cup flour	1/2 cup brown sugar
1/2 cup butter	

Mixture No. 2

2 eggs	1 cup brown sugar
2 tablespoons flour	1/2 teaspoon baking powder
1/2 cup nutmeats cut fine	1/4 teaspoon salt
1 teaspoon vanilla	1 cup coconut

No. 1 Sift flour and sugar, cut in butter, and press into 9 X 9 pan and bake slightly.

No. 2 Beat eggs until light. Add sugar, flour, baking powder, and salt sifted together. Beat. Add rest and pour over first mixture. Bake 20-25 minutes at 350°.

Lutheran cooks were famous for furnishing BARS for ladies aide, Luther League, church suppers, and funeral lunches. Dream bars were one of my favorites and Mom made them often.

Clarice Carlson Orr

Disciple Lemon Bars

1 box of lemon cake mix	1 stick of margarine
4 eggs	8 ounces of cream cheese
1 box of powdered sugar (3 cups)	

Melt margarine and add cake mix and 1 egg. Blend until moistened. Spread into 9 X 13 pan and set aside.

Blend softened cream cheese and 3 eggs. Add 3 cups powdered sugar until creamy. Pour over first mixture. Bake at 350° for 35 minutes until light brown on top. For glass baking pan bake at 325°.

Eunice Cade
Lincoln, Nebraska

B oth Grandma Demerath and Grandma Orr make these lemon bars, so I might enjoy them in the city or on the farm when we visit Nebraska. We're lucky to have grandmas who keep us well-fed. When I was in the Army stationed in Germany, they all felt sorry for me at Christmas. And everyone sent me popcorn.

Mark Orr
My Grandson
Akron, Ohio

Lemon Bars Deluxe

Crust:

2 cups flour	1/2 cup powdered sugar
1 cup butter	

Sift the flour and sugar and cut in the butter. Press into a 9 X 13 inch pan. Bake 20-25 minutes until light brown.

Filling:

4 eggs	2 cups granulated sugar
1/3 cup lemon juice	1/4 cup flour
1/2 teaspoon baking powder	

Beat the eggs until light colored. Add the sugar gradually and then lemon juice. Sift the flour and baking powder together. Add to egg mixture. Pour over baked crust and return to oven for 25 minutes or until a light golden brown. Sprinkle with more sifted powdered sugar if you like.

Chocolate Chip Bars

2 eggs
2/3 cup oil
1 1/2 cups flour
1 1/2 teaspoons baking powder
1/2 cup oatmeal
1/2 cup chopped pecans or walnuts

1 1/2 cups brown sugar
1 teaspoon vanilla
1 teaspoon salt

Marguerite Demerath
My Orr Grandsons' Other Grandma
Creighton, Nebraska

Coconut Crisps

1/2 cup butter
1/2 cup white sugar
1 teaspoon vanilla
1/2 teaspoon soda
2 cups corn flakes
Walnut halves

1/2 cup brown sugar
1 egg
1 1/4 cup flour
1/2 teaspoon salt
1 1/4 cups flaked coconut

Cream the butter, add sugar, egg, and vanilla, creaming until light and fluffy. Sift together dry ingredients, stir into creamed mixture. Stir in flakes and coconut. Chill slightly for easy handling. Shape in small balls and drop about 3/4 inch apart on cookie sheet. Lightly press a walnut half in the center of each. Bake in 350° oven about 10 minutes. Makes 5 dozen.

Clarice: When my Grandson John III was little, he called me his Reading Grandma and Grandma Demerath was his Cookie Grandma. Matthew, Mark, and John are my only grandsons, out of seven, who have another living grandmother. However, they are indeed fortunate to have Grandma and Grandpa Demerath who raised their family of six children on a farm in northeastern Nebraska. They keep in close touch with their 20 grandchildren and one great-grandchild. When they were all together for Ed and Marguerite's Golden Anniversary, there were 37 family members. That crew can eat a lot of cookies!

Grandma Demerath was always cooking and baking, but these Coconut Crisps were one of my favorites. When we visited their farm near Plainview, Nebraska, there were a lot of cousins who lived nearby. Some were my age and there were a lot of little ones running around. We slept downstairs and, when we came up for breakfast, Grandma had some nice sticky rolls for breakfast and sugared cereal. Mom never gave us sugared cereal, but Grandma would take us down to the fruit cellar and let us choose our favorites. I liked Peanut Butter Captain Crunch.

Tim and Bill were my same age and had fun with a basketball hoop in the hayloft. But, I felt somewhat like the city greenhorn since I didn't grow up on the farm. One time I remember going to Uncle Jim's to see the new baby pigs. I reached out to touch one of the pink noses, and got bitten on the end of my finger. Grandpa and I rode around in the pickup and he showed me the farm. There was a center pivot in the middle of the field and all I could see was corn.

Matthew Orr
My Grandson
Columbus, Ohio

27

This recipe has been chosen from the files of the Washington Apple Commission and is one that I like because it is easy to prepare and is representative of a healthy and nutritious lifestyle. These bars make a great snack for those family hikes!

If someone had told me a few months ago that I would soon be traveling all over the country as the spokesgranny for the Washington state apple growers, I most likely would have thought they were from outer space! But once in a blue moon, heavenly things do happen to earth people!

Each year, the Washington Apple Commission conducts an annual search to find the World's Greatest Grandma. The commission teams up with supermarket chains in the United States and Canada to invite the children, grandchildren, spouses, and friends of outstanding grandmas to write an essay describing what makes their nominee special. The goal is to honor women who represent today's grandmothers: women who are active with their families and their communities, who are involved in exciting activities and who live busy, healthy, active lifestyles.

In his nomination letter, my husband Thom wrote about my grandchildren Brooke and Kelsey calling me "Grandma Toast," my activism and volunteer work in the community, my pas-

Granny Smith's Apple Cranberry Nut Bars

1 cup all-purpose flour
2/3 cup brown sugar
1/2 teaspoon salt
2/3 cup buttermilk
2 large egg whites
1 Granny Smith apple, cored and chopped
1/2 cup dried cranberries or raisins
1/4 cup chopped nuts
2 tablespoons flaked coconut (optional)

1 cup quick oats
2 teaspoons baking soda
1/2 teaspoon cinnamon
3 tablespoons vegetable oil

1. Heat oven to 375° F. Lightly grease a 9 inch square baking pan. In large mixing bowl, combine flour, oats, brown sugar, baking soda, salt, and cinnamon; stir to blend.
2. Add buttermilk, oil, and egg whites; beat just until blended. Stir in apple, dried fruit, and nuts. Spread batter evenly in pan and top with coconut, if desired. Bake 20 to 25 minutes or until cake tester inserted in center comes out clean. Cool and cut into 10 bars.

Nutrition information per bar with coconut
Protein: 4g; Fat: 7g; Carbohydrate: 39g; Fiber: 2 g;
Sodium:298mg; Cholesterol: .6mg; Calories: 232

Compliments of the Washington Apple Commission

sion for hiking in the Grand Canyon, and my recent academic success as a college graduate. Eventually, I was selected as a regional winner from the Midwest, then chosen from more than 7,500 entrants from across the United States and Canada for the title of Granny Smith 1999. Receiving this title is a tremendous honor, and one that I will cherish forever. As the winner of the Search for Granny Smith, I will be making TV and other personal appearances promoting Washington apples and the role that grandmothers play in the world today.

It is essential that a narrative of my activities and my perspectives about life be preserved for my grandchildren.

When I am reading my mother's written memoir entitled "My Childhood Days on the Farm," I am reminded of the importance in keeping written records of family history. Mom wrote this little book of memories in 1988 for my sister and me, as well as her three grandchildren. This work was her effort to keep her memories of life's experiences alive, including her perspective of my grandmother's life.

My grandma died when I was two years old, yet because of my mother's diligent efforts to keep history alive with the written word, I have a very clear and precise visual of my grandmother as she went about her daily chores. I can see her comforting her children, driving the buggy to town in order to sell her farm products, harvesting and canning the fruits and vegetables from her orchard and garden, preparing homemade tonics for her children, churning butter, and making cottage cheese.

Mother told of her mother grabbing the shotgun as she marched to the hen house to find out what was disturbing the chickens, making feather beds and feather pillows, using her apron as a "basket," washing the clothes on the washboard in a large washtub, and singing hymns as she sewed new clothes and mended the old. I am keeping with this tradition of preservation by providing a similar accounting of my experiences for my daughter and grandchildren, including a scrapbook that records my outlook as Granny Smith 1999.

As I prepare for the busy year that lies ahead of me, I am reminded that two pairs of small eyes will be watching every move that I make, whether I am speaking about the challenges facing victims of domestic violence, the importance of women's contributions to our historical narrative, or the need for a wholesome, healthy lifestyle as represented by the nutritional value of apples. Brooke and Kelsey will be observing how I solve problems, how I meet the challenges that are placed in front of me, and how I accept the responsibility of representing the Washington state apple growers and all of the "greatest grandmas" in this world. This opportunity to teach my family by example excites me a great deal, as well as the chance to take it one step further to the national level.

Melba Cope
GRANNY SMITH 1999
Lincoln, Nebraska

Clarice: Although I had read that Melba had been named Granny Smith, we had not met. Through a series of coincidences, we became acquainted and learned that we have other interests in common, besides grandchildren. We are both looking forward to exciting times ahead.

29

Another favorite treat my mother made were these forgotten cookies. They were so light and delicate, one batch didn't last very long in our family of six. They didn't keep well anyway, since if there was any humidity in the air these cookies were tough and rubbery.

Clarice Carlson Orr

Forgotten Cookies or Meringues

2 egg whites
2/3 cup sugar
1 cup of chopped walnuts and/or 1 package chocolate chips
1 teaspoon vanilla

Beat egg whites until stiff. Add sugar gradually. Add nuts and/or chocolate chips and vanilla.

Put on well-greased cookie sheet by teaspoonsful. Put in preheated oven 375° and immediately turn off the oven. Leave in oven 4-6 hours. Do not open the oven door during this time.

Many times I am at Bonnie's house when one of her kids is making cookies. At our house, similar cookies will be too brown, too flat, too raw, but at Bonnie's, they're always perfect. I think this recipe has won the purple ribbon for each one of their kids when it was their turn to try baking for the Seward County Fair. Cookies don't stick around very long, so if you want to keep some for the Fair, put them in the freezer. That way, you won't have to do any last minute cooking.

Alex Reisinger
My Grandson
Seward, Nebraska

Bonnie's Chocolate Chip Cookies

1 cup sugar
1 cup shortening
2 eggs
1 1/2 cups flour
1 teaspoon salt
1 cup chocolate chips
1/2 cup brown sugar
1 teaspoon vanilla
1 tablespoon hot water
1 teaspoon soda
1/2 cup oatmeal

Combine sugars, shortening, vanilla, eggs, and water. Mix in flour, soda, salt, oatmeal and chips. Bake at 350° for 10-12 minutes.

Clarice: I've been to Bonnie's and I can vouch for the fact that cookies probably don't last long there with three big guys, their sister Jill, and all their friends who like cookies as much as Alex. I'm glad that Alex and Tony are friends.

Dixie Doughnuts

1 package granulated yeast	2 cups milk, scalded
2/3 cup sugar	1/2 cup shortening
1 teaspoon salt	1 teaspoon vanilla
2 eggs	7 1/2 cups flour
2 teaspoons nutmeg, if desired	

Dissolve yeast in 1/4 cup lukewarm water. Add sugar, shortening, and salt to scalded milk. When milk has cooled to room temperature, add beaten eggs, yeast, flour, and flavoring. Mix thoroughly and set aside to raise double in bulk. Using only a small portion of the dough at a time, roll out on floured board to about 1/2 inch thickness and cut. Let the cut doughnuts stand until doubled in bulk. Fry in deep fat.

Glaze: Use a very thin mixture of powdered sugar and water to which a few drops of vanilla has been added. Orange extract may be substituted for the vanilla for variety.

Raised Orange-Flavored Doughnuts

1/2 cup scalded milk	3 tablespoons shortening
2 tablespoons sugar	1 teaspoon salt
2/3 cup water	
1 package yeast dissolved in the water	
1 egg	3 cups flour
1 tablespoon grated orange (or lemon) rind	3/4 teaspoon nutmeg

Mix together. Dough will be sticky and soft. Let rise until double. Roll to 1/2 inch thickness on floured board. Cut and let rise. Then fry in deep fat at 375°.

Roll finished doughnuts in granulated or powdered sugar or dip in glaze of powdered sugar and water.

For five or six years when I was growing up, I would go visit my favorite Aunt Odessa during the summer. Sometimes I would ride the bus by myself; other times Aunt Dessa and Uncle Bill would be visiting family and take me home with them or my folks would go for a visit. They lived three hours away from my family. Each summer while I was visiting, we would have two foods to eat—homemade ice cream which I really didn't like, but Uncle Bill did because he ran a dairy farm—and the other was freshly made doughnuts. Aunt Dessa would stir up the dough and I would roll, cut, fry and glaze them. When they were cool, I would fill the cookie jar with them. I now have that same cookie jar. Uncle Bill, at 79, still asks me when I am coming to visit and make those good doughnuts. They probably wouldn't taste as good today!

Phyllis Staats
Lincoln, Nebraska

As a child, whenever there was a heavy snow and we were unable to go to school, my father would have my mother mix up a batch of doughnuts after he finished the morning farm chores. Then, my brother, sister, and dad would fry the doughnuts and the whole family would enjoy eating the doughnuts together, all day long. As my children grew up, I continued this snowy day tradition with them.

Cheryl Jurgens
Lincoln, Nebraska

I was able to enjoy Grandma's cooking more than most children since she lived with us on the farm. Saturday was bread baking day at our house, and in the wintertime, Grandma also made doughnuts. When we took our Saturday night bath in the galvanized tub, the kitchen was filled with the enticing aromas of bread baking, wood burning in the old black range, and soap from our baths.

After we finished bathing, Grandma dropped her doughnuts in a pan filled with heated lard, turned each one to brown it on both side, carefully drained it, and then rolled it in granulated sugar. The large doughnuts were saved for possible Sunday visitors, but we were allowed to eat the doughnut holes immediately. I can still remember the taste of those warm, sugar-coated morsels. I thought then, and still do, that it was truly food fit for a king.

Although we have Grandma's recipe, we've never been able to exactly replicate her doughnuts because Grandma had a habit of adding extra ingredients, such as leftover mashed potatoes. Perhaps what is really missing is Grandma's touch.

Luella Corliss-Sphon
Lincoln, Nebraska

Grandma's Saturday Night Doughnuts

2 packages yeast*
1 teaspoon sugar
1/2 cup lukewarm water
2 cups milk
9 1/2 cups flour
1/2 cup butter or stick margarine**
1/2 teaspoon salt
1 cup sugar

Dissolve the yeast and the 1 teaspoon sugar in lukewarm water. Scald the milk and add just enough flour to make a light batter. Beat well and let cool. Then add the yeast mixture, beat well, adding more flour if necessary. Let this rise until light. Cream the margarine, sugar, and salt; add beaten eggs. Then add this mixture to the raised batter and mix well. Let the dough rise until double in size. Roll out dough on a floured surface and cut with floured doughnut cutter. Cover and let rise until double in size, about an hour. Heat vegetable oil (about 2 inches deep) to 375° in a deep-fat fryer or heavy saucepan.*** Put doughnuts in hot oil and turn when they come to the top. Fry until golden brown, drain, and roll in granulated sugar while still warm.

* Grandma used cakes of yeast

** Grandma used lard

*** Grandma used hot lard in a cast iron skillet

Stuffed Doughnuts

Mix together the following:

    1 cup sugar
    3 teaspoons salt
    1 tablespoon lard (heaping)
    1 teaspoon butter

Heat to boiling 1 1/2 cups water and pour over the above mixture. Let cool until lukewarm.

Add:

    1 1/2 cups milk
    2 packages baker's yeast. (I'm sure you can substitute
      2 tablespoons granular yeast moistened in
      1 tablespoon water)
    1 teaspoon sugar
    1 beaten egg
    Enough flour to make a sticky dough.

Prune mix:

    1 cup cooked, chopped pitted prunes
    2 teaspoons grated orange rind
    3 tablespoons sugar

This dough will almost pour out of the mixing bowl. Let rise 2 hours and then punch down. Pinch off the dough about the size of a baseball and flatten into a circle. Put a teaspoon of prune mix into the center and pull up the edges being careful that the mix stays in the center all around. If you do not, when the doughnut fries, you cannot make it turn over as one side is too heavy. Place these on a floured surface and let rise 1 hour. Deep fat fry. Drain on a rack, roll in powdered sugar. To manage the sticky dough, spray your hands with vegetable oil.

Before cholesterol, before women were liberated by commercial mixes, Mom made stuffed doughnuts. We lived on the edge of a Czech community that made lots of kolaches but not a lot of stuffed doughnuts which really is a variation of that sweet roll. One summer, LaDene Essman (of Czech descent) helped Mom and taught her to make these doughnuts. Thereafter, it was a mini-celebration when Mom made stuffed doughnuts.

We all remember one summer afternoon when our cousin from Boston was staying with us. Harry was 12 or 14 at the time, a growing teenager who was already 6 feet tall. Mom made stuffed doughnuts and the smell of deep fat frying doughnuts would draw anyone into the house. Harry came in as Mom was finishing the frying and exited with a doughnut on each finger. I don't think it ever occurred to Mom to ration the fruits of her labors, but Harry certainly took more than his share.

Ellen McCallum
Lincoln, Nebraska

Doughnuts

1 cup sugar
2 tablespoons melted butter
2 eggs beaten
1 1/2 cups milk
1 teaspoon vanilla or nutmeg
2 teaspoons baking powder
Flour to make a soft dough

My mother got this recipe from a neighbor when I was a little girl. She made this recipe with great success. But, you have to know what "a soft dough" is. Mine turned out like hockey pucks.

I was a newly-wed in July 1956. As a young bride, I wanted to impress my new husband with my cooking abilities. My mother was an excellent cook, and Loren had tasted many of her meals during our three-year courtship. Loren's mother died when he was five years old, so he really cherished home cooking.

On my day off from work, I was going to show him I could make the above doughnut recipe. My mother had made it many times in my growing up years, and I had helped her. I mixed and followed the recipe carefully, then I began to fry the doughnuts and I tried one. Wow! Not like my mother's. The cooking smell was good, but they were not tasty! What to do...I decided the easiest way to get rid of this large amount of dough was to go ahead and fry them, then throw them away. I was finishing up when Loren came home from work. He thought the doughnuts smelled wonderful and reached for a sample. I said, "Don't eat them, you will get a bad stomach ache." Did he listen? No!! My gullible young husband ate several...and yes, he got a stomach ache. Never again did I make a recipe that had inexact measurements and, after that, Loren listened more carefully to my warnings.

This next recipe is a good one, but since it is such a large recipe, you may want to cut it in half, or even fourths.

Twila Wilson
Lincoln, Nebraska

Doughnuts
This is for a BIG family

3 cups sour milk
      with 1 teaspoon soda dissolved in it
2 eggs
1 teaspoon each salt, baking soda, and nutmeg
2 tablespoons melted lard
1 1/2 cups sugar
2 quarts or 8 cups of flour

Mix lightly and handle very little. Roll and cut with doughnut cutter and fry in deep fat.

Twila Wilson

Clarice: Twila is a wonderful grandmother who takes care of her four grandchildren every day. Trent, Taylor, Tyler, and Tessa help make jelly from wild plums and then deliver the jelly jars to neighbors for Christmas.

COMFORT FOODS

True friendship begins only when people share a common memory and can say, "Do you remember?"

Table Talk

Our kitchen table was the most important piece of furniture in our South Dakota farmhouse. Three times a day for many years, our family of six and the hired men were not only fueled and nurtured by the food, but by the conversation around the table.

If that oilcloth-covered table could talk, it could have told lots of stories. All the neighborhood news of babies, weddings, deaths, and rumors was related, as well as The War News. When the folks spoke Swedish, we knew something was happening—some scandal, youthful dalliance, or marital discord not appropriate for children's ears. Later, I learned those stories that I'm certain were once hot topics.

Mom read the letters from her brother and sisters aloud at the supper table. Uncle Carl was a professor at the University of Texas and Aunt Hilda taught at nearly every school in the Black Hills. I think their letters motivated us to go to college. Aunt Lillie and her family moved from the Midwest Dust Bowl to the Bitteroot Valley in Montana. Pa's brother and sisters were all farmers who lived nearby. We kids got an education as we learned about family relationships, geography, and off-the-farm careers.

Sitting around the kitchen table, we learned about Life. Our parents let us talk and express our opinions. On busy days, Mom might get a little short and Pa would be very quiet when his emphysema was troublesome. However, I treasure the memory of the clever retorts, a lot of laughter, and hundreds of good times together.

When my family comes to dinner, I try to recreate that happy climate. My grandchildren love to talk and I can hardly get a word in edgewise. But that's what grandmas are for...to listen...I don't learn anything if I do all the talking.

Pa's "Rice Puhdding"

3 cups milk	1/2 cup raw rice
1/2 teaspoon salt	2/3 cup sugar
1 1/2 teaspoons vanilla	Cinnamon
Raisins	

Place milk, rice, salt, sugar, vanilla, and raisins in a 1 1/2 quart greased casserole with cinnamon sprinkled on top in a preheated 300° oven. Bake, uncovered, for 2 hours; serve hot or cold.

Mom's Baked Rice Pudding

Put 2 1/2 tablespoons rice in a 1 1/2 quart greased casserole. Pour in milk until about 3/4 full. Add sugar to taste, 1/2 to 2/3 cup. Bake in preheated 300° oven for two hours. If it isn't thick enough by the time the rice is done, add a little cornstarch mixed with milk. Let this boil up again. The pudding thickens as it cools.

The only way to have a friend is to be one.
—R. W. Emerson

My dad's favorite comfort food was "Rice Puhdding." Mom usually made this in the winter when the cook stove purred all day long. She might also put a roast in the oven, surrounded with potatoes, carrots, and onions. A nobby, green Hubbard squash-half, filled with butter and brown sugar, might also fit in the big, black oven. I can still smell the wonderful aroma that filled the kitchen.

Clarice Carlson Orr

I attribute my enjoyment of cooking to Mom. She was always patient in letting me experiment and working with or beside her. She encouraged me to be creative and try new recipes on the family. Many times there were no recipes; we just used common sense. Years later, she would tell me how she enjoyed having the granddaughters in the kitchen.

Even though she was in South Dakota and I was in Arizona, I could always visualize a familiar scene of her in the kitchen on the Carlson homestead, encouraging little bodies to stir, measure, and create treats for Grandpa Jim.

Marcia Carlson Rislov
A Carlson Cousin
Green Oaks, Illinois

Clarice: Amanda Tilberg was one of my father's sisters and Dorothy's mother. Everyone knew that Aunt 'Manda was the BEST cook. Mel Pooley, Amanda's great-nephew, was one of the relatives who requested Aunt 'Manda's recipes. Thank you, Dorothy, for remembering this Custard recipe; I don't know of any more comforting food.

Aunt 'Manda's Custard

4 eggs, beaten
3 cups milk
little salt

3 tablespoons sugar
1/2 teaspoon vanilla

Put milk in saucepan to heat with the sugar and salt. Heat, but don't boil. Remove and add beaten eggs and vanilla. Beat again. Pour into casserole or baking dish. Sprinkle on top with nutmeg. Place casserole in pan of warm water. Put in 350° oven. To test for doneness, insert silver knife in center. When it doesn't stick to the knife, it's done. May also be baked in custard cups.

Dorothy Tilberg
A Carlson Cousin
Ethan, South Dakota

This recipe was handed down from my great-grandmother to my grandmother to my mother and on to me.

It was always served for Thanksgiving and Christmas.

My grandmother died at home on Christmas night having been ill for several days. When we went to their town for the funeral, we had dinner at my grandparents house. Grandpa made date pudding for dessert. He proudly added that "he could cook, too!"

Jean Hammond
Publisher's Mom
Crete, Nebraska

Date Pudding

1 1/2 cups sugar
2 eggs
1 1/3 cups flour
1 (12 oz.) package dates

1/2 cup nut meats
1 teaspoon soda
1 1/2 cups boiling water
2 tablespoons butter

Mix soda with dates (cut up). Then add the boiling water and butter. Beat egg yolks separately and add them. Add sugar, flour, and nuts. Add beaten egg whites and bake in 8 X 12 pan at 350° for 30-40 minutes.

Bread Pudding

2-3 cups bread crumbs
1/4 teaspoon salt
1 teaspoon vanilla
1/2 cup raisins
1/2 cup chopped nutmeats

1/2 cup brown sugar
1 teaspoon cinnamon
2 1/4 cups milk
2 slightly beaten eggs
2 tablespoons butter

Combine all ingredients except butter. Mix lightly. Turn in greased 1 quart baking dish. Dot with butter. Bake at 325° until inserted knife comes clean, about 45 minutes.

Elenora Pierson
Mitchell, South Dakota

Lemon Sauce

2 cups boiling water
1 cup sugar
2 tablespoons margarine

6 tablespoons cornstarch
Juice of 2 lemons

Combine ingredients and boil until thickened.

Clarice: I like this recipe that Elenora submitted to the cookbook, "Someone's in the Kitchen at New Home," from the Lutheran Church in Mitchell, South Dakota, the church where I grew up.

Cousin Joan sent me this Swedish recipe that is much like the recipe my mother served over bread pudding, Grandma Rosenquist's Steamed Molasses Pudding, gingerbread, or yellow cake.

Clarice Carlson Orr

I came from a family of seven boys and three girls. Five boys and one girl were born before me and one girl and two boys after me.

During the Depression, there wasn't much money. We didn't have fancy desserts or, as a matter of fact, much else. Mother raised chickens and always had a large garden. I remember making this recipe many, many times—usually right before a meal. At the end of the meal, it was gone! We didn't have to worry about the bananas turning brown.

The spoon we used for stirring has the edge worn off—I still have this spoon and I still use it. I wanted this spoon because it brought back many good memories. It has M E C on it—I think the letters stand for Methodist Episcopal Church—m-m-m-I wonder how it ended up at my mother's house. Hope God forgave her.

My sister has the recipe book and the pages are splattered, turning brown and brittle. It's a notebook with Mother's recipes hand written.

Eunice Cade
Lincoln, Nebraska

Clarice: Eunice continues to furnish cakes and cookies for many Methodist affairs. That worn spoon has paid its penance.

Large Cake

1/2 cup butter (I'm sure we used margarine)
1 1/2 cups sugar   4 eggs
2/3 cup milk   2 1/4 cups flour
1 1/2 teaspoons (rounded) baking powder
Vanilla flavoring

There were no instructions for making it, but we creamed the butter and sugar, added the eggs. Sifted the flour and baking powder and alternated it with the milk. We baked it in a greased and floured 9 X 13 pan at 350°, probably for 30 to 35 minutes (until it sprang back when touched with a finger). We used a broom straw for testing, too—of course, inserting the unused end. My sister and I now wonder how sanitary that was!

Then comes the good part. We mashed three bananas, added a little sugar and spread on the cake, and then sliced bananas to cover the complete cake. UMM!

Sister Irene's Pumpkin Pie

2 cups pumpkin   1 1/2 cups sugar
4 eggs   1 1/2 cups milk
2 tablespoons melted oleo 1 teaspoon ginger
1 teaspoon cinnamon   Dash of salt
1/2 teaspoon allspice   1/2 teaspoon nutmeg
1/4 teaspoon cloves   Unbaked pie shell

Make 1 1/2 times the recipe for two pie tins.

Maxine Nickel
A Carlson Cousin
Fulton, South Dakota

Clarice: Irene was our oldest cousin, the oldest of seven children with four sisters. Maxine didn't want her sister Irene left out of the book, so she sent this favorite. Irene and her husband, Park Pooley, always had a big truck patch and I'm sure they grew their own pumpkins.

Apple Roly-Poly

Place caramelized brown sugar and butter on the bottom of a pan and add apple slices.

Pat sweet roll dough into an oblong adding butter, sugar and cinnamon and roll up as you do cinnamon rolls. Slice into 1/2 inch pieces and place cut side down on top of brown sugar and apple slices. Let the dough rise, then bake and serve.

Clarice: When we moved to Lincoln more than 40 years ago, we lived in one of the new houses on the land where Elinor's father had raised grain. It's curious that both our fathers were grain farmers and, though I didn't know Elinor until 15 years ago, we lived in the same neighborhood at different times in our lives.

We lived between Havelock and University Place before those villages were annexed to Lincoln. My father, a farmer, planted grain on the land now occupied by hundreds of homes, and several churches and schools. Mother made bread every day to feed our family of six. On Saturdays, our house was like Grand Central Station, when friends and neighbors often dropped by.

I remember the wonderful smell of bread baking when we came home from school. We really wanted to get home right away because we knew there might be hot Apple Roly-Poly waiting for us. Mother worked hard to keep us fed and happy. We knew we could always bring our friends home. Even the ornery boys in the neighborhood.

The boys sometimes played ball on Sundays in the field on the University Place side of 56th Street although they knew it was against the law in that strict Methodist town. Then, a young prankster would telephone the police in Uni Place to report the deed. A policeman was dispatched on his bicycle to the scene of the crime. When he arrived, the insolent and defiant boys were standing on the Havelock side of 56th Street.

Elinor Caves
Lincoln, Nebraska

Mother's Caramel Rolls were so great, my brother Darrell even got in trouble over them. It seems he was to stay after school for some reason. We lived only two blocks from school, so because he knew Mother was baking Caramel Rolls, he ran home to eat rolls. Then, back to school he went, and the teacher asked, "Where were you?" After telling her he went home for some of his mom's fresh baked rolls, the teacher said, "Why didn't you bring me some?" So, I have enclosed her famous Caramel Roll recipe.

Ken Hanson
A Carlson Cousin
Custer, South Dakota

Mother's Caramel Rolls

Dissolve together

2 packages dry yeast
1/4 cup warm water

Melt 3/4 cup shortening in 3 cups scalded milk. Cool to luke-warm.

Add 2/3 cup sugar and 2 teaspoons salt.
7 cups flour

Mix 3 cups flour with the first six ingredients. Let rise about 10 minutes.

Add enough remaining flour to make soft dough. Knead on floured board 2 or 3 times.

Let rise until double and punch down.

2 cups brown sugar.

Spread 1 cup of brown sugar in the bottom of each of 2 9 X 13 pans. Cut dough in chunks and layer on top of brown sugar. Let rise until double.

Just before putting in the oven, pour 1/4 to 1/2 cups cream over each pan of rolls.

Bake at 375° about 20 minutes or until golden brown. Invert pan on waxed paper.

Clarice: Ken's mother, Minnie Hanson, was one of my father's sisters. A remarkable woman, she raised five children all by herself during the depths of the Great Depression and she mothered Earl, Ida Louise, and Joyce when their mother, Aunt Elna, died at a young age. Her circumstances were often difficult, but Aunt Minnie always seemed contented with her lot in life. It is interesting that Aunt Minnie outlived her six brothers and sisters as well as each of their spouses.

Sister Gladys' Sticky Buns

2 packages active dry yeast
1/2 cup warm water (105° to 115°)
1/2 cup lukewarm milk (scald and then cool)
1/2 cup sugar
3/4 teaspoon salt
2 eggs
1/2 cup butter, margarine, or shortening,
    softened but not "lite"
4 1/2 to 5 cups all purpose flour
2 scoops vanilla ice cream
3/4 cup butter or margarine, softened
1 cup brown sugar
4 teaspoons cinnamon
3/4 cups chopped walnuts or pecans

Dissolve the yeast in warm water. Stir in milk, sugar, salt, eggs, shortening, and 2 1/2 cups of the flour. Beat until smooth. Allow this mixture to rest for a minimum of 20-30 minutes before proceeding. Mix in enough remaining flour to make the dough easy to handle.

Turn the dough onto a lightly floured surface and knead until smooth and elastic. Lightly oil the mixing bowl. Return the dough and cover. Place in a warm place until doubled. At this point, it can also be covered and refrigerated for up to 3-4 days. One half of the dough is required to make one 9 X 12 pan of rolls.

Melt 1/4 cup butter or margarine in a 9 X 12 baking pan. Add the vanilla ice cream and stir until melted. Sprinkle 1/2 cup of brown sugar over the melted mixture.

Take 1/2 of the dough and roll into a very thin rectangle approximately 15 X 9. Spread the dough with butter and sprinkle with cinnamon, brown sugar, and nutmeats. Roll up, beginning at the wide side. Pinch the dough to seal into a roll. Cut the roll into 15 slices and place into the 9 X 12 inch pan. Cover with a cloth and let rise until double. Bake 25 to 30 minutes in a 375° oven. Invert on a large tray or board immediately after removing from the oven.

Catholic nuns are known for their educational and teaching abilities, their pious devotion, and simple lifestyle. Sister Gladys came to Creighton after I had finished my education there and gone on to college, but my mother and sisters spoke fondly of her. Her job was to cook for the other Sisters and she quickly became known in the community for her unpretentious ways, her humor, and her outstanding capabilities in the kitchen. She introduced a secret for making any recipe of "sticky buns" truly outstanding because, with the secret ingredient, they will never turn into a hard, break-your-teeth experience. Her secret: ice cream! One scoop of ice cream, vanilla of course, gourmet or low fat, melted with the brown sugar and butter in the bottom of the baking pan was the trick.

Marilyn Demerath Orr
My Daughter-in-law
Peninsula, Ohio

Clarice: My "daughter-in-love" is as excellent a cook as her mother, Marguerite Demerath. Since her days as a 4-Her, Marilyn has always been resourceful and willing to tackle any project. My mother gave her approval for her grandson John's marriage to Marilyn when she learned that Marilyn could dress and cut up a chicken.

My grandchildren, Lisa and Tyler, prefer these rolls rather than cake, cookies or candy. We all enjoy them at all holidays and any other time.

Hazel Hendrix
Lincoln, Nebraska

I like to serve macaroni and cheese with a crunchy salad. For meat lovers, green beans with ham or bacon added tastes good.

When I was a bride in 1950, my husband did not want to eat casseroles. He was a "meat and potato" kind of guy. However, I felt the need to economize. Knowing that he enjoyed anything with cheese in it, I tried serving macaroni and cheese. He liked it!

My children have grown up with this favorite dish. My five children and eight grandchildren continue to ask for it at family dinners as the main dish or as a side dish. As soon as they showed an interest in cooking, each of my children learned to make macaroni and cheese. They say theirs never tastes the same as Mom's. I like to think it must be the un-measured ingredient—love—that I stir in.

Marilyn Gates
Lincoln, Nebraska

Super Cinnamon Rolls

1 1/2 cups scalded milk	2 sticks butter
1 2/3 cups sugar	1 cup cold water
3 packages yeast	3 eggs, well beaten
2 teaspoons salt	7 cups flour
1 tablespoon cinnamon	

Scald milk and melt 1 stick butter in milk. Add 2/3 cup sugar and cold water. Mixture should be lukewarm; add yeast. Stir well and let stand for 15 minutes or until bubbles are formed. Add eggs, salt and flour. Stir real good!

DO NOT KNEAD! Let rise in warm place 1 hour. Roll out and spread with 1 stick softened butter, the other 1 cup of sugar and 1 tablespoon cinnamon. Roll up and slice into rolls. Place in a greased pan. Smash down when put in pan, making the size of rolls you prefer. I make them small. Let rise for 1 hour or until doubled in size. Bake at 350° for 15 to 20 minutes. Frost with your favorite recipe. This recipe makes a lot of rolls. They freeze well.

Macaroni and Cheese

Cook 8 ounces (2 cups) macaroni and drain.

Make a white sauce over medium heat. Mix together until smooth:

3 tablespoons of butter or margarine
3 tablespoons flour

Gradually add 2 cups milk. Cook and stir until it comes to the boiling point.

Add grated or chunks of 8 ounces of cheddar cheese to the sauce until the cheese is melted.

Stir the cheese sauce into the macaroni.

Place mixture in buttered baking dish. Sprinkle a little bit of grated cheese on top. If you like a crunchy topping, sprinkle with crushed soda crackers or Ritz crackers.

Bake at 300-325° for 30 minutes.

Cheese Grits Casserole

4 cups boiling water
1 teaspoon salt (garlic salt, if desired)
1 cup grits
1 cup grated cheese
    or 1 tube Kaukauna Club garlic cheese
2 eggs
1/2 cup milk
1 stick melted butter
Cornflakes crumbs

Bring water and salt to a boil. Stir in grits and cook slowly for 15-20 minutes, stirring frequently. Then add cheese, blending thoroughly. Beat eggs with milk, stir in butter, and add to grits and cheese. Place in buttered casserole dish and top with buttered cornflakes crumbs. Bake 35 minutes at 350°.

Being a Southerner, born and reared in Knoxville, Tennessee, was a big plus for me when I moved to Lincoln, Nebraska in 1977. People loved my Southern accent and my Southern cooking. I soon made friends with several lovely Lincoln people and decided to host a Southern Brunch for some of them.

My menu was:
Fried ham slices
Cheese grits casserole
Fluffy biscuits
Fried apples
Generous cups of coffee

One of my friends liked the grits casserole so well she asked for the recipe. She made grits for breakfast so often she gained 10 unwanted extra pounds. The moral of the story is: Never say grits are for the birds, until you try Cheese Grits Casserole.

Barbara Patronsky
Lincoln, Nebraska

I remember cold, winter mornings in the 1940s on the farm. A cook stove filled with wood and corncobs warmed the kitchen. The table sat beside the stove and I can feel the heat on my side now!

Mom would make big pancakes. I put homemade churned butter on the pancake first, then some syrup, and spread Chew-It on top. Then, I'd add a "little" more syrup. Did that ever warm the body before those cold walks up the hill to our country school!!

Joanne Noe
Lincoln, Nebraska

Chew-It

Boil a pork roast with salt added. Remove meat from the bone and grind it. Cook an equal amount of oatmeal as ground meat in the meat liquid. Mix meat and oatmeal together and season to taste with salt and allspice.

I got this recipe from a co-worker at the Rainbow Shop—a craft and fabric shop. It's wonderful to have prepared and ready to heat up when you come home after work. Even though there is no meat, it's really tasty and filling.

Betty Bruner
A Shirt-tail Relative
Mitchell, South Dakota

Potato Soup

Put all ingredients in a heavy kettle and cook about 2-3 hours.

6-8 potatoes cut in small pieces
2 onions   2 carrots
2 ribs of celery   4 chicken bouillon cubes
1 tablespoon parsley flakes   5 cups water
1 teaspoon salt   Dash of pepper
1/3 cup butter or margarine

Then add (1) 13-ounce can evaporated milk and cook 1/2 hour more.

Top with chives and serve.

Dill Soup

Peel and dice as many potatoes as you want for your family. Chop up the tender green tops of dill—about 1 tablespoon. Cover with water and add 1 teaspoon salt. Cook until potatoes are tender. Do not drain. Mix 1 cup of cultured sour cream with 1/2 cup flour. Mix some water with this so you can add this to the hot potato mixture without getting lumps. Bring to a boil and serve. Enjoy!

Oh, the smell of that Dill Soup when I came into Grandma's kitchen! It would make any mouth water. I just knew if I stood by the old wood-burning cook stove long enough smelling the potatoes and dill cooking, I would get invited to stay for dinner. My Grandma was a tall serious woman with a heart of gold. My Grandpa was a short, jolly man who loved to play jokes on everyone. People still talk about "Old Joe's tricks."

When the soup was about finished, she would have me help to set the table. Her soup bowls, with the crackled finish, had a lovely pink rose in the center. The silver had an old tarnished look, but in my eyes it was the best. I even have one of the bowls and a spoon to this day. We would have a prayer, said in Bohemian, before we could eat. We ate this creamy soup with a thick slice of home-made bread spread with butter and white syrup. My family still eats it this way and it is always a first request when the children and grandchildren come home to visit.

This is how I remember her making it. It must be right, because it is always as good as Grandma's!

Marlys Christensen
Arlington, South Dakota

Corn Chowder Soup

4 slices bacon, chopped finely
1 medium onion, sliced
4 cups cubed potatoes
2 (10-ounce) packages frozen whole kernel corn

1 cup heavy cream	1 teaspoon sugar
1/4 cup margarine	2 1/2 teaspoons salt
1/4 teaspoon pepper	2 cups milk

Sauté bacon until golden; add onion, potatoes, and 1 cup water. Cover. Bring to a boil and simmer 10 minutes or until potatoes are tender. Remove and set aside. In medium pan combine corn, cream, sugar, butter and simmer covered over low heat 10 minutes. Add to potato mixture with remaining ingredients. Cook over low heat. Do not boil.

When Chad and Matt were at home, we had soup at least once each week. They liked this one, and my mother, Gladys Carlson, liked to make this soup for winter days on the farm.

Marcia Carlson Rislov
A Carlson Cousin
Green Oaks, Illinois

Most favorite family recipes came from friends and relatives. Over the years, I have tried to modify these basic recipes to reduce fat and sodium, yet increase flavor with herbs and spices. Son Matt described our favorites as "heavy on spice and flavor." The *Ladies Home Journal Cookbook* (a bonus for buying an entire set of Wearever just before getting married) continues to be my guide in knowing what seasoning to use with various meats, poultry, and vegetables. I enjoy creating my own recipes; cooking has been my therapy while working outside my home.

Marcia Carlson Rislov
A Carlson Cousin
Green Oaks, Illinois

Wild Rice Soup

Wash and boil 1/2 cup wild rice 15 minutes, then drain.

Fry 1 pound bacon until crisp, saving 3 tablespoons of bacon drippings.

Sauté, in the bacon drippings, 3/4 cup chopped celery, 1/3 cup green pepper, and a 4-ounce can of mushrooms. Add (2) 14 1/2 ounce cans of low sodium chicken broth and 2 cans cream of mushroom soup.

Put all in a large kettle. Cook on low heat for 1 hour. DO NOT ADD SALT. If desired, add a few tablespoons cooking sherry.

Clarice: Yes, Marcia loves to cook. She learned from a master—her mother. I enjoyed this Wild Rice Soup in her home one evening before we saw the Will Rogers Follies, one of my favorite stage productions.

This is an old family recipe from Hollis's mother. Of course, I double the recipe for us. One of our sons is sure to show up when he knows we're having cream of wheat!

Opal Steinbeck
Grand Island, Nebraska

Cream of Wheat Dessert

4 cups water
2 cups milk (I even use dried milk)
Sprinkle of salt   1/2 cup sugar
1/2 cup cream of wheat   2 eggs beaten
2 whole sticks of cinnamon

Bring water and milk to almost boiling. Add cream of wheat, salt, and sugar. Keep stirring! Add cinnamon sticks. To the beaten eggs, stir in a little of the hot mixture so the eggs won't curdle when added to the cream of wheat. Cool.

This is a meal in itself for us at suppertime. We like it with grape juice!

Apple Mush

Apples—Wealthy or McIntosh, if possible
Sugar
Spices—cinnamon, nutmeg, allspice, ground
    cardamom—any or all—or none,
    if you prefer.

Peel and core apples, cut into small pieces. Add sugar. I use about 3/4 cup of sugar to six cups of apples, but I like mine tart. Add water to about an inch below the level of the apples in the pan, bring to a boil and let simmer 15-20 minutes. While cooking, add spices. My mother rarely measured spices, and I don't either, but start with about 1 teaspoon of cinnamon and 1/8 of a teaspoon of the others, if you use them. Taste and adjust. Add more sugar if needed. Add water if it's too thick or cook longer if it's too thin. You might like to add a dash of black pepper or substitute cranberry juice for some of the water. You can't hurt it. Chill thoroughly (although it's also good warm). Eat with thick cream or sour cream. This is especially good on waffles or Swedish pancakes.

We used to go to my uncle's farm, where my mother had grown up, in late summer to pick apples. The orchard was old and was never sprayed or pruned, so the yield and quality varied. We didn't wait until they had ripened fully because by that time they would all have fallen or been attacked by worms. But they had mellowed and acquired a blush of red.

They were soft but flavorful apples, which cooked quickly into a mushy applesauce. In a good year, Mom canned quarts and quarts of it. We ate it with cream—real cream—for dessert or we put it warm on pancakes, again with cream, on cold winter mornings. Sometimes the cave, where the canned goods were stored, was so cold the applesauce was almost frozen. This made it better than ever. And the more thick, cold cream the better. We had apple pie, too, but mostly I remember Apple Mush.

Marleen Johnson
Lincoln, Nebraska

49

I have my Grandma to thank for the love of chocolate and Husker football. Grandma always consoled me with a pan of brownies when I was feeling down, sick, or had a broken bone. But, she also had a pan of brownies ready for me whenever I starred in a musical, won a school election, or just because. Grandma's brownies are especially special to me because I am the only one in my immediate family who ever got a whole pan all to myself...and believe me, I didn't share.

Amy Schmitt
Crete, Nebraska

Chocolate Fudge Brownies

2 sticks margarine	2 cups sugar
4 eggs	1 teaspoon vanilla
4 ounces unsweetened chocolate	
1 cup flour	
1/2 cup chopped walnuts (optional)	

Melt chocolate and cool.

Cream sugar and margarine; add eggs and beat until fluffy. Add cooled chocolate and beat. Add flour and walnuts (if desired). Bake for 25 to 30 minutes at 350º.

Frost while hot with the following chocolate frosting:

Frosting

Chocolate:

1/2 cup brown sugar	1/4 cup margarine
2 tablespoons milk	1 square chocolate
	or 2 tablespoons cocoa

Boil all for a few minutes. Add 1 cup powdered sugar and beat well until of spreading consistency.

You can also use this recipe to make white or caramel frosting which are favorites, too.

White:

| 1/2 cup white sugar | 1/4 cup margarine |
| 2 tablespoons milk | 1/2 teaspoon vanilla |

Boil all for a few minutes. Add 1 cup powdered sugar and beat well until of spreading consistency.

Caramel:

| 1/2 cup brown sugar | 1/4 cup margarine |
| 2 tablespoons milk | |

Boil all for a few minutes. Add 1 cup powdered sugar and beat well until of spreading consistency.

"RECEIPTS" FROM HARD TIMES & PIONEER DAYS

The way I see it, hard times aren't only
about money,
or drought,
or dust.
Hard times are about losing spirit,
and hope,
and what happens when dreams dry up.

—Karen Hesse in *Out of the Dust*, 1997
A Newbery Medal Winner

Taste Buds From The Depression Era
Gordon's Story

When I think of the Great Depression, I think of food. My folks ran a dairy, so we ate well and generally lived well when many people were experiencing economic hardships. The centerpiece of most of our meals included dairy products—milk, cream, butter, and cheese. My younger sister and I always knew when Mom was to bake bread; my sister and I would hurry home after school so that we might have some of her freshly baked bread while it was still warm. Mom would bake a special loaf just for us to eat while it was warm; she would pull a chunk of bread from the beautiful, golden loaf and we would spread butter on it and sprinkle it lightly with sugar and be transported immediately into taste-bud heaven. If sour cream were available, we would sometimes use it instead of butter on the warm, fresh bread; this provided a little variety to our treat. I still savor the memory of these special occasions.

Cornmeal mush was another dish that we had often during the Thirties. Mom was especially creative in how she served this dish to her family. Mush was made fresh to top off our evening meal—we ate it while it was hot with cream and sugar. Mom made the mush in one of her largest kettles so she could make a large batch and have a lot left over for breakfast the following morning. For breakfast, Mom would fry the sliced sections of mush, and we would eat it with butter and homemade sugar/maple syrup or with fresh pork tenderloin and eggs.

But Mom had another way of preparing leftover mush that especially tickled my taste buds. She would chop the cold mush into small, bite-size pieces, place the chopped mush in a saucepan, cover the mush with whole milk; and place the pan on the stove. We liked the mush lightly sweetened, so Mom added sugar to the milk and mush combination before placing it on the stove to heat. The mush was cooked just until it reached the scalding stage (a film formed on the top) then removed from the heat. She ladled the hot, sweetened mush into cereal bowls and served it to her eager family. I treasure my memories of those breakfasts.

To this day, several times a year, I hunger for cornmeal mush. And when I do, I make it myself and eat it by myself. My wife, Sid, wants no part of it—too many unpleasant memories for her. The urge for mush usually strikes me when we're at our Colorado home. I think this is because then I'm in a rural, somewhat rugged, setting and childhood memories tend to crowd my mind. It's also in Colorado that my hunger for cornbread surfaces; so we make cornbread. My Oklahoma childhood again shows up in how I like to eat it. I'm transported into culinary heaven if I can eat my hot cornbread crumbled in a glass of milk. This is living!

Gordon F. Culver
Lincoln, Nebraska

Making Corn Meal Mush To "Piece Out Our Income"
Sid's Story

During the early years of the Great Depression, my mother sought ways "to piece out income." Knowing that her sister-in-law had made and marketed cornmeal mush to a local grocer in her city, Mother wrote to her requesting advice and the recipe. My aunt obliged (by sending the following recipe) although she tried to convince Mother that cakes would sell better and be more profitable.

Cornmeal Mush

To one gal. of water take 1 1/2 lbs. of fresh corn meal, one tablespoon sorghum molasses or sorghum syrup and 1 1/2 oz. of salt.

Process: To make 10 cent rolls take 24 gals. of water, 36 lbs. of meal, 36 oz. of salt and 2/3 quart of sorghum. Get the 24 gallons of water hot then take out 8 gals of it and add salt and sorghum to the 16 gals still left in your boiler. Now take 1/3 or 12 lbs. of the meal and mix it with 2 1/2 gals of the 8 gals you have taken out. It must be only lukewarm. Let this mixture stand from 3 to 5 minutes. Have water in cooker steaming hot all the time and add the meal mixing slowly, keeping the water steaming hot all the time. Cook this 20 min., then mix the balance of the meal, with the balance of the water (5 1/2 gals.) Add this as before keeping the mixture boiling hot. Steam three hours, stirring well.

In 1932, my parents invested in the necessary equipment and began to manufacture and distribute one- pound cylindrical packages of mush molded for slicing. It was sold in the little town of McPherson, Kansas, under the brand name, "Millie May Mush." (Mother's name was Mildred Mayfield.) After purchase, the mush was usually sliced, fried, and served with butter and syrup for the families.

Making the mush was hard work for very little profit. It took five hours to make a batch, and sold for 35 cents per pound. Mother measured the ingredients into a 25-gallon lard can, which was set in a tub of boiling water. She stirred the mixture constantly with a large wooden paddle. The mush was then poured into metal tins which made molds of one pound each. When the batch cooled, the molds were emptied and wrapped in "oil paper." Mother delivered the product to the grocery story early the next morning. What did not sell in two days was picked up and replaced. My six-year-old brother peddled the leftovers around the neighborhood at a reduced price. (I tried, but just couldn't do it. I was too shy!) Our family ate a lot of mush that winter, too.

Mother's journal added this note about the corn meal mush venture: "I found a piano teacher who would take Sidney Lee for 50 cents per lesson. I earned the money by taking a batch of mush to McPherson every two weeks. I would clear $1 on this which paid for two weeks of lessons. These were difficult days for all of us. ...I won't recount too much of this period. We got through it."

Sid Hahn Culver
Lincoln, Nebraska

Sven Carlson and an American Blessing

In 1882 a young man from Sweden came
In search of a life that might bring him fame.
He wasn't tall in stature, only five feet tall,
And proud to stand on his head away from the wall.

Both of his parents died before he was ten years old
And he had to live with people who were very bold.
Life got so bad that he ran away from that life
And he immigrated to America with his pretty wife.

They rented a farm and a family they planned.
By the time it was finished their thirteen kids stand.
Nine boys and four girls made for him a wonderful plan
And when they all had families, 'twas a happy clan.

At Christmas it was a very grand event
The food they had, had to be heaven sent.
The table had to be about twenty feet long
To hold all the kids that to this clan belong.

Then the Swedish baloney and lutefisk were brought in.
And the ostkaka with lingonberries made you grin.
Then they said a blessing and it got very quiet.
For about thirty people eating was a wonderful sight.

Alexis "Lucky" Spader
Lincoln, Nebraska

Clarice: Lucky is a Poet Elder who commemorates significant events in his family with poetry. This poem is about his father-in-law. Although her maiden name was Carlson, Helen and I are not related.

Korv Swedish Potato Baloney

3 pounds potatoes cooked with skins on
3 pounds pork, uncooked   2 pounds beef, uncooked
2 small onions ground   3 tablespoons sugar
2 tablespoons salt   2 teaspoons pepper
1 pint (2 cups) scalded milk.

Peel the cooked potatoes and grind all ingredients together adding the milk last. Mix well and stuff into casings. Cook about 1 hour slowly. Be careful not to break the casings when turning.

I remember always having Swedish Potato Baloney at Christmas time, and I still make it sometimes. Although it's getting more difficult to find the casings to stuff the meat mixture, ask at a super market that makes their own sausage.

Helen Carlson Spader
Lincoln, Nebraska

Sylte (Head Cheese)

4 pounds of pork, from head or shoulder
8 pounds of side pork
Seasoning of salt, pepper, allspice, and bay leaves

Boil both kinds of pork until extremely tender in separate kettles. A layer of fat will come to the surface. Skim this off. While the meat is still hot prepare head cheese. Spread a piece of muslin in shallow pan. Then use cooked rind of pork to line pan and alternate fat and lean, fitting pieces together and seasoning each layer heavily with salt and pepper and lightly with ground allspice. Put pork rind on top. Tie cloth over top with string. Place pan in larger pan. Press with a heavy weight. Keep cold when pressed.

I found this recipe in my mother's lined, faded pencil-written "composition book." The covers are gone and the brown pages are tattered and spattered. The recipes reveal Mom's searching and longing to make the most of what little was on hand.

I remember my folks talking about Head Cheese, how tasty it was and all. But I probably turned up my nose at the thought of eating something with such a disgusting name. Or maybe I ate it and didn't know what it was.

A warm day in the winter was a good day to butcher. This occurred during school, so I seldom witnessed the big event. I didn't see the meat until the big pork or beef halves appeared on the back porch ready to be cut up into smaller pieces.

Pa would help Mom with this task after he had sharpened all the butcher knives on a grindstone. I helped cut the pork fat into smaller pieces to be put in big pans and kettles, heated on the stove, and rendered into lard. The cracklings, or residue after the fat was cooked out, were tasty, brown and crispy, especially good on the bottom of cornbread. The fat was drained off into crocks and turned into creamy white lard that made wonderful cookies and pies.

Clarice Carlson Orr

💟 55

This has been a tradition in our family to have at Christmas for several generations. It just wouldn't seem like Christmas without this very delicious dessert!! It is rather a long process to make, but it is worth every minute of it. I can remember when I was a little girl I stood by Grandma making it on her coal and wood burning stove and it would smell so good! Then our mother taught us girls the way to make it, and we are so very grateful. Without Ostkaka, it just wouldn't seem like Christmas. "Once a Swede, always a Swede."

Karen Ahrendts
Lincoln, Nebraska

Clarice: Ostkaka means cheese cake. Ost is Swedish for cheese and kaka is cake.

Ostkaka

1 gallon whole Vitamin D milk
1/4 rennet tablet, dissolved in a little cold water

1/2 cup flour	1/2 cup cream (optional)
2/3 cup sugar	4 egg yolks beaten
1 teaspoon vanilla	1 teaspoon cardamom seed

Have milk lukewarm. Mix flour with a small quantity of milk and then stir into all of the milk. Pour in the rennet tablet you dissolved in water and mix thoroughly. Let stand until a solid mass. Cut with a knife or wire whisk so the whey can separate from the curd. Drain until the curd is very dry. (Some people like the texture better if a little whey is left.) This will take 3-4 hours to become the consistency you like.

Mix the egg and sugar and add to the curd, then add the cream. Pour into a greased casserole baking dish and bake as a custard in an oven of 325° approximately 1 1/2 to 2 hours, until it puffs up and is slightly brown on top. Serve warm with either strawberries or lingonberries which is the Swedish way of eating it.

A Swedish Table Prayer

I Jesu navn går vi til bords
Å spise og drikke på ditt ord.
Deg Gud til aere, oss til gavn
Så får vi mat, in Jesu navn.

In Jesus' name to the table we go,
To eat and drink according to His word.
To God the honor, us the gain,
So we have food in Jesus' name.

Ostkaka

Russian Adaptation of Swedish Cheese Cake

2 cups creamed cottage cheese
2 tablespoons flour
3 eggs, beaten
1/2 cup sugar
1/2 teaspoon grated lemon rind
1/8 teaspoon pulverized cardamom seeds
1 cup whipping cream
1/2 cup golden raisins, soaked in brandy

Preheat oven to 350°.

Blend cottage cheese, flour, beaten egg, sugar, lemon rind, and cardamom in blender. Add cream, stir in raisins. Pour into buttered 1 1/2 quart casserole. Set casserole in large pan and pour boiling water around to a depth of 1 inch. Bake at 350° about 1 1/2 hours. Serve warm or cold with raspberry or cherry sauce if desired.

Christina Oldenburg
A Rosenquist Cousin
Mill Valley, California

Clarice: Christina, who was named for our Grandmother Anna Christina, has immersed herself in Swedish culture; she was a wonderful tour guide when we traveled in Sweden. But, when I asked for her Ostkaka recipe, she surprised me with this "Russian" adaptation! However, I know this is a good recipe, because I make a similar version that satisfies my Swedish roots. My recipe uses 4 eggs but no whipping cream and 1/4 cup of flour, not 2 tablespoons. The lemon rind, cardamom, and raisins are all flavorings that our grandmother would have used, but are not in my recipe.

I like to make an Americanized Ostkaka for a Christmas Coffee or buffet. I fill holiday cupcake liners in a muffin tin with the cheesecake batter and place the tin over hot water to bake. Usually, I can find lingonberry (a mini-cranberry) sauce or jam to put a dab on each little Swedish sweet. This is GOD JUL—or Happy Christmas—for me.

Lingonberry Sauce

1 quart lingonberries
3 cups sugar

Pick over berries and wash. Add 1 cup water, cook about 15 minutes, add sugar. Cook slowly until it thickens. Stir often, so it will not stick to pan. Lingonberries are the Scandinavian cousin to the American cranberry. Traditional sauce for Ostkaka.

From *Lutheran Favorites*, July 1955,
4th printing
St. Paul's Lutheran Church
Osceola, Nebraska

Grandma said, "Never make a double batch."

My Grandma could make the best Danish Kringler—or so I thought. She usually made them at Christmas time. With such a large family, they didn't last long. I really wanted to be able to make them just like she did. After she had gone to the Arlington Care Center, we weren't sure she could still remember her recipe. It wasn't written down anywhere that we could find. We brought her out to our home so she could help my sister and me learn to make them. She knew just how the dough should feel, but she couldn't remember the exact amount of each ingredient. She never measured. It was usually just a dump of this and that. So we measured as she put it in. The recipe card look like this: 1 cup flour + 3/4 cup + 1/4 cup until she thought it felt just right. The best part was when we would each make one, bake it, and test it! It was a day I will never forget. And I can make pretty good Kringler myself—or so my dad says. This is the recipe that we came up with on December 21, 1979.

Lorinda Christensen Royer
Aurora, Colorado

Danish Kringler

Cream together

1 cup butter or margarine   1/4 cup lard
1/2 teaspoon baking powder wet with water
3/4 cup sour cream   1/4 teaspoon vanilla
2 cups flour (You may need a little more–
    until it feels right and handles easily.)

Mix this like pie crust, cutting in shortening. Roll dough in flour and roll out to ¼ inch thick. Cut in narrow strips and form into a figure eight. Dip in foamy beaten egg white and then in sugar. Bake at 350° until light brown.

Frukt Soppa
(Swedish Fruit Soup)

1/2 pound prunes	1 cup raisins
1/4 cup dried apricots	4 tablespoons tapioca
1 lemon, sliced	1 orange, sliced
1 can cherries	2 apples, diced
1 cup sugar	1 stick cinnamon

Soak dried fruits, tapioca, sugar, cinnamon, orange, and lemon in enough water to cover, overnight. In the morning, add diced apples and water, cook until fruit is soft. Add canned fruit last. This soup (or sauce) may be served either hot or cold.

From *Lutheran Favorites*, July 1955
4th printing
St. Paul's Lutheran Church, Osceola, Nebraska

Clarice: Mom changed this fruit soup recipe a little in that she used 1/2 cup maraschino cherries instead of pie cherries. Pa always liked a small dish of fruit sauce, pudding, or Jell-O to finish off a meal. He enjoyed Frukt Soppa in the fall and winter.

Danish Ableskiver

2 cups of flour	1/2 teaspoon baking powder
1/2 cup sour cream	3 egg yolks beaten
1 1/4 cups milk	

1/2 teaspoon soda added to sour cream
3 egg whites stiffly beaten

Mix in the order given. Fold in the egg whites last. Bake in ableskiver pan.

Ableskivers are like pancakes only they are round like a ball. The pan is a cast iron skillet with round indentations, like half a baseball. You fill them with the batter and when they brown and bubble, you take a fork and flip them over, so they become round on both sides. Some people fill them with cooked apples or applesauce. We like ours plain. You can serve them with syrup or jam; whatever you prefer.

Years ago, my husband and I and another couple, Norm and Norma Boeka, were youth sponsors for our church. As a part of this program, we attended a recreation retreat in Dannebrog, Nebraska. For supper one night, we were served Danish Ableskivers, and found them to be delicious.

After returning home, Norma and I each bought the special cast iron skillet necessary to prepare them. With eleven kids between us, we had to make quite a few batches. We would get together on Sunday evenings and cook heaping stacks of ableskivers, keeping them warm in the oven until all were ready. They melt in your mouth.

Our kids renamed them "Baseball Pancakes" because of their round shape. To this day, they still ask for Ableskivers, when they come home for a visit.

Helen Seymour
Lincoln, Nebraska

If you can't say something nice, don't say it at all.
—Thumper's mother in "Bambi"

When I was a little girl, my Grandmother, who lived with us, would make lefse at Christmas time. Lefse is a Norwegian, soft, flat unleavened bread. It is similar to a flour tortilla. She would mix up the batter and bake them on top of the old cook stove while I sat and watched. Then, she would let me prepare one to eat. I would spread it with butter and sprinkle it with brown sugar. I would roll it up and eat it. It was yummy!

I still make lefse at Christmas to share with my family, (who are good Norwegians) and they all love them.

Violet Nesheim Carlson
My Sister-in-law
Williamsport, Maryland

My father told in glowing terms about the Norwegian Flat Bread his mother made. My mother, not Norwegian, didn't know how to make it. Eventually, when I grew up, with home and family of my own, I found a neighbor who gave me this recipe.

Starting with my grandmother, six generations of our family, including my great-grandchildren, did, or still do enjoy Norwegian Flat Bread. You can make our family tradition yours!

Ferne C. Liebsch
Arlington, South Dakota

Norwegian Lefse

4 cups potato flakes	1 cup Crisco
1/4 cup sugar	3 1/2 cups hot water
1/2 to 3/4 cup light cream	3 teaspoons salt

Mix all ingredients together. Let stand in refrigerator overnight. Add 2 cups flour. Roll about 1 tablespoon of dough into a ball. Dip in flour, roll thin, and bake on hot lefse griddle. Cool between tea towels or paper towels. After baking they need to be refrigerated or can be frozen. Can be rolled up and eaten with tuna or chicken salad, cheese spread, etc.

Norwegian Flat Bread

7 cups white flour	3 cups whole wheat flour
1 cup melted shortening or oil	1 quart buttermilk
1 teaspoon soda dissolved in buttermilk	
1 cup sugar	1 teaspoon salt

Mix dry ingredients together with the shortening like pie crust. Add the buttermilk with the soda. Roll a small piece of dough as thinly as possible, place on cookie sheet and prick with a fork so it will stay flat. Bake at 350° for 15 minutes or until crisp. But, not burnt! When cool, break in serving pieces and store in airtight tins. Keeps well.

This is a large recipe and takes hours to do even though I bake two pans at a time and keep four in operation. Eating this, with or without butter, is a treat everyone can enjoy, even those watching calories and/or sugar.

The first time you make it, I recommend dividing the recipe in half but, after that, you and your family will want the whole recipe. It is wonderful for snacks as well as meals and makes great Christmas gifts.

Ompankaka Swedish Oven Pancake

Mix:

4 eggs	2 cups milk
1 cup flour	Salt
Butter	

Preheat oven to 450°. Usually, fry bacon and pour the fat in a 9 X 13 baking pan. Bake until fluffy and slightly brown. Cut into squares and serve with butter and syrup.

Ron's mother served this for Sunday Brunch and the "kids"—the adult children—and grandchildren looked forward to this meal.

Sally Johnson
Lincoln, Nebraska

My Bohemian Grandma's Noodles

I sat next to Grandma when she made her noodles for a soup of leftover pork roast. It seemed strange and wonderful to see Grandma using the counter instead of a bowl. She made a pile of flour directly on the counter, then hollowed out the center. Several raw eggs were added to the middle, then a little salt and melted butter joined the eggs. With her hands she mixed it all together adding more flour if necessary to make a stiff dough. She divided it into three portions and rolled each into a thin layer on a floured board. All the dough rested while we cut up the other ingredients for the soup. When the dough began to change to a lighter color, we rolled it up like a jelly roll and cut it into strips. We decorated the wooden clothes rack with streamers of noodles until late afternoon when they were dry. We added some of them to the soup and sealed the rest in wax paper bread wrappers for the next soup.

Ingredients for modern use:

3 whole eggs	1 teaspoon salt
3 tablespoons melted butter	
2 1/2 cups all-purpose flour plus more flour for cutting board	

Roll 1/8 inch thick, cut 1/2 inch wide strips. Strips will need to dry several hours before cutting into 2" lengths. Store in glass jars in the refrigerator. Cook 20 minutes in soup, broth, or water.

Emma Pavlik Safarik worked hard all her life as a housewife, cooking Bohemian fare of fine quality—potato dumplings, sweet and sour cabbage, and heavenly kolaches with prunes, cherries, and cottage cheese dotted with raisins. Though she had cookbooks, her best recipes came from her childhood on the farm near St. Paul, Nebraska.

Being the oldest, I got to stay with them in Omaha in their little clapboard house near Grandpa's work at Union Pacific. We washed and hung clothes on the line together and aired the feather bed after a long winter of use.

Jeanette Safarik Richoux
Lincoln, Nebraska

Clarice: I wanted to include this old fashioned steamed pudding recipe of Grandma Rosenquist's, so I was pleased when my cousin, Joan, sent it. It made me feel good to know that Joan was also familiar with it. One Christmas, I had a series of Plum Pudding Parties (patterned after my friend Jacqui's gatherings). I prepared steamed pudding and served it with a hard sauce or a lemon sauce and a red or green maraschino cherry on top. It was easy to make and stayed fresh for several days, but most of all, I felt connected to my pioneer heritage.

Grandma Anna Christina Rosenquist's Steamed Pudding

1/2 cup molasses	1/4 cup butter
1/2 sweet milk	1 egg
1 cup raisins	
1 teaspoon each of nutmeg, cinnamon, and soda	
1/2 teaspoon salt	1 1/2 cups flour

Mix all together and place in pan within a pot of boiling water. Steam for 2 hours.

Joan Martin
A Rosenquist Cousin
Concord, California

Chocolate Steamed Pudding

1/2 cup sugar	2 tablespoons butter	1 egg
1/2 cup milk	1 cup flour	1 teaspoon baking powder
1 square chocolate	Pinch of salt	

Cream butter and sugar. Add egg and beat by hand until smooth. Alternately add milk and dry ingredients. Finally add melted chocolate. Steam 40 minutes or so. The recipe serves six or so. Sometimes I add walnuts.

This was my mother Amanda's recipe. We had it often and I considered it everyday fare. I remember that I was embarrassed that my mother served it as dessert when we entertained our country school teacher. I was wishing Mama had made something fancier. After I married, I found the old recipe and made it. My family loves it and expects it, especially on Christmas Eve. I was only seven when Mama died, so I must have been in the first grade with Ella Grout as my teacher.

Mama had a steamer (a kettle with holes in the bottom) that she placed over a pan of boiling water. She put the pudding into small jelly glasses inside the steamer.

Mildred Gulberg Gilbertson
Clarissa, Minnesota

Old Fashioned Cream Pie

1 unbaked pie shell
2 slices white bread, crusts removed

2/3 cup sugar	2 1/2 tablespoons flour
2 tablespoons butter	1/2 pint (1 cup) coffee cream
1/2 pint (1 cup) milk	Nutmeg

Dot bottom of pie shell well with butter. Crumble bread over the butter. Mix flour and sugar; sprinkle over bread and butter; pour cream over this and add enough milk to fill pie shell. Sprinkle top with nutmeg. Bake about 45 minutes at 350°.

During the Thirties, for a really special occasion and at my pleading—would you believe begging!—my mother would make a cream pie that was out of this world. My mother would remove it from the oven just before the custard-like filling was completely "set"—there was a thin, slightly milky topping on the pie. We've tried to duplicate this pie, but it has never come up to my mother's standard. We tend to overcook it. We're still trying! One of my six sisters provided me with our mom's recipe; I hope you enjoy it.

Gordon F. Culver
Lincoln, Nebraska

Applesauce Cake

2 cups flour	1 cup sugar
3/4 cup water	2 level teaspoons soda
3 tablespoons cocoa	3 tablespoons corn starch
1 teaspoon cinnamon	

1/2 teaspoon each cloves and nutmeg

Toss in 1 cup nutmeats, 1 cup raisins, and mix. Add 2 cups applesauce, 1 cup melted butter or 3/4 cup lard or meat fryings.

Bake in paper lined tin for 45 minutes at 350 °.

This is a very old recipe, but it is still delicious. I think I'd like the melted butter better than the lard or meat fryings.

Twila Wilson
Lincoln, Nebraska

A favorite recipe that Grandma Stephanie Urban made was Apple Strudel. Grandma used the whole kitchen table to roll out the crust. I've taught this recipe to our daughter, Stephanie, (Grandma's namesake). It is now a Christmas breakfast treat also enjoyed by Grandma's grandson, Samuel, who never met her personally, but has come to know and love her through this recipe.

These days, my five-year-old grandson, Traeben, enjoys helping me in my kitchen. He especially likes eating the strudel with frosting, whipped cream, or even ice cream on it when it is hot. I am planning on teaching him about Grandma's kolaches, also.

I've come to appreciate the talents of my grandparents which they developed from their farming and gardening creativity and resourcefulness. What they have passed down to me, I can continue to pass down. In this busy world, with more of its bread machines and delicatessens, I confess that I search out places like the Grain Bin bakery where I can smell and sample real bread with real butter, linger awhile, and remember Grandma Urban's warm and fragrant kitchen.

Jenifer Kuester Nelson
Lincoln, Nebraska

Apple Strudel

2 1/2 cups flour	1/2 teaspoon salt
3/4 cup warm milk and water mixed	
1 egg, beaten	Melted butter
1/2 cup browned cracker crumbs	
1 gallon peeled and sliced apples	
2 cups sugar	1/2 cup chopped nuts
1 cup raisins	Cinnamon to taste
2 tablespoons melted butter	

Put flour, salt, and melted butter in bowl and work together. Add milk mixture and beaten egg. Work dough well in the bowl and then put on a lightly floured bread board and knead and pound until tiny bubbles appear on it. Leave on the board, cover with a heated bowl, reheating the bowl when it cools. Leave it under the bowl for 1/2 hour or until rest of the ingredients are prepared. Then pick the dough up and thrust your fists into the underside and stretch it a little. Place the dough on a floured tablecloth and keep stretching and pulling the ends gently until you have a large, paper-thin circle. Sprinkle melted butter and the browned cracker crumbs over the dough. Spread the sliced apples over the dough, then sugar, raisins, nuts, and cinnamon. Coconut flakes can be used, too. Roll the entire circle like a jelly roll and place it in the form of a horseshoe on a well-greased cookie sheet. Brush the roll generously with melted butter. Bake at 350° for 45-50 minutes. When it starts to brown, brush with a mixture of milk and melted butter. (I've used corn oil or margarine in place of the butter successfully.) Serve warm or cold. ENJOY!

Kolaches

2 packages dry yeast
1 1/2 cups milk
1 1/2 teaspoons salt
6 egg yolks, beaten
1/2 cup lukewarm water
3/4 cup butter
3/4 cup sugar
6 cups flour
Fruit Filling (Solo fruit filling can be used.)
Powdered Sugar Icing is optional

Scald milk. Stir in butter, salt and sugar. Cool and add egg yolks, which will give the finished dough a golden appearance. Sprinkle yeast into water with 1 teaspoon of sugar. Let stand to dissolve. Add to milk mixture and 1 1/2 of the flour; beat until smooth. Stir in additional flour. Place in greased bowl; cover with cloth. Let rise until doubled in size. Divide dough into walnut-size pieces; shape into balls and place apart on greased pans. Brush with butter. Let rise 15 minutes; press center of each roll to make indentation and fill with filling. Let rise until doubled.

*My grandmother makes me think
that God is her best friend.*
—Charlie Shedd

As a child, a visit to my maternal grandparents was best described as never going away hungry. Vincent and Stephanie (Klimes) Urban retired from years of farming into the Czech community of Clarkson, Nebraska.

Their sunny west kitchen had the aroma of either canning or baking. Out those kitchen windows was a large, well-kept vegetable garden from which Grandma canned for winter. Grandma baked every week. She kept a supply of baked goods in the freezer. As soon as we came, she would get some kolaches out and put them out on a plate to thaw while we visited. (This was before microwaves!) If they needed to be warmed, they were placed in a brown paper bag and placed in the oven at low heat while the coffee (made with a raw egg stirred in with the coffee grounds) perked on top of the stove.

During the time spent with Grandma, I learned about sewing and baking. She taught me about kneading bread and how the dough felt. I remember she used potato water in her bread dough. She told me to keep the dough out of the draft while it was raising. And she always covered the dough with her hand-embroidered tea towels.

Jenifer Kuester Nelson
Lincoln, Nebraska

Growing up with a 100 percent Czech background, kolaches are a big part of every celebration. When we go over to Grandma Oborny's for family get-togethers or holidays, we always enjoy her freshly made kolaches. Grandma makes kolaches with every type of filling possible, and sometimes she adds sprinkles on top. Grandma never wrote down her recipe for it was passed down verbally from generation to generation. When Grandma explains how to make kolaches she says, "You add a little of this, a splash of that, then mix in some of this."

My grandma's recipe is somewhat different from this one, but this is the recipe Mom uses and what I learned from. I've made kolaches by myself, and have always favored the poppy seed filling.

This recipe can also be used for rich rolls, made the same way, minus the filling. Mom also uses this recipe to make cinnamon rolls, a famous recipe of hers. Mom makes cinnamon rolls whenever the five of us girls come home. The aroma of her baking is heavenly! We love to have coffee with our cinnamon rolls, sometimes dipping the roll into coffee for extra flavor. My four sisters and I will always treasure the taste of these delicious Czech foods.

Barbara Sladky
Waverly, Nebraska

Kolach/Cinnamon Roll/Rich Roll Dough

4 packages yeast	1/2 cup warm water
2 cups warm milk	1 cup sugar
3 teaspoons salt	4 eggs
2/3 cup lard (melted)	10 cups flour

Mix ingredients and three cups of flour together. Let rest 30 minutes. Then add the remaining seven cups. Grease and cover dough. Let rise for one hour, or until dough doubles.

Kolaches:

Divide dough in half. Cut into small pieces and roll into 1 1/2 inch balls. Place on greased pan two inches apart. Grease top of balls. Immediately flatten balls with fingers. Let rise. Make an impression in each ball. Add filling and let rise slightly. Bake for 10 minutes at 400°. Remove from pan immediately and lightly grease dough.

Poppy Seed Filling:

1/2 pound poppy seed (2 cups ground poppy seed)	
1 cup milk	1 small egg
3/4 to 1 cup sugar	1 tablespoon syrup

Beat milk and egg together until well mixed, then add poppy seed. Add sugar until sweet, then add syrup. Boil well. Add vanilla. Fill kolaches.

Cinnamon Rolls:

Glaze: In two 9 X 13 cake pans, melt 1/4 cup margarine and 1/4 cup brown sugar in each.

Filling:

Mix 1/2 cup sugar and 1 teaspoon cinnamon in a small bowl. Spread half of dough onto a baking/cutting board. Roll dough out across board, until dough is approximately 1/4 inch thick. Drizzle 1 tablespoon melted margarine and 1 teaspoon vanilla over the dough. Spread sugar and cinnamon mixutre over dough. Follow with 1/2 cup raisins.

Roll dough up and pinch edges together at the top. Cut into pieces about 1 1/2 inches thick, and lay sideways in pan. Bake 10 minutes or until golden brown, at 400°. Remove from pan by flipping pan upside down onto cooling rack. Pull rolls apart. Repeat all steps with other half of dough.

Kolaches

Part 1

2/3 cup sugar	2/3 cup shortening
1 1/2 teaspoons salt	1 cup hot mashed potatoes
1 1/2 cups hot potato water	

Part 2

1 cake yeast or 1 teaspoon dry yeast
1/2 cup lukewarm water   3 egg yolks
7 cups flour

Put sugar and salt in large bowl and add shortening. Put hot potato water over all and mix. Take 1/4 cup lukewarm water, and 1 teaspoon sugar, add yeast and mix well.

When yeast rises to the top of the cup and the other mixture is lukewarm, mix together and add egg yolks and 2 cups of flour. Mix well with mixer at high speed about 7 minutes. Now, add other 5 cups, 1 cup at a time, until it is well blended. Oil a large bowl and pour dough into it. Brush top with oil and cover with plastic and a towel that has been wrung out in warm water.

Set in warm place of 85° for about 2 hours. When risen, work down with a spoon and let rise again.

Cut small pieces into a circle; you might use a small, round cookie cutter. Put in a baking pan and, when risen to double in size, make a hole in the middle and add filling, like a thumbprint about 1/4 inch deep. Let rise 20 or 30 minutes more and bake in hot oven (400°) until brown, 15 to 20 minutes.

Prune Filling: Combine 1 cup cooked prunes with 3 tablespoons sugar, 1/4 teaspoon cinnamon, and mix.

Poppy Seed Filling: Grind poppy seed and boil in just enough water to keep moist. Add sugar and a few raisins.

Bill is Czechoslovakian and enjoys Czech food—especially kolaches. Every time we went to a family gathering at his parents, we were served kolaches. So, I decided to learn to make them.

The first few times they weren't very tasty. In fact, one time they didn't raise, so I dug a hole in the garden and buried them. In the spring, Bill was digging up the garden and came in the house with some white stuff on the spade.

"I just can't figure out what this is," he told me. I began to laugh as he had discovered my secret!

Sylvia (Iwanski) Chalupsky
Burwell, Nebraska

Perogies are something I enjoyed eating at Grandmother's house back in the late '30s. It was an all day job making them but they were oh, so good.

After we three girls grew up, married, moved away, and had children—it was my children who enjoyed eating perogies at their grandmother's house. I remember my son running up to my mother, giving her a hug, and asking, "Nana, did you make us perogies?"

Well, now my children are married, and their children got used to eating them at my house in Elkhart, Indiana.

I have since moved to Lincoln to be near my daughter Stephanie who is married to Nebraska Governor Mike Johanns. My grandson has asked me on several occasions if I made perogies! This past Christmas, along with the ham, etc., I decided to surprise him with an extra dish of perogies. It wasn't much of a surprise though, because he smelled the sautéed onions when he entered the house.

The only big change over the years is that I now buy Mrs. T.'s Frozen Perogies. My Grandmother must turn over in her grave each time I make them!

Joan N. Suther
Lincoln, Nebraska

Perogies

Filling:

Boil peeled potatoes in salt water. Drain when soft. Lay lots of sharp cheddar cheese on top to melt and mash again.

*Hide this filling—or everyone will eat it up.

Dough:

Beat 1 egg and 1 cup of water together. Add 2 cups of flour and 1 teaspoon salt.

Work the dough with extra flour until dry and can be rolled out.

To Make Perogies:

Roll dough thin and cut into small squares. Put potato mixture in the middle of each square. Fold dough over and pinch ends until you have little triangles left.

Let perogies dry out a little in the air. Turn each perogie while drying.

Sauté chopped onions in butter until they turn dark brown.

Boil perogies in salt water until they float. Drain.

Cover with the butter and onion mixture and ENJOY!.

OR, Buy Mrs. T.'s Frozen Perogies

Potato Dumplings

5 cups riced potatoes
1 teaspoon salt

4 eggs
3 cups flour

Cook potatoes in the jackets (do not peel) and put through a ricer or grinder. (A ricer is a sort of colander that you force the potatoes through so they look like rice.) Cool potatoes before mixing in eggs, salt, and flour. Form into balls the size of a tennis ball. Drop in boiling water and cook until they float to the top, about 15 minutes. Makes about 20-25 dumplings.

Serve with cream gravy and, of course, fried chicken. Leftover dumplings can be sliced and fried in butter until brown and crispy.

My Grandmother, Pauline Metzger, was widowed twice before I was even born.

Grandmother always wore a dress and apron and well-worn shoes. When she came to visit us, my sister and I would help her make potato dumplings. We would attach the old food grinder to a wooden chair and grind the potatoes into a dishpan. She never used a recipe and always added ingredients until it looked or tasted right. My Mother learned to make dumplings the same way, but has actually written this recipe for me.

Karen Pooley
A Carlson Cousin
Mitchell, South Dakota

When I was a kid and we lived on a farm, the noon meal was the big meal of the day; meat, potatoes, vegetables, and bread. The jack-in-the-sack was our evening meal, as most of our evening meals were smaller and simpler. Many times it was a one-item meal like pancakes (no eggs), macaroni and cream and sugar, rice with cream, sugar, and cinnamon, milk soup with sugar, leftovers from dinner, or jack-in-the sack.

I can still visualize this round jack-in-the-sack sitting in the center of the table. It would sit nicely on the platter on the knot end. Because of the knot, one side was much flatter and the smooth part of the flour sack makes a perfectly round ball shape. Mother would slice it like an angel food cake, each one of us got the size to our liking. Mother usually served it with the syrup sauce. With three older siblings and my parents we usually ate "the whole thing" at one sitting. It was the only thing we had to eat with all the milk we could drink.

As I look at the list of things we ate, most everything was served with sauce or gravy and a lot of sugar. (Guess this is German cooking.) Is it any wonder that Grandma Metzger didn't think we "looked healthy" unless we were just a little overweight. (Wonder what she would think today with all the emphasis on thinner.)

German Grosen Klump
(Jack-in-the-Sack)

Mix together:
- 3 eggs, beaten
- 1 quart of milk
- 1 tablespoon melted shortening
- 1/2 cup sugar
- 2 teaspoons baking powder
- Pinch of salt
- Raisins, as many as you wish
- Flour enough to make a stiff dough, just so it drops easy off spoon.

Put the dough in a cloth the size of a small white flour sack that has been dipped in hot water and sprinkled on the inside with flour. Now, bring the corners together and tie, but leave space for the dough to rise. Cook 1 1/2 hour in plenty of water to cover.

Serve with browned butter or syrup sauce.

Syrup Sauce

In a frying pan, put brown Karo syrup, add water (I believe this is to increase the volume), a pinch of salt and cornstarch to thicken.

Karen Pooley
A Carlson Cousin
Mitchell, South Dakota

Clarice: Karen plans to host a "hands-on" Metzger family reunion and make jack-in-the-sack, can beef and pork in a pressure canner, find a cream separator to separate milk from the cream, and churn butter. That sounds like a whole summer's schedule to me.

Meat, Vegetable, and Prune Tzimmes

1 large onion sliced thin
1 tablespoon canola oil
2 1/2 pounds boneless beef chuck, cubed and trimmed of fat
1 1/2 cups chicken broth
1 level tablespoon honey
1/2 teaspoon salt or to taste
5 large carrots, scraped and cut into 1 inch pieces
4 white potatoes, peeled and cut into 1 1/2 inch pieces
3 yams, peeled, cut into 1 1/2 inch pieces
20 dried pitted prunes

1. In a large Dutch oven or pot, brown the onions in hot oil.
2. Dry beef with a paper towel. Push aside the browned onion and brown the beef.
3. Add chicken broth, honey, and salt. Cover and simmer the beef until almost tender (about 2 hours). Remove beef to a large plate. Skim the fat from the pan juices, do not use.
4. Add the vegetables and prunes to the pan. Place the beef on top of the vegetables.
5. Cover and simmer until vegetables and beef are tender (about 1 to 1 1/2 hours).

Makes about 8 servings. Nice served with a green salad.

My Grandmother Mary came to this country from Germany when she was 17 years old. She met Morris Krentzman and shortly thereafter they were married. They were blessed with twin girls, one of whom was to be my mother. As the story goes, Grandfather's hair turned gray overnight upon hearing he was the father of twins!

Grandmother Mary was a wonderful person and cook. This special casserole dish stands out in my memory. Grandmother never wrote her recipe down so I'm giving my version of what she made. It is delicious even when reheated. Enjoy!

Harriet Kohn
UNL Home Economist
Lincoln, Nebraska

*The German word "Frau" is formed
from the words "Froh" and "weh"
which mean joy and woe.*

This is a German dish that my Mother always fixed in the summertime. But Mother never wrote things down much in her cooking of things such as this; she went by how it tasted. Sometimes she was so busy on the farm, she didn't take the time to remove the skin and bones from the cooked chicken. It was up to each of us to pick it apart with our fingers and suck the jellied broth off the bones. Mother always seemed to get the neck. I wonder if she really liked the neck.

Years passed and I got hungry for the taste of this pickled chicken so I had to create this recipe to the taste that I remembered as a child. I wrote it down after many tries.

Betty Vanosdall
Grand Island, Nebraska

Pickled Chicken

Cook a whole chicken until done, cool, skin, and debone.
Take 2 1/2 cups chicken broth
1 1/2 cups vinegar
1 medium onion (sliced)
6 bay leaves
1 tablespoon sugar
1 tablespoon pickling spices…(may tie in a cloth)
Salt and pepper to taste

Bring this brine to a boil until the onions are nearly tender (about 10 minutes)

If you put the pickling spices in a cloth, remove it now.

Add the cut-up chicken to broth and boil for 5 minutes. Pour into a serving dish. Chill until broth is jelled.

German Style Chicken

One old hen cut in pieces and boiled in brown vinegar and H_2O (more vinegar than H_2O). Add 1 scant cup sugar, 1 large onion, 1 tablespoon pickling spice and 1 tablespoon bay leaves and salt and pepper to taste. Eat hot or cold; may be put in pan with fat of the chicken poured over. Keeps indefinitely.

M. L. Swanson
Osceola, Nebraska

Clarice: Browsing through the Men's Wares section of a 1952 edition of Lutheran Favorites of St. Paul's Smorgasbord, *I was surprised to find some of the Swedes, including M.L. Swanson, made this same kind of German Pickled Chicken.*

Paglialongas' Pizza

1 cup plus 2 tablespoons water
2 tablespoons olive or vegetable oil
3 cups flour
1 teaspoon sugar
1 teaspoon salt
2 1/2 teaspoons regular active or quick-acting active dry yeast

Follow your bread machine directions.

Heat oven to 400°. Divide the dough into eight equal pieces. On a floured surface, let the kids roll their dough to any shape they like. Thick or thin, circle or a P for Phillip, the shape is the fun part. The final step before the oven and toppings is to rest the dough on a surface of cornmeal. This will help the pizza not to stick. Now, add your individual favorite toppings. Phil and Mike always make thick layers of pepperoni and cheese—no veggies and just a dash of sauce. Lou likes a lot of sauce and light meat and vegetables. The veggies—eggplant, onions, mushrooms, and peppers are my favorite.

Meat—your favorite selections like cooked sausage or pepperoni

Cheese—it must be mozzarella; I plan a ration of one pound of cheese for one pound of dough.

Vegetables—sautéed or raw onions and bell peppers, eggplant, zucchini—whatever you enjoy.

Sauce—your favorite

Clarice: Cheryle has gracefully adapted her Midwest Scandinavian cooking heritage to her Italian husband's California food preferences. But, she often tries Swedish recipes, too.

Twenty years ago, I would have written a recipe from memory of spaghetti sauce, because that is what we made. We made gallons of it, twelve quarts at a time, enjoying it with all kinds of pasta, but most of all on Friday night, as pizza. My mother-in-law would have told you about the fifty years she made pizza on Mondays. That was bread baking day in her family and the last pound was made into pizza. Jennie Paglialonga's pizza was like the old country, for she was raised in Abruzzi, east of Rome. Her pizza contained all the leftovers and lots of kinds of meat. Lou's memories are of thick pizza and sausage that hung from the rafters in the cellar.

Today, we enjoy a sauce from the jar; it's the convenience mostly. I know that if we would make the sauce, it would be wonderful. We do still make pizza—so use your favorite sauce, and even your favorite bread machine makes pizza dough. And let the kids help you.

Cheryle Orr Paglialonga
My Daughter
Atascadero, California

When I went back to South Texas to visit my old neighbors and friends, this recipe was going all over the area. Everyone was fixing it.

Gladys Woods
Lincoln, Nebraska

Tortilla Soup

Brown 1 pound ground beef with 1/2 cup chopped onion. Add:

1 large can tomatoes
1 small can tomato sauce
1 can pinto beans, undrained
1 can kidney beans, undrained
1 can whole kernel corn, or hominy, undrained
1 small can chopped green chilis
1 package dry ranch dressing mix
1 package taco seasoning mix, mild or spicy
1 quart water

Bring to simmer in large kettle, simmer one hour. It's good the first day, but if the flavors have a chance to meld, the second day it is really good. Serve with tortilla chips, if desired.

Hush Puppies

I first tasted hush puppies at the annual YMCA/YWCA Fish Fry at Ft. Hays Kansas State College in Hays, Kansas, when I was a college freshman in 1951. They are delicious!

Twila Wilson
Lincoln, Nebraska

2 cups cornmeal
1 tablespoon baking powder
1/2 teaspoon soda
3 tablespoons chopped onion

1 tablespoon flour
1 egg, well beaten
1 teaspoon salt
1 cup buttermilk

Sift dry ingredients and mix. Add onion, egg, and buttermilk. Drop by spoonsful into hot fat. Fry until golden brown. Drain on paper.

Enchiladas

1 1/2 pounds ground beef
1 can Old El Paso enchilada sauce
1 can tomato soup
1 can cream of mushroom soup
1 cup shredded cheddar cheese
10 corn tortillas

Brown the ground beef. In a sauce pan, combine 1 Old El Paso enchilada sauce, 1 can tomato soup, 1 can cream of mushroom soup. Heat and add 1 cup shredded cheddar cheese. Pour half of this mixture into the ground beef. Dip the 10 corn tortillas in hot oil briefly, stack on layers of paper towels, and keep warm. Spoon ground beef filling mixture onto tortillas. Fold in thirds, and lay in baking pan. Pour remainder of sauce mixture over the top with more shredded cheddar cheese. Bake at 350° 30 minutes uncovered.

This meal is one of my all-time favorites! Dad grew up in Mexico so he always likes enchiladas. We always serve enchiladas with "Green Stuff," our family's favorite lime Jell-O recipe. If the Mexican food seems too spicy, the lime gelatin will take the heat right out! One tip: drink milk, not water! It's fun to serve enchiladas for company and see how many gallons of milk people go through!

Claire Elizabeth Reisinger
My Granddaughter
Seward, Nebraska

Clarice: Claire's interests are international. She went to school in Wurzburg, Germany, for the last half of her high school junior year. She lived with the same family that her father, Nick, lived with as an exchange student thirty years ago. Claire also visited Iris, an exchange student from East Germany who had lived with her family in Seward two years ago. In addition, Claire has a penpal, Claudia, in Slovenia. She has also kept in touch with families her mother, Becky, knew in Melbourne, Australia.

While living in Tucson for 17 years, we acquired a taste for Southwestern cuisine. This was the first recipe added to our collection. It was shared by Kathy and Evelyn Raab, friends of mutual friends from when we lived in DeKalb, Illinois. Over the years, we've added cooked chicken to the sour cream mixture and it has become known as Chicken Enchiladas.

Marcia Carlson Rislov
A Carlson Cousin
Green Oaks, Illinois

Sour Cream Enchiladas

Mix together 4-ounce can green chilies, 1 can cream of chicken soup, and 1 cup sour cream

Grate together 8 ounces of Monterey jack cheese and 8 ounces of longhorn cheese—(I substitute cheddar or a mixture of cheeses.)

Chop one bunch of green onions, including about half of tops

Soften 1 dozen corn tortillas in hot grease for a few seconds. You can eliminate fat calories by spraying with PAM and heating each tortilla.

Put a spoonful of the sour cream mixture on each tortilla and place in pan in overlapping fashion. Put remainder of sour cream mixture over all and sprinkle rest of cheeses over that, then sprinkle with remaining onions.

Bake in 325° oven for about 30 minutes or until cheeses are hot and bubbly.

Being of German descent, I never quite figured out why my mother had this recipe for Spanish Eggs. When I asked her, she said it was one she found in the *Dakota Farmer*, which was popular when I was a kid. My mother is 88 years old and she always was trying new recipes. She still does today; never uses the same recipe to bake chocolate chip cookies.

Karen Pooley
A Carlson Cousin
Mitchell, South Dakota

Spanish Eggs

1 dozen hard-boiled eggs	1 tablespoon butter
1 good-sized onion	1 tablespoon flour
1 tablespoon salt	1/2 teaspoon red pepper
1 can tomatoes	2 cups sour cream

Put butter, onion, flour, salt, red pepper, onion, and tomatoes in a frying pan and cook for 5 minutes. Add the sliced eggs and sour cream. Serve over mashed potatoes. A very good Lenten dish. About 10 servings.

Clarice: My mother added onion and a jar of home canned tomatoes to scrambled eggs and I think she called that dish Spanish Eggs. Maybe the Spanish or Mexican influence was making its way into our culture more than 50 years ago. Because we usually had an abundance of eggs, we often had some variety of eggs for supper along with our fried potatoes. My mother also found new recipes in The Dakota Farmer.

Clarice: In 1967, in celebration of Nebraska's Centennial, Nebraska's First Lady, Maxine Morrison, worked with Catherine J. Hillegass to publish the Nebraska Centennial First Ladies' Cookbook.

This editor's note was included in the section on Nebraska's Pioneer Families:

We found it very interesting that the following 8 recipes were submitted to us by people of several different ethnic origins. These delightful concoctions are all called by a different name but are very similar in nature. Try them—they will intrigue your family, as they did ours. It's no wonder these recipes have been handed down from mother to daughter—the grandchildren undoubtedly saw to that.

The names of the recipes included: Number One Fried Cakes and Celestine Crusts from Czech kitchens, Grebel from a German/Austrian family, Schtritzell, Bozi Milosti (Heavenly Love), Knee Patches, and Kuechlie (recipe of Mary E. Sandoz, the mother of Mari Sandoz who was of Swiss background).

Celestine Crusts

2 cups flour
1 cup sweet cream
2 egg yolks
1 whole egg beaten
1/4 teaspoon salt
1 teaspoon sugar

Mix and knead well on floured board. Roll as thin as a knife blade with a rolling pin. Cut in strips 2 X 4 inches and pierce with fork in several places or make 2 slashes with knife. Fry in deep hot shortening until golden brown. Remove from deep fat, sprinkle with powdered sugar. A quick snack with coffee. (Delicious.)

Recipe of Mrs. Frantisek Chab
Submitted by Mrs. Bessie Chab
Wilber, Nebraska

Kuechlie (Fat Cakes)

5 eggs, slightly beaten
5 tablespoons cream, sweet or sour, but heavy
5 tablespoons sugar
3/4 teaspoon salt
Flour

Mix all ingredients, adding enough flour to make a stiff dough. Chill. Roll very thin, cut into 2 X 4 inch pieces. Deep fat fry as doughnuts. Dust with sugar and cinnamon while hot.

Recipe of Mary E. Sandoz,
mother of author Mari Sandoz
Submitted by Mrs. Fritz Sandoz,
Lakeside, Nebraska

Clarice: I have since realized that my Swedish grandmothers used a similar combination of ingredients in a recipe called Fattigman, (fah-tee-mon).

Fattigman

11 egg yolks, well beaten
Add 5 tablespoons of cream
8 tablespoons sugar
1/4 teaspoon salt

Add flour enough to make a stiff dough, about 3+ cups. Chill slightly and roll out on floured board quite thin. Cut in diamond shapes and make a one inch slit in the middle. Fry in deep fat. Drain and sprinkle with granulated or powdered sugar.

This recipe uses 11 or 12 egg yolks and frequently was made at the same time my mother made an angel food cake that included 11 or 12 egg whites. Although we usually had a plentiful supply of eggs, my thrifty mother never threw any food away if she could help it. Whenever I break an egg, I instinctively use my finger to wipe out every bit of egg white in the shell adding it to the recipe...just as my mother always did.

My dad loved Mom's cooking. And when she made old-fashioned Swedish recipes like Fattigman, he was in his glory. I can see him smiling as he hunched over his creamy cup of coffee stirring carefully to make sure the sugar on the bottom was dissolved, ready for him to dunk his cookie, doughnut, or Fattigman.

This recipe that used all those egg yolks brings to mind my main job of gathering eggs. I didn't mind it much, except in the spring when the hens were broody, wanting to nest and raise a batch of chickens. I would approach the old Rhode Island Red with a stick and hold her pecking head against the side of the nesting box and reach under her feathers to retrieve the egg she had laid that day. That would be a little success for my day! I remember also that my brother Paul, who later became an engineer, taught me about centrifugal force. I learned I could rotate the egg bucket very quickly with a swing of my arm over my head and the eggs wouldn't fall out.

Clarice Carlson Orr

Indian Fry Bread is another recipe that is very similar to the Nebraska Pioneer Family recipes.

Indian Fry Bread

Cornmeal or flour for dusting board
1 1/2 teaspoons baking powder
2/3 cup warm water (approximately)

2 cups flour
1/2 teaspoon salt
Lard for deep frying

Lightly dust a board with cornmeal or flour. Combine 2 cups flour, the baking powder, and the salt. Add a little warm water at a time and stir constantly—a wooden spoon works best—until it's the consistency of bread dough. Knead thoroughly until smooth and elastic, then cover the bowl and let the dough rest for 10 minutes. Heat 2-3 inches of lard (you could use oil) in a large deep frying pan to 400°. Tear off 2-inch pieces of dough and roll out 1/4 inch thick and 8-10 inches in diameter on the flour or cornmeal dusted board. Poke a hole in center of each piece with your finger. Fry the bread rounds one at a time on each side until golden, (about one minute per side). Makes about 15. Serve hot, drizzled with honey or sprinkled with powdered sugar or cinnamon/sugar combination.

Clarice Carlson Orr

Knee Patches

3 eggs, beaten
3 teaspoons sugar
1/4 cup milk

1 tablespoon butter
1/2 teaspoon salt
Flour

Beat the eggs and add all other ingredients. Add flour to make a dough like noodles (very stiff). Roll out very thin and cut into squares. Fry in lard, stretching the dough before you drop it into the hot fat. Watch so that it doesn't get too brown—it only takes a minute. Sprinkle with powdered sugar if you wish.

Mrs. James Federnuitz
Submitted by her daughter, Mary Hubka

Clarice: Recently, I visited with Maxine Morrison, the wife of former Nebraska Governor Frank Morrison, who compiled the recipes for the Nebraska Centennial First Ladies' Cookbook *along with Catherine Hillegass. Mrs. Morrison and the cook at the Governor's Mansion tested some 100 recipes that were included in the cookbook. She remembers when they tried this recipe for Knee Patches. They followed the instructions and stretched the dough over the knees of their jeans before dropping it in the hot fat!*

"For everything there is a season,
and a time for every matter under heaven."

—Ecclesiastes 3:1

Everything under heaven has its season. There is a time of glory for everything. The time of triumph comes and it goes, leaving behind the memories.

This is true of many houses across the plains of South Dakota. They had their season. At one time they were new. Some man proudly planned and built that house and moved the family in with great excitement.

Those houses could tell many tales of the lives that were lived within the four walls. They could tell of christenings, graduation parties, new brides, birthday celebrations, Thanksgiving dinners, Christmas present openings, and all sorts of joyous occasions.

They could also tell of the flu epidemic, broken legs, pneumonia, cancer, and maybe even a shooting. They could tell of rain and wind and snow and hail they withstood.

I suppose those old houses knew of the nights spent walking with a fussy baby; secrets written in diaries hidden under the eaves; outgrown toys and clothing stashed in the attic; lizzards that lived in the cellar; cobs hauled in from the pig pen; and the furniture that came in new and was cast off as it wore out.

Old houses that now sit abandoned on farms could tell a lot of tales. Maybe they are trying to as they creak and groan. Maybe if we listened, oh, so carefully, we could get a message from the winds that blow through the broken windows and rustle the torn wallpaper.

Ecclesiastes 1:4 sums it up:
A generation goes, and a generation comes, but the earth remains forever.

—-Chrys Daniel
from *Patches*

BREAKFAST & COFFEE TIME

GOOD MORNING!
THIS IS GOD!
I will be handling all
of your problems today.
I will not need your help.
So, relax and have a great day.
—From God@Work

Coffee: The Great American Tradition

Americans drink more coffee than any other people in the world, and not just because they like the taste.

A cup of coffee, "Norwegian Geritol," in the morning starts the day for most Americans. Most adults rely on a cup of coffee to "get going" in the morning.

"Come on in for a cup of coffee" is the standard invitation. It is an invitation to sharing; sharing not only the coffee but the moment. Over the coffee cups people share interests, ideas, emotions, news, all sorts of things. Coffee is a gesture of friendship.

The phone rings. "I'm having coffee on…," invites the voice on the other end. Now that doesn't mean the hostess is merely making a cup of coffee on Tuesday of next week as it may sound. That invitation means PARTY.

When the hostess says, "I'm having coffee for…" it means a celebration. It usually honors a special guest with a shower, welcome, farewell, congratulations on a success, birthday, anniversary, visit from out of town, or any other legitimate excuse for a get-together.

"Come for coffee after…" is an invitation to prolong some event. Friends have gone to a movie, a play, a concert, or an athletic event. The excitement runs high and the conversation is going strong. Thus, the coffee invitation extends the joy for a longer time.

"There will be coffee after the meeting," is an advertisement of sorts. It gives added appeal to an event. It means there will be fellowship after the business.

Coffee is a reward for when the ironing is done, after the floor is scrubbed. Coffee is relaxing, soothing. It offers the drinker an excuse to sit and rest and relax.

Coffee is a beverage made by combining boiling water and little brown beans? Hardly! Coffee is an American institution—one of the nicest ones we have!

—Chrys Daniel
From *Gleanings*

Chrys' Country Kitchen Muffins

2 cups boiling water poured over 2 cups All-Bran

3 cups white sugar	1 cup butter or margarine
4 eggs	1 quart buttermilk
2 teaspoons salt	5 cups flour
5 teaspoons soda	4 cups bran flakes

Pour the boiling water over the all-bran in a five-quart ice cream pail and stir. I usually add the shortening at this time so it can melt nicely into the mixture. Let cool a bit. Add sugar, eggs, buttermilk, and salt, mixing well with electric mixer. Add the flour and then the soda, mixing well. Then stir in bran flakes, with or without raisins.

This mixture can be kept in the refrigerator for six weeks. Stir the mix and spoon into muffin tins (about half full) and bake for 15-20 minutes in a 350° oven.

Even though the CEO of this farm operation has retired, the home place is still considered the headquarters. The main shop is located on this farmstead. The younger women are gone most of the day, teaching in nearby towns, so the CEO's wife becomes the telephone operator and receptionist.

Cattle buyers, feed and seed representatives, insurance salesmen, loan officers, and neighbors stop by often to discuss business in what has become known as Chrys' Country Kitchen. Someone, somewhere, came up with a lifesaver for those winter days when assorted boots line the back door. Hot muffins are welcome by one and all.

Chrys Daniel
My "Adopted Sister"
Wentworth, South Dakota

Clarice: Many times I have parked my feet under Chrys and Bill's big oval table at the end of their Great Room I call Nordic Hall. And many are the times I have savored these muffins, piping hot. I know why Daniels have so many cattle buyers, feed and seed representatives, insurance salesmen, loan officers, and neighbors who just happen to stop by! If their olfactory radar doesn't detect Hohwieler's coffeecake or baking powder biscuits, it's these great muffins.

Ode to Mom

My mom, this recipe she gave me
To make and eat with glee.
I can mix up some batter to keep
In the refrigerator for many a week.
I can take some batter and bake a few
Or more if I'm feeding a crew.
I like to eat them day or night,
To have with a meal
Or as a snack, bite after bite.
I'm glad this recipe she shared.
She showed me she really cared.
I enjoy whipping up a big batch,
There is no other recipe or mom to match.

Sara Carlson Oxendine
My Niece
Frederick, Maryland

Clarice: Sara has learned baking and cooking from a master cook and baker—her mother, Violet Nesheim Carlson.

Raisin Bran Muffins

10 to 15 ounces Raisin Bran cereal
5 cups flour
3 cups sugar
2 teaspoons salt (optional)
5 teaspoons baking soda

Mix the above in a large bowl and add the following:

1 quart buttermilk
4 eggs, beaten
1 cup oil

Bake in muffin papers 15 minutes at 400°. Makes 5 dozen. Batter will keep in the refrigerator up to 2 months. Peaches, apples, etc., may be added to batter.

Clarice: The recipe for Raisin Bran muffins and The Muffin Lady's Muffins have exactly the same ingredients with a few exceptions. Sara's recipe called for a 10-ounce box of cereal and Nadyne's called for 15-ounces. In addition, Nadyne adds 1 teaspoon cinnamon and 1 teaspoon vanilla. Nadyne uses foil cupcake liners and the muffins don't stick to the paper.

The Muffin Lady's Muffins

I've been known as the Muffin Lady for many years, since I have been baking and delivering muffins to shut-ins at church, and friends at different holidays. My friends always enjoy the visit a well as the muffins. I have found it to be a very rewarding experience.

Nadyne Bauer
Lincoln, Nebraska

Mini Pecan Muffins

1 packed cup of brown sugar   1/2 cup flour
1 cup chopped pecans   2/3 cup oleo
2 eggs, beaten

Combine brown sugar, flour, and pecans and set aside. Combine butter and eggs, mix well and stir into flour mixture just until moistened.

Fill mini muffin pans 2/3 full (use liners). Bake at 350° for 20 minutes. Yields 3 dozen

Marge Jessee
Lincoln, Nebraska

Clarice: Marge is famous for providing tasty homemade tidbits. She is a gracious hostess and can always find a reason to have a party. Knowing she would be gone over my birthday, she planned a surprise dinner party a couple of weeks before my day. Marge is also a wonderful long distance grandmother. Marge provides emotional and spiritual nourishment along with her mouth-watering muffins.

Swedish Tea Ring
(This makes 2 large rings)

2 cups milk   2/3 cup sugar
2 teaspoons salt

Scald the milk and add sugar and salt. Cool to lukewarm and stir in 2 cakes of crumbled quick yeast.

Add 2 beaten eggs, 1/2 cup softened shortening or margarine, 3 cups flour, 1 tablespoon grated orange rind, 1/2 cup raisins. Mix well. Add 4 cups flour.

Mix and turn out on a floured board. Knead until smooth and satiny, but keep dough as soft as possible. Let rise until double, knead lightly, and let rise again until double.

Divide the dough in half. Roll half the dough until it's an oblong 9" X 18". Spread with 3 tablespoons softened butter or margarine; sprinkle with 1/2 cup sugar mixed with 2 teaspoons cinnamon. Roll up tightly, beginning at the wide side. Seal by pinching dough together and place sealed edge down on lightly greased baking sheet. Join the ends by sealing. With scissors, make cuts 2/3 of the way through, at one inch intervals. Turn each of those sections on its side. Cover. Let rise until almost double. Do this with the other half of dough, too. Bake at 375° for 25-30 minutes.

While still warm, frost with powdered sugar icing and decorate with candied fruits and nuts for Christmas or as desired.

My mother made 6 or 8 of these at Christmastime and gave one to each of her children to have on Christmas morning. Sometimes her neighbors got one too.

Marj Meyer
Lincoln, Nebraska

85

This is excellent for breakfast—especially if guests are coming. You can make it the day before and warm it before serving.

Helen Kunze
A Carlson Cousin
Huron, South Dakota

Clarice: I hardly knew Helen when we were growing up, but it's fun to know her now that we're all grown up! This recipe intrigued me so I tried it and found it a wonderful oatmeal coffee cake. I added some brown sugar and butter streusel topping to satisfy my sweet tooth.

Baked Oatmeal

4 cups old fashioned oats	1/2 teaspoon salt
1 1/2 cups milk	
1/2 cup brown sugar (dates or honey may be used instead)	
2 beaten eggs	1/2 cup melted butter
2 teaspoons baking powder	2 teaspoons cinnamon
1 large Granny Smith apple, peeled and chopped	
1/2 cup raisins	

Mix in order given. Bake in lightly sprayed 8 X 8 inch pan. Bake at 350º for 30-45 minutes for metal pan and 325º if using glass. Do not overbake.

I have had a joyous journey on this great planet earth; and some of that joy comes from having so many loving relatives, all of whom were good cooks. How could I miss with that combination? I think that good food is one of the celebrations of life.

Years ago, I was selected as Mrs. Arizona. One part of that contest was to submit your favorite recipe. This was my prize winning recipe. In fact, I published a cookbook from that contest since so many people have enjoyed this old recipe which originated in Hungary.

Gayle Edinger Harmon
Mesa, Arizona

Hungarian Coffee Cake

1 cup shortening (margarine or butter)	
1 cup brown sugar	1 cup white sugar
2 cups flour	2 eggs
1 teaspoon soda	1/2 teaspoon salt
1 cup sour cream	

Cream the shortening and sugar, add the flour, and crumble the two mixtures together. Set aside one cup of this mixture. Mix two eggs, soda, salt, and sour cream together. Combine the two mixtures and pour into a 9 X 12 cake pan or two layer pans. Sprinkle the top with the one cup you have set aside. Bake 9 X 12 pan 40 minutes at 350°, or layer pans, 30-35 minutes at 350°. This recipe stores for a week; it freezes well, too.

Clarice: I became reacquainted with Gayle and her husband, Jerry, when I went to my 50th high school reunion at Mitchell, South Dakota.

Overnight Crunchy Coffee Cake

2/3 cup margarine	1 cup white sugar
1/2 cup brown sugar	2 eggs
1 cup buttermilk	2 cups flour
1 teaspoon baking powder	1 teaspoon soda
1/2 teaspoon cinnamon	1/2 teaspoon salt

Cream together margarine and sugars; add the eggs one at a time and mix well after each addition. Sift dry ingredients together and add alternately with the buttermilk. Put into 9 X 13 inch pan.

Sprinkle with this topping:

1/2 cup brown sugar	1/4 cup walnut meats
1/4 teaspoon cinnamon	1/4 teaspoon nutmeg

Put in the refrigerator for 8 hours or overnight. Bake at 350° for 35 minutes.

Hohwieler Coffee Cake

2 cups flour	1 cup sugar
1 teaspoon baking powder	4 eggs
1 cup oil	1 can prepared pie filling

Mix dry ingredients in a bowl with electric hand mixer. Add eggs and oil. Put half of the batter in a 9 X 13 inch pan. Spread the pie filling evenly over the batter. Cover with the remaining dough, which is very thick. Bake 35 minutes in a 350° oven. Dribble powdered sugar over the top when warm, or drizzle a thin powdered sugar icing when slightly cooled, or serve with whipped cream topping depending on the occasion.

This has been served many times for coffee hour at New Home Lutheran Church.

Mildred Backlund
Mitchell, South Dakota

Clarice: Mildred is one of the great cooks who continues to furnish for coffees and church suppers at New Home, the church where I grew up.

Farmers are known for helping one another in good times when they need an extra hand to step in and take over chores when an accident or illness strikes. So it was that sons Dale and Dave went to help put up hay at the neighboring farm.

They came home with smiles on their faces and a challenge to their mother. "We had the best lunch. I don't know why you can't cook like the Hohwieler women," they commented.

So, I went right to the phone to see what neighbor Jan had made for them. She gave me this recipe that is so good. The very best part is that it can be stirred up from a few ingredients, easy to keep on hand, and can double as a bar or dessert as well as Hohwieler Coffee Cake.

Chrys Daniel
My "Adopted Sister"
Wentworth, South Dakota

My grandparents lived in Gradenhutten, Ohio. My grandma was the daughter of the Methodist minister, but she still married a Moravian! She obviously learned to bake the Moravian way. I have fond memories of sitting at her oilcloth-covered kitchen table eating Moravian sugar cake. My family lived about three hours from Gradenhutten, but Grandma always insisted we have something to eat before "that long ride home." The something to eat was usually Sugar Cake. Grandma lived to be 91 in spite of cooking with lard, eggs, and a lot of processed sugar! Her recipe lacks the exactness of today's recipes, but it seems to give the basics.

Lynn Nickol
Eagle, Nebraska

My sister and her husband were visiting us. Betty can tolerate only a small amount of milk and no whole wheat bread. I wanted to make something special for breakfast and thought of my recipe using white bread cubes, sausage, eggs, and milk. I had no white bread, but I had three left-over Pillsbury Grands biscuits, a carton of Egg Beaters, 1% milk and a package of frozen pre-cooked sausages. The result was delicious and we all said it was worthy of a repeat.

Marge Young
Lincoln, Nebraska

Moravian Sugar Cake

Put in a bowl: 1 cup mashed potatoes and 1 cup white sugar. Add 1 cake yeast dissolved in 1 cup warm water. Let rise until light. Then add 1 egg and 3/4 cup melted shortening and 1 teaspoon salt. Add about 3 cups flour and let it rise until quite light. Then divide it into portions, probably 3 or 4, and put it into greased pans (7 X 11 inch or round cake pans.) Smooth it out with hands. Cover. Let rise again until very light and you can make dents on the surface. Into each dent put a small lump of butter, some cinnamon, and plenty of light brown sugar. Sprinkle surface with granulated sugar. Bake at 375° about 20 minutes.

My grandma said, "Do not make the dough as stiff as for bread."

Breakfast Casserole
(Somewhat low cholesterol and low fat)

Spray an 8 X 6 X 2 inch Pyrex pan. Set oven to 350º.

Slice three Pillsbury Grands biscuits in half crosswise and place a single layer in bottom of pan. Place a package of frozen pre-cooked sausages on top of the biscuits. Mix a carton of Egg Beaters with one cup of milk and add salt and pepper. Pour this mixture gently over the top of the biscuits. Let stand about five minutes to let the liquid soak into the biscuits. Bake until puffy, perhaps 20-30 minutes.

This serves 4 small appetites.

Orange Butter Coffee Cake

1 packet Red Star Active Dry Yeast
    or 1 cake Red Star Compressed Yeast
1/4 cup warm water
1 cup sugar
1 teaspoon salt*
2 eggs
1/2 cup dairy sour cream
1/2 cup Land O'Lakes Butter, melted
1 3/4 to 3 cups Pillsbury's Best Flour
1 cup coconut, toasted
2 tablespoons grated orange rind

Soften yeast in warm water in mixing bowl. Stir in 1/4 cup sugar, salt, eggs, sour cream, and 6 tablespoons butter. Gradually add flour to form a stiff dough, beating well after each addition. For first additions of flour, use mixer on medium speed. Cover, let rise in warm place (85° to 90°) until light and doubled, about 2 hours.

Combine 3/4 cup sugar, 3/4 cup coconut, and orange rind. Knead dough on well-floured surface about 15 times. Roll out half of dough to a 12-inch circle. Brush with 1 tablespoon melted butter. Sprinkle with half of sugar-coconut mixture. Cut into 12 wedges. Roll up, starting with wide end and rolling to point. Repeat with remaining dough. Place rolls, point-side down, in 3 rows in a well-greased 13 X 9 inch pan. Cover; let rise in warm place until light and doubled, about 1 hour. Bake at 350° for 25 to 30 minutes until golden brown. Leave in pan. Pour Orange Glaze over hot coffee cake. Sprinkle with 1/4 cup coconut. Serve warm or cold.

* For use with Pillsbury's Best Self-Rising Flour, omit salt.

Orange Glaze

Combine in saucepan 3/4 cup sugar, 1/2 cup dairy sour cream, 2 tablespoons orange juice, and 1/4 cup Land O'Lakes Butter. Boil 3 minutes, stirring occasionally.

This recipe was the Best of Show for the 1990 New Mexico State Fair.

Jackie Sykes
Albuquerque, NM

Recipe for a Good Day

Start out with the basic ingredients of the family, mother and father. Add assorted children of various coloring, temperaments, and stages of growth. Mix well in the pasture by the lake. Allow them to mellow in the sun as they gather driftwood, polished stones and dried weeds. Sprinkle liberally with "Come here and see..." Spice with a foot race up the hill. This is an economical recipe that serves everyone adequately.

—Chrys Daniel
From *Patches*

My husband Mel makes pancakes for his grandchildren every time they come to visit. They always want to help. As tiny tots, their mother has always allowed them to sit on the kitchen counter and help her cook, and Grampa also lets them. He even lets them break the eggs (their mother does not) into the bowl.

Grampa has lots of help—Cole 4, Mady 2, and Jilli 6. What is that saying "Too many cooks spoil the broth?"—not in this case. Grampa makes many kinds of pancakes—bears, bunnies, dinosaurs, and Mickey Mouse. Sometimes you need a creative mind to figure out what it is. The kids really enjoy Grampa's pancakes.

Karen Pooley
A Carlson Cousin
Mitchell, South Dakota

Grampa's Pancakes

1 egg
1 1/4 cups buttermilk or soured milk
2 tablespoons vegetable oil   1 1/4 cups flour
1 tablespoon sugar   1 teaspoon baking powder
1/2 teaspoon soda   1/2 teaspoon salt

Blend egg, milk, and oil. Blend dry ingredients together. Add to liquid, batter will be lumpy. Grease heated griddle. Turn pancakes when puffed to brown other side. Makes 16 pancakes.

Old Fashioned Buttermilk Pancakes

1 egg, beaten
1 cup buttermilk
2 tablespoons vegetable oil
  (could be melted bacon grease)
1 cup flour
1 teaspoon baking powder
1/2 teaspoon baking soda
1/2 teaspoon salt
1 tablespoon sugar

Blend beaten egg, buttermilk and vegetable oil together. Combine other ingredients and sugar; add to buttermilk mixture, blending only to combine ingredients. Drop mixture by spoonfuls onto a lightly buttered preheated griddle or skillet. Cook until bubbly, turn and brown other side. Yield 10 4-inch cakes.

My childhood was spent in Holt County, Nebraska. We lived in the country 25 miles from the nearest town. Our home was an original homestead and is still in the family. I was one of three girls in the family and being the youngest I got to experience a number of wonderful opportunities. My childhood was a happy one and many times I think of the beautiful times we had on the ranch. Helping my Dad drive cattle and working with my horses was probably the highlight of growing up! As far as food is concerned, my mother did a great deal of cooking to provide for the men who helped my Dad operate the ranch. Probably the food I remember most were the buttermilk pancakes.

As was the custom, in the old days, the men folk always slipped outside early to do the chores. Whether it was milking the cows, saddling the horses, or harnessing the work horses; the men's work started early. We three girls got to sleep in. Mother prepared a hearty breakfast for the men before they left for the fields. I can still hear her beating the batter for the buttermilk pancakes. Not long afterwards you could hear the horse and buggy going by the window of our bedroom, on their way to the hay field. This is the recipe I am sure my Mother used to mix up those pancakes so many times. I hope you will try them.

Betty Stewart
Lincoln, Nebraska

Clarice: Betty is in her 70s and has lived in the city for most of her life. However, since the ranch remains in the family, she often loads up her horse, Peanuts, and goes back home to ride. I guess you can take the girl away from ranch life, but you can't take ranch life out of the girl.

91

This is one of my favorite Holiday Breakfasts. We could come to the table and eat whenever we were ready. That might be after opening Christmas gifts, finding our Easter eggs, going out early on July 4th to watch Dad set off a stick of dynamite, or whenever else. Yes, he actually set off a stick of dynamite—way out in the pasture, away from buildings or animals. We would watch it blow up a lot of dirt, and of course it woke up neighbors all around us! They weren't upset; they just expected Fred to wake them up on that day, and sometimes some of them would come over for Mom's Baked Omelet.

Early on, Mom made her own cheese soup and then she didn't need the can of milk because the soup already had that. And when some of us had time, she would use fresh mushrooms we had gathered. But today, it is easier to just buy a can of mushrooms and a can of cheese soup. This is a really good recipe and there is a lot of room for changes and additions. Today, it is served at many brunches and breakfasts.

Amy M. Franklin
Lincoln, Nebraska

Baked Omelet

Fry and drain some bacon (however much you want to use)
Melt 1 stick (1/4 pound of margarine) in a 9 X 13 pan
Add 8 slices of bread, cubed (can be white or whole wheat)
Mix:

5 beaten eggs	2 cups milk
1 1/2 cups diced ham	Crumbled bacon
Pepper to taste	

Pour over the bread cubes.
Add the following that is mixed together:

1 can mushrooms	1 can cheese soup
1 can of milk (fill the empty cheese soup can with milk)	

Pour over the mixture in the pan. Bake uncovered at 350° for 1 hour.

Betty's Quiche

1 9 inch deep dish pie crust
1 cup grated Swiss cheese
1 can cleaned and deveined small shrimp
1 can mushroom stems and pieces, drained
1/2 cup broccoli cuts, thawed and drained
2 tablespoons chopped green onions
3 eggs, lightly beaten
1 cup half & half—or evaporated milk
1/2 teaspoon salt
1/2 teaspoon lemon juice
1/4 teaspoon dry mustard
Dash of allspice
1/4 cup sliced almonds, toasted

Prepare pie crust or use premade one. Sprinkle cheese over bottom of pie shell. Add shrimp, broccoli, and green onion. Combine eggs, half & half, salt, lemon juice, mustard, and allspice. Pour over shrimp, broccoli, and green onions. Top with more cheese and add sliced almonds. Bake at 375° for 45-60 minutes or until knife inserted in the center comes out clean. Serve with fruit and rolls.

Betty Stewart
Lincoln, Nebraska

STAFF
OF LIFE

Bread is the staff of life,
without which we do not live,
but, if bread is all we get,
we do not live at all.

——From an old cookbook

Anna Sofia's Tunnråbröd—Unleavened Thin Bread

Stone Ground Flour, probably rye and barley		Water
A little salt	A little sugar	A little shortening

We don't know the ingredients and we don't know how to make it. But here is the story of my Great-Great Grandmother Anna Sofia and how she supported her family.

Anna Sofia's Cottage Industry: Making and Marketing Tunnråbröd

My Swedish Great-Great-Grandmother, Anna Sofia, was born in 1828 in Härlöv, Småland, Sweden. Her husband sailed to America and died, leaving her with three children, Ida, Anna Christina, and Carl. Her father, Carl Swenson, bought a little house next to his and fixed it up for her and her family. Work in the hayfields was too hard; she tried unsuccessfully to have a little store and she couldn't earn a living making matchboxes. Her next venture was making tunnråbröd, a thin unleavened bread, and over the years she developed a considerable trade.

Christina, Mom's first cousin, has helped define tunnråbröd. *Tunn* is thin, *rå* is fresh, and *bröd* is bread. So it is thin, fresh bread. If it is tunnbrod, without the *rå* denoting freshness, it is a little like hard tack or Ry-Krisp. (Grandma Edna Carlson loved Ry-Krisp.) We think that it is the Swedish cousin of Norwegian lefse, somewhat like a flour tortilla (a wrap when fresh and a shell when dry) of the Southwest, or pita bread of the

Middle East. Perhaps tunnbrod is like the chapati, (without the spices) I experienced in Bombay as an AFS student in India. It is an unleavened dough that is shaped into a ball, flattened and baked in an oven.

I've read the story in the writings of my grandmother's sister Hilda and her brother Carl—the father of Cousin Christina. Anna Sofia baked for one or two days and the next day walked nine miles to the town of Växjö. She often started at two in the morning and arrived at five-thirty. Fru Hammarquist helped her secure orders from other towns. She shipped the tunnbröd in wooden boxes which were then returned for refilling. Sometimes she got a ride home, but more often she had to walk the long, difficult way. One night she fell and hurt her knee on a stone and "screamed all night so no one else could sleep." The next morning her daughter, Anna Christina, went to Munsagård, another farm, to get help. Once, while chopping kindling to bake the tunnråbröd, a piece of wood flew up and hit her over the eye, leaving a permanent scar.

In 1886, when she got too old to bake and sell tunnbröd, she went to America, (Mitchell, South Dakota) with her daughter, Anna Christina, to live with her brother, John, and her daughter, Ida.

Mom, Christina, and I went to Sweden in 1994. It was thrilling and meaningful to see the land where my forebears lived and worked; to be in the churches and stand by the ancient fonts where my ancestors were baptized was touching. I was moved to see the cottage where Anna Sofia and her three children lived. The little yellow house with white gingerbread trim still stands on the shores of Lake Furen, surrounded by aspen and fir trees. The ground is mossy with colorful mushrooms and tiny wildflowers everywhere. You might expect a tomten, troll, or gnome to peek out from behind a rock.

I peeked through the white lace curtains and saw the spis, kitchen stove or fireplace, where Anna Sofia made the tunnråbröd. We wandered around behind the house and saw a covered well, just like the well of the "Old Oaken Bucket" where Anna Sofia drew her water. At the bank of the lake was an old fishing boat—not hardly one that my grandmothers used.

That tranquil scene gave me a sense of the strong lineage I have from my foremothers. This heritage journey will long stay in my memory.

Becky Reisinger
My Daughter
Seward, Nebraska

Clarice: A postscript to Becky's story is that, after we saw Anna Sofia's charming cottage, we went to Växjö for supper. We stopped at a "Quick and Fast Drive-In" (that really was the name of it). To our surprise, "tunnråbröd" was on the menu, so of course we ordered it. The "cook" took what appeared to be a soft, thin tortilla shell and rolled it into a cone—the size of a waffle ice cream cone. He plunked in a blob of mashed potatoes and stuck a hot dog in the middle and asked, "Ketchup or mustard?" As I recall, I chose ketchup. I doubt that Anna Sofia ever had a hot dog in her tunnråbröd; we learned that the culture of food changes through the years, even in the Old Country.

Almost Like Grandma Rosenquist's Heavy Rye Bread

Grandma Anna Christina's rye bread still lingers in my memory as the best tasting bread of my childhood. For several years I have searched for her recipe. I talked with my brother Loren about it and his answer was, "I never cared for Grandma's bread; it was too heavy."

After several tries and juggling of ingredients, this is close to satisfying my grown-up taste buds. Cousin Irene's recipe for Swedish Rye Bread has a glaze put on the top of the bread before baking and again just before the loaves are done. The glaze is a syrup of 1 teaspoon of molasses and 2 teaspoons hot water. That sounds like a little trick Grandma Rosenquist may have used.

Clarice Carlson Orr

3 cups warm water
4 packages dry yeast
1/2 cup molasses
2/3 cup brown sugar
1 tablespoon salt
1 teaspoon anise seed, crushed
5 cups rye flour
2 tablespoons grated fresh orange rind
   or 1 tablespoon dried orange peel
4 tablespoons oil
5 to 6 cups white flour

Dissolve dry yeast in warm water. Stir in molasses and sugar. Mix remaining ingredients as listed; you may use a mixer with dough hooks or add last 4 or 5 cups of flour by kneading it in. Let rise for two hours, punch down, and shape into 4 loaves. Let rise until doubled. Bake at 375° for 30-40 minutes or until the center makes a hollow sound when tapped.

Kay Orr's Swedish Rye Bread

Combine:

4 cups rye flour	4 cups hot water
1 cup sorghum	2/3 cup brown sugar
1 tablespoon salt	4 tablespoons shortening
Plus 7 cups white flour later	

Soften:
4 tablespoons dry yeast in 1/2 cup water

Mix all of the above together to make a "sponge." Put in warm place and let rise for 1 hour. Knead in 7 cups of white flour. Divide dough into four loaves and let rise until double. Bake at 350-375° about 40 minutes.

Clarice: While his wife Kay was Governor, Bill Orr compiled the First Gentleman's Cookbook *published in 1989, the proceeds from the sale of which were used to establish the Governor's Mansion Restoration Foundation, a permanent, non-profit endowment for future restoration and redecoration of the State of Nebraska's official residence in Lincoln, Nebraska. In the summer of 1998, First Lady Diane Nelson opened the Mansion to the public to view the newly redecorated residence. Incidentally, Bill and Kay Orr are not relatives of ours.*

This recipe has been made for generations of Swedes in Kay's family. It was given to her by her Grandmother Skoglund. While I was in college, Kay's mother would send one or two loaves of the bread to me at the Fraternity where I lived. It was so good that the entire Fraternity became fond of it. Therefore, I was lucky to get one or two slices to toast. With Kay and her mother, Sadie, tempting me with Swedish Rye Bread, I didn't stand a chance. Later, the only trouble with Kay being Governor was she didn't have time to make rye bread often enough.

William D. Orr
Nebraska's First Gentleman
1986-1990
Lincoln, Nebraska

Did you know sliced bread was first introduced in 1928?

It seems to me that my mother made this wonderful rye bread every Saturday when I was a child. I also remember eating a slice of it topped with scrambled eggs for a quick Saturday night supper before we went to town on summer nights. But when I spoke of that to my sister, she said, "I don't remember ever doing that!" Perhaps we had it once and I liked it so well that it stays in my memory as something we always did.

When my mother's health began to fail, I learned to make rye bread under her supervision and found it very hard work! I still do, but I love to make it, at least at Christmastime. I can still hear her telling me things like, "You can just feel when you have enough flour." There are many slightly different recipes for rye bread and they're all good. But this one is the best because it reminds me of my mother.

Marleen Johnson
Lincoln, Nebraska

Clarice: Cousin Joan found this recipe in her mother's files. When Aunt Lillie and her family moved to the Bitteroot Valley in Montana, she took along many recipes from old neighbors and relatives from South Dakota.

Mother Johnson's Swedish Rye Bread

2/3 cup molasses
2 1/2 cups water
2/3 cup brown sugar
1 tablespoon anise seed
1 teaspoon salt
2 tablespoons grated orange rind
2 tablespoons lard
2 tablespoons caraway seed (optional)
4 cups rye flour (approximately)
7 cups white flour (approximately)
1 package dry yeast

Boil the first 7 ingredients 5 minutes (with anise seed in a cheesecloth bag) Remove anise, add caraway seed if using. Add yeast dissolved in a little warm water. Stir in flour, a cup at a time, rye and white alternately, beating well after each addition. When no more can be stirred in, turn out and knead in more flour. Stop adding flour when dough pulls away from itself in layers. Knead thoroughly. Let rise until double. Form into loaves and brush tops of loaves with beaten egg white. Let rise again. Bake at 400° for 10 minutes and 350 for 50 minutes. Brush tops of loaves with butter.

Mrs. Backlund's Graham Bread

A pinch of ginger activates the yeast

In a bowl, put 1/3 cup sugar, 3 cups lukewarm water. Sprinkle 2 packages of yeast over the top.

Do not stir. Add 3 teaspoons salt, 1/4 cup shortening, 1/4 cup molasses, 3 handsful of graham flour, 1 handful of wheat germ, about 3 pints of white flour. Knead until non-sticky. Place your hand on the dough and, if it sticks after counting to 30, it needs more flour. Let it rise. Shape into 3 loaves and let rise again. Bake 3/4 hour at 375° or 350°.

Joan Martin
A Rosenquist Cousin
Concord, California

Mae's Brown Bread

4 cups water
1/2 cup brown sugar
1/2 cup molasses
10 to 12 cups white flour
1 cup graham flour

1/2 cup lard or shortening
1 tablespoon salt
3/4 cup uncooked oatmeal
2 packages dry yeast

Bring to a boil the water, lard, sugar, salt, and molasses. Remove from heat, add the oatmeal. Set aside to cool to lukewarm. In mixer bowl, combine 1 cup white flour, yeast, and 1 cup graham flour. Add liquid and beat for 2 minutes at medium speed of mixer. Add 2 cups white flour and beat about 1 minute. Transfer this mixture to a larger mixing bowl and stir in enough white flour to make a dough stiff enough to handle with your hands. Turn onto floured board and knead until smooth and elastic, adding remaining flour if needed. Place in greased bowl, turning once to grease top. Cover and let rise in warm place until double. Punch down. Let dough rest for 10 minutes. Divide dough into 5 equal portions, shape into loaves, and place in greased pans, 8 X 5 X 2 inches. Let rise until double. Bake at 350° about 35 minutes until golden brown. Don't overbake. Turn out of pans to cool on wire racks. Brush tops with melted butter, if desired.

My recipe for Mae's Brown Bread is an old recipe. My husband Glenn's aunt gave this recipe to me a LONG time ago when I first began to bake bread from scratch. It has earned me blue ribbons at the County Fair every time I enter it!!

When I took care of Kaleb, he always wanted to "help" in the kitchen. The bread goes over very well with that family. Now that they have moved to Indiana, I bake it whenever we go to visit them.

Joy Hagen
Webster, South Dakota

Clarice: If you stay at the Hagen's Lakeside Farm Bed and Breakfast, you may find Mae's Brown Bread on the table!

As we trudged through the snow and ice on our way to my parents' home, we reflected on the crippling ice storm we had experienced. It was 1948, and the worst ice storm in a decade had hit southern Oklahoma. Power lines were down, trees were broken and hanging low, water pipes were frozen, the town businesses had shut down, no school—everything had come to a standstill. My husband and our four-year-old daughter, Kaye, and I were moving to my parents' home for a few days because our little home in Vet Village was very cold.

Through the five days that followed, we enjoyed a wonderful family time—eating and playing cards by candlelight or a kerosene lamp. Bathrooms were a bit of a problem, but my father and my husband dutifully brought in snow and ice and melted it; then used it to flush. When we ran out of bread, my mother rose to the occasion and made delicious homemade rolls. (Fortunately, our gas stoves were working.)

Many years have passed, but I still remember our "fun ice storm."

Marjory Jessee
Lincoln, Nebraska

Mother French's Wonder Rolls

1 cup cool water	2 packages dry yeast
1 cup Crisco	2/3 to 3/4 cup sugar
1 and 1/2 teaspoons salt	1 cup boiling water
2 eggs, beaten	6 cups unsifted flour

Crumble yeast into cool water with 1 teaspoon of sugar. Let stand at least 5 minutes. Put sugar, shortening, and salt in large bowl and add boiling water. Stir until shortening is dissolved. When that mixture is cool (be sure), add beaten eggs and yeast. Add flour, 2 cups at a time, mixing well each time.

Cover tightly and refrigerate at once. Let stand at least 6 hours in refrigerator before baking. This will keep from 7 to 10 days. To bake: Take from refrigerator 3 hours before baking. Roll out a piece the size and shape of a pie.* Spread soft butter on top and cut into pie shaped pieces. Starting at the outer edge (the wide side of the piece) roll up...with the butter on the inside. Let rise 3 hours and bake at 400° for 10-12 minutes. (Watch the oven, as the time varies.)

*Note: If dough is too thin, or sticky, sprinkle a small amount of flour on wax paper and roll out the dough.

Clarice: Marge has brought these feather-light rolls to our Ladies' Potlucks and they are WONDERful.

Sweet Roll Dough in a Bread Machine

1 cup milk, warmed a bit
1/2 cup butter or margarine, cut up
1/3 cup sugar
2 large eggs, lightly beaten
3/4 teaspoon salt
4 cups white bread flour (or 3 cups white and 1 cup wheat)
2 teaspoons rapid-rise yeast.

Put the ingredients in the bread machine bucket in the order that your particular machine requires. Use the dough setting for raising. When completed (usually 1 1/2 hours), remove dough, squeeze to remove air bubbles and shape as desired on two baking sheets. Cover with towels, raise about 20 minutes in a warm (not hot) place. Bake in a pre-heated 375° oven until a golden brown. Remove from pan to a cooling rack and you'll have 20-24 rolls ready to eat or frost.

In her small kitchen on a ranch in northern Nebraska, my future mother-in-law shared with me her recipe and method of making dinner or sweet rolls. Over the years, this recipe has helped me turn out MANY dozens of rolls to feed a large, growing family. Today, a bread machine has taken over the mixing operation, using almost the same recipe as originally given to me by Clara Lind.

Janet Harms
Lincoln, Nebraska

Uncle Ralph's Rolled Oat Muffins

Soak together for 1 hour:
    1 cup rolled oats
    1 cup buttermilk
Mix together thoroughly:
    1/2 cup soft shortening (part butter)
    1 egg
    1/2 cup brown sugar
Sift together:
    1 cup flour
    1/2 teaspoon soda
    1 teaspoon baking powder
    1 teaspoon salt

Stir in alternately with oat-buttermilk mixture. Bake at 400° for 20 to 25 minutes. Yields 12 medium-sized muffins.

I remember Mom talking about her Uncle Ralph's muffins. He liked to bake them for the men's meetings at church. I don't make them very often, but I'm glad we still have the recipe to pass on.

Linda Dageforde

One of my early dates with the man who was to become my husband was a late fall family supper on the farm. I was pleased, thinking it meant I met the approval of his parents.

Soon after the meal, I learned the true reason—they needed help "catching chickens." The pullets that had been running free through the summer needed to be rounded up and put in the chicken house before the weather turned bad.

The menfolk reached into the trees, grabbing the protesting birds by their feet, handing them down. The rest of us carried these flapping, clawing, squawking creatures to their new home. That night nearly ended the romance.

Before that chore could be completed, most of the "old hens" of the preceding season had to be reallocated to make room for the pullets in the chicken house. Some were sold for a pittance on the market, and others were canned for winter meals. Dressed, cleaned, and cut up, the parts were put in quart fruit jars and processed in the pressure cooker.

There's nothing handier than a jar of chicken that can be quickly opened, the meat stripped from the bones, immediately ready for a variety of hot dishes. And so creamed chicken on biscuits became my staple.

We had a student pastor who often managed to stop by our house about suppertime. While he and friend husband discussed the latest concern of the congregation, I would slip down to the basement for my coveted chicken. As it heated, I stirred up a batch of baking powder biscuits and filled in with whatever I was planning for the family. He probably thought that was all I knew how to make. But he kept on coming until he finished his pastorate here.

Though I do not can chickens anymore, I have kept the biscuit recipe close at hand because it is the only thing in the world I can make better than my mother-in-law, Agnes Daniel, one of the great cooks of the Century.

Fresh, hot bread of any kind can make a simple meal into something special. Canned stew over these biscuits makes a quick, satisfying main course. They are also good buttered and topped with jelly.

Chrys Daniel,
My "Adopted Sister"
Wentworth, South Dakota

Baking Powder Biscuits

2 cups flour	4 teaspoons baking powder
1 teaspoon salt	2 teaspoons sugar
1/2 teaspoon cream of tartar	1/2 cup shortening
1 slight cup milk	

Mix dry ingredients together in a bowl. Cut in shortening until coarsely crumbled. Stir in milk. Turn out on lightly floured surface and knead about 10 times. Cut into rounds and bake for 10 to 12 minutes in a 450° oven.

(If you use butter for shortening and add another teaspoon of sugar, you have shortcake—'swonderful served warm with strawberries or rhubarb sauce with half and half as "pour cream" over the top!)

Grandma's Twelve Fluffy Biscuits

3 cups flour
4 tablespoons sugar
1 egg

4 teaspoons baking powder
1 cup milk

Mix with a fork. Knead a little. Pat out about 3/4 inch thick on counter surface or cutting board. Cut with biscuit cutter or use an empty, clean soup can for a cutter. You can also cut the biscuits with a knife. Put on baking sheet and bake at 350° for 12 to 15 minutes.

I remember so well when I was a child going to my grandmother's house. At that time, it was a long trip. My dad checked the car to be sure it had enough water, gas, oil, and air in the tires. We would leave early in the morning and get to Grandma's about 11 A.M.

My grandmother usually had hot baking powder biscuits with fresh home-churned butter and syrup and sometimes sidepork for breakfast. She mixed the biscuits, then baked them in her big, black oven. She served them piping hot with the fresh butter that she kept in a crock in a bucket that hung in the well. Just the thought of these big, fluffy, hot biscuits dripping with butter and syrup would get any hungry child or grownup to the table pronto to relish these treats.

Mother was a wonderful Southern lady who raised her own five children by herself after her husband was killed in an accident. She picked cotton by hand to get food for the table. After she moved back to Nebraska, she also took care of her three grandchildren when their mother died at childbirth. She is gone now, but I'll never forget her and her biscuits.

Irene Essink
Lincoln, Nebraska

Aunt Nellie's Cornbread

1 cup yellow cornmeal
5 tablespoons sugar
1 egg
1 teaspoon soda
3 teaspoons melted shortening

1 cup flour
1/4 teaspoon salt
1 cup sour milk
1 teaspoon baking powder

Mix and beat 3 minutes. Pour into well-greased pan (8 X 8). Bake at 350° for 25 minutes.

One of my favorite meals when I was growing up was ham and beans served with this delicious cornbread. We always put the beans and ham on top of the cornbread and generously covered it with bottled chili sauce.

When my grandma died and Mom and her 3 sisters took turns making meals for my grandpa, this was a favorite of his, too.

Linda Dageforde

103

Serve this in the dish it was baked in, spooning it onto the dinner plates. This should be eaten with a dinner fork and can be used as a substitute for potatoes or pasta. Many enjoy a small amount of butter on it. Originally served in the South, it became a favorite of my New England-born mother and she served it often in her home in Illinois. In Nebraska, we enjoy it with roast pork, shrimp, or fried chicken dinners.

Cynthia Pemberton
Lincoln, Nebraska

Crusty Spoon Bread

2 tablespoons butter or oleo
1/2 cup yellow cornmeal
1/4 cup flour plus 1 teaspoon baking powder
1 tablespoon sugar plus 1/2 teaspoon salt
1 large egg or 2 small
1 3/4 cup milk

Put butter in an 8 X 8 pan or medium-size casserole. Heat this in 375° oven while you mix the batter. In a bowl, combine cornmeal, flour, sugar, salt, baking powder. In a small bowl, combine beaten egg and 1 cup of the milk. Add this mixture to blended dry ingredients. Mix quickly. Pour batter into pan with hot melted butter. Pour remaining 3/4 cup milk over the top. Bake at 375° for 50 minutes. Serve at once. Yield 4-6 servings.

As a family, we have moved 17 times. This is a recipe from a neighbor in Okemos, Michigan. It was her mother's, who was a farmer's wife. I bake it in double batches in half-size loaf pans, topped with pecan halves. I have welcomed new neighbors with a gift of this wherever we have lived. My family's favorite sweet bread, it freezes well. Let it ripen in the refrigerator a few days before serving.

Beryl Boerner
Lincoln, Nebraska

Clarice: It will keep if you can hide it until the baking fragrance dissipates. It is moist and it toasts well.

Polly's Yummy Banana Bread

1 cup crushed bananas
1 cup granulated sugar
1/2 cup shortening (1/2 butter and 1/2 margarine)
2 eggs beaten
1/2 teaspoon soda
1/2 teaspoon baking powder
1 3/4 cups flour
1 cup nutmeats, chopped

Cream sugar and shortening. Measure dry ingredients together and alternately add crushed bananas. Add nuts, chopped coarsely, and add eggs last. Bake in a regular loaf pan that has been greased and sugared. Bake at 350° for 60 minutes.

Banana Oatmeal Bread
(low fat, low cholesterol)

1 cup brown sugar
7 tablespoons vegetable oil
2 large egg whites plus1 large egg
1 1/3 cups mashed banana (about 2 large)
1 cup regular oatmeal   1/2 cup fat-free milk
2 cups all-purpose flour   1 tablespoon baking powder
1/2 teaspoon baking soda   1/2 teaspoon salt
Cooking spray

Combine sugar, oil, egg whites, and egg and beat well with a mixer. Add banana, oats, and milk to the sugar mixture, beating well. Combine flour, baking powder, baking soda, salt, and cinnamon; mix dry ingredients and add to the sugar mixture, beating just until well moistened. Spoon batter into a 9 X 5 inch loaf pan or 2 mini-loaf pans coated with cooking spray. Bake at 350° for 1 hour and 10 minutes in the larger pan or 45 minutes in the mini-pans, or until a toothpick inserted in the middle comes out clean. Cool ten minutes before removing from the pan.

I found this recipe in a magazine and adapted it to my tastes. I've always loved oatmeal bread and to combine it with bananas in a healthy recipe makes it all the better. All grandchildren are bound to like this treat, even health conscious sports-minded teens. The oatmeal will help to fill them up.

Clarice Carlson Orr

Sanka Decaffeinated Coffee was first introduced in 1923.

People Still Neighbor

We often hear the complaint that people don't "neighbor" like they used to. This is true in some ways. We don't load all the kids in the car and go to the neighbors for a visit with their family like we used to when I was a kid...Although we don't play cards or dominoes with neighbors like folks used to in the olden days, I think rural folks still "neighbor" in the true sense of the word...

If you have need of a neighbor, he or she is there. And if a neighbor is in a bind, you go there to help. Neighbors always show up with food in hand when there is sickness or death in a family...They will drop anything to help out in case of an emergency such as a fire or accident.

Neighbors still "send the boy over" to finish up a field if you've had a breakdown and it looks like rain.

They will come over and sympathize if you get more hail or the wind blew harder at your place. They always seem to have time to help get the livestock back in after it has gotten out...

Neighbors in the country still share. If you need something for a party, your neighbor will give or loan it even if she hasn't been invited. Folding chairs, coffee pots, lace tablecloths, snack trays, and rose bowls are carted around the neighborhood so often it is hard to establish original ownership.

Neighbors watch neighbors—not just to be nosy. They watch for lights and unusual activity. If the neighboring farmer hasn't been out to do his chores at the usual time, it is a pretty good sign that he or someone in the family is sick. The good neighbor checks in to see if he can be of any help.

Though we do not socialize with our neighbors as much as in the past, we still "neighbor" with one another when there is need for a neighbor.

—Chrys Daniel
from *Prairie Panorama*, 1988

SUNDAY DINNER

*Pray as if everything
depended on God
and work as if everything
depended on you.*
—Cardinal Francis J. Spellman

Company Roast Beef and Gravy

When my family is coming for Sunday Dinner, I shop for a 6 to 7 pound piece of lean boneless beef—preferably a rolled rump roast, eye or heel of round, sometimes called "watermelon cut," or in San Luis Obispo County, California they call this Tri Tip. These cuts are boneless, easy to slice when cooked, and there's no waste. (I love a standing rib roast, too, but that's another celebration. For everyday, I might use a cheaper blade cut of meat with a big bone.)

Season the meat rubbing the outside with salt and coarse pepper and brown well in a little hot oil in a Dutch oven or heavy stew kettle that can go into the oven. This initial browning, without any water, is what makes the good brown drippings for gravy. I like to put a bay leaf and several onion slices on top of the meat. (Mom taught me to use the bay leaf; it makes the meat slightly sweet.) Put the covered kettle in the oven at 350°.

Peel 5 or 6 large carrots and cut each in 2 or 3 pieces and put around the roast. When the meat gets brown and needs moisture, add a little water and continue cooking in the oven until it's very tender, smells heavenly, and the family is nearly ready to eat.

To make the gravy, take the roast and vegetables out and put on a pan or platter keeping it near the warm oven. Put the Dutch oven on the stove top burner and add about 2 cups of water. Heat while scraping the brown from the sides into the pan. In a small mixing bowl add 1/2 to 1 cup tap water to 1/2 to 3/4 cup flour, stirring to make a smooth paste and adding a little more water until it's pourable. Add some of the hot liquid drippings from the roasting pan to the flour and water mixture, stirring to keep it smooth and ending by pouring the drippings/flour mixture into the pan on the stove, still stirring to keep it smooth. Let the mixture bubble until it is of the consistency you like, adding more water or flour. Pour into the gravy boat.

Carve the roast and place the carrots around the meat on the same platter. Meanwhile, someone has mashed the potatoes and put a heaping glob of butter or margarine on top. Everyone helps carry the food to the table and is seated.

When my family comes to my house, I like to use my best china, crystal, silver, some kind of a centerpiece, cloth napkins, and my lace tablecloth—they wash like a dream and never need ironing. It seems as though the children are better behaved—all of us for that matter—when we sit down to a pretty table. No one eats until we've asked the blessing. Sometimes I pray an old prayer in Swedish and then in English. Sometimes I ask a son-in-law to pray. Sometimes we hold hands around the table and sometimes we don't. After the Amen, hands reach for the roast beef platter and vegetable bowls and the conversation flows, only to be interrupted by someone going back to the kitchen for refills.

We have a wonderful tradition that the women prepare the food and the men clean up afterwards. When the work is done, we move on to the ritual battle of the guys against the gals playing Trivial Pursuit.

Recently, my Grandma Orr stayed for two weeks on the farm with my brother and me. I thought the only reason we needed her was to drive us back and forth to school. She tried really hard to have food ready for us, but meals were usually squashed in between track and practices after school, concerts, and other events at night. One night we were home and Grandma treated us to the best roast beef dinner ever! I didn't know roast beef could taste so good and her mashed potatoes were even better than Mom's. Thanks, Grandma, and I want you to put your recipe in the book so Mom will always have it.

Patrick Reisinger
My Grandson
Seward, Nebraska

Clarice: I didn't know my roast beef was such a hit that night. I do know that a home cooked meal is a gift for my grandkids and their parents who live their lives on the run. Perhaps I add a bit of calm and respite—a lull in their hectic activity—with my slower pace. I must always remember the Roast Beef Phenomenon.

Cuzzin Elaine Stack has a tip on how to make lumpless gravy. She says to add a pinch of salt to the flour before mixing it with the water.

Nebraska Minute Steaks

Dredge minute steaks in flour and brown in oil. Add salt and pepper to taste and add 1 cup water. Then, layer the steaks with mushroom soup, chopped onions and canned mushrooms in an oven-safe skillet such as an old-fashioned iron skillet. Cover and bake at 350° for 1 1/2 hours, but it can wait for you. The longer it is in the oven, the more tender it gets. When ready to eat, put the meat on a platter and a wonderful gravy is already made for you in the bottom of the skillet.

This is Grandma Demerath's recipe for the very best Minute Steak. She always fixes it on Sundays when we visit. She puts carrots and potatoes in with the steak before we go to church and it smells so good when we come home. My uncles on the farm butcher their own beef and pork and Grandma has access to that wonderful Nebraska-grown meat in her deep freeze.

John Orr III
My Grandson
Columbus, OH

Clarice: Marguerite Demerath and I frequently are together for special occasions like graduations and weddings at the family home of our mutual three grandsons. Marguerite makes everyone happy when she fixes this great Minute Steak.

This recipe is from a friend in Iowa where I formerly lived. After moving to Maryland, the church women began making and serving it to the Senior Fellowship group at church. Everyone enjoyed eating it so much the seniors wanted to buy the leftover ham loaves. We decided to have an annual Ham Loaf Sale each spring. Last year, we made over 300 pounds of ham loaves to sell.

Violet Nesheim Carlson
My Sister-in-law
Williamsport, Maryland

Ham Loaf

1 pound ground smoked pork	3/4 pound ground pork
3/4 cup cracker crumbs	2 eggs
1/2 cup milk	1/8 teaspoon pepper

Mix all together and bake at 350° for 1 hour.

Topping (if desired)

3/4 cup brown sugar
1 1/2 teaspoon prepared mustard
1/4 cup water
1/4 cup vinegar

Heat to boiling and cook 10 minutes. Pour over meat. Bake for 30 minutes more.

Clarice: Violet is one of the best cooks I know. She is the longtime overseer/director of the kitchen at Trinity Lutheran Church in Hagerstown. Many years ago my brother Paul had five heart-by-passes. Violet creatively revised their eating patterns to help him enjoy several more years.

This is the only kind of dressing we had when I was growing up. I did not know about other kinds of dressing until I went away to college. The quantities are just guesses because I never have measured any of the ingredients when I have made the dressing.

Marie E. Knickrehm
Lincoln, Nebraska

Clarice: Marie gained much experience in being resourceful when she was the dietician responsible for feeding the men on a hospital ship in the South Pacific during World War II.

Dried Fruit Dressing for Turkey (or other poultry)

13 pound turkey

6 cups toasted dry bread cubes
Any combination of dried fruit, such as:

1 cup prunes	1/2 cup apricots
1/2 cup apples	1/4 cup Muscat raisins
1/3 cup dried peaches and pears	

Toast the bread cubes in a small amount of fat in a heavy skillet. Add the dried fruit and some water; cover to steam the fruit. Add water as necessary. When the fruit is rehydrated add to the bread cubes and put the dressing in the turkey and roast as usual.

Swedish Meatballs

1 pound each hamburger, ground ham, and ground pork
2 eggs beaten   1 cup cracker crumbs
1 cup milk   Salt to taste

Combine meats, eggs, crumbs, milk, and salt; form into balls. Place in a baking dish.

Mix together: 1 teaspoon dry mustard, 1/2 cup diluted vinegar, 1 cup brown sugar. Pour over meatballs and bake at 350° for 1 hour.

Clarice: I've feasted on Carol's Swedish Meatballs and they are great...the brown sugar sauce is wonderful, much like my sister-in-law Violet's.

Homemade Shake and Bake

4 cups of fine bread crumbs   1/2 cup of vegetable oil
1 tablespoon salt   1 teaspoon of pepper
1 tablespoon garlic salt or 1/2 tablespoon of garlic powder
1 teaspoon paprika   2 tablespoons parsley flakes
1 tablespoon oregano

Mix and store in container in refrigerator.

Dip chicken or pork into water, then into mix. Bake 1 hour at 375°.

Midge Hole Carlson
My Sister-in-law
Vermillion, South Dakota

My mother, Hattie Reed Frazee, was a special mother, grandmother, and great-grandmother. She held her family together as their numbers grew and grew. We remember her best for the good times at the farm just north of Lincoln. She loved to have her family all come for Sunday dinner and holidays—sometimes 60+ folks. The food was always terrific. She could cook with all the best—Swedish meatballs, pumpkin pecan pie, applesauce, nutbread, holiday sugar cookies, and always, chocolate chip cookies filled the canister.

We especially like this recipe for Swedish meatballs, which she made quite often. She could make them ahead and freeze them, then pour the sauce over them when she was ready to cook for a family dinner or a potluck supper.

Mother also loved to sit and sew for hours. She never used the sewing machine. Sewing by hand was her only way; she used many scraps of fabric to make beautiful quilts for her five children, 22 grandchildren, 40 great grandchildren, and 1 great-great-granddaughter.

Carol Frazee Lantz
Lincoln, Nebraska

When I asked Chad, Matt, and Ken about favorite recipes each one said we had to include Barbecued Spareribs. The Secret is in the sauce, using country style pork ribs, and I like to cook them in a crock pot. I double or triple the barbecue sauce so there is extra to heat and serve on the side or set aside and save in the refrigerator for later use.

Marcia Carlson Rislov
A Carlson Cousin
Green Oaks, Illinois

One day I was making this chicken recipe for dinner and my grandson, Cole, aged 4, asked what I was cooking. When I said chicken, he asked "King Super Chicken?" (King Super's is a large grocery chain in Denver, where he lives.) I said, "No, Grama's Chicken."

That day at dinner, after his third helping of chicken and not eating anything else, he announced, "This is better than King Super." I guess that makes this recipe one of his favorites.

Karen Pooley
A Carlson Cousin
Mitchell, South Dakota

Barbecued Spareribs

Country-style pork ribs
Barbecue Sauce:

1/2 cup ketchup
1 tablespoon brown sugar or honey
1 tablespoon soy sauce
1 tablespoon Worcestershire sauce
1 tablespoon vinegar
1 teaspoon chili powder
1 teaspoon liquid smoke
1/4 teaspoon dry mustard
1/2 teaspoon onion salt or powder
1/2 teaspoon garlic salt.

Slow cooker method: It's not necessary, but you may braise the ribs in a broiler before putting in the slow cooker. May add a few drops of liquid smoke to each rib. Cook on high until it's hot and then to low for all-day cooking.

Baking method: Place the ribs in a shallow baking pan and brush generously with barbecue sauce. Bake in a slow oven, 300° for 1 to 1 1/2 hours, until meat is tender. Turn the ribs once so they brown on both sides and continue brushing with additional barbecue sauce. Drain any excess fat that accumulates in the pan before serving.

Grama's Chicken Delight

6-8 chicken breast fillets, cooked and cooled
Mix together:

2 cans cream of chicken soup
1/2 cup mayonnaise
2/3 cup milk
2 teaspoons lemon juice
1/2 cup grated American or cheddar cheese

Pour mixture over chicken and bake at 350° for 1 hour.

Lisa's Mashed Potato Casserole

5 pounds of potatoes or 9 large
8 ounces of cream cheese
1 cup sour cream
1 teaspoon onion salt
1/4 teaspoon pepper
2 tablespoons butter
1/2 to 3/4 cup of Velveeta cheese
Chives, optional

Cook potatoes and mash. Add ingredients and mix well. Bake at 350° for 30 minutes. Sprinkle the top with paprika. Top with butter when ready to serve.

Tyler's Favorite Sweet Peas

1 can of sweet peas   Salt to taste
1 tablespoon butter.

Heat and serve—anytime—for a snack, lunch, or dinner.

I make sure that there are always cans of peas in my cupboard, since Tyler frequently is at my house before or after school. Need I say that he is the only one in his family that likes peas?

In cooking for my two grandchildren, I have found they are pleased with these simple recipes. As a rule, when I try a time-consuming or fancy recipe, it won't even be tasted. Eating any kind of meat requires some urging from their parents. However, they love homemade cinnamon rolls and cherry or pumpkin pie.

Hazel Hendrix
Lincoln, Nebraska

Sweet Potatoes

3 or 4 large sweet potatoes cooked and peeled
1/2 can (small) crushed pineapple with juice
6 or 7 maraschino cherries   4 tablespoons cherry juice
ham drippings or bacon slices little bit of syrup
3/4 cup brown sugar   1/2 stick margarine

Slice and layer potatoes and other ingredients. Bake at 350° for 30 minutes. Cover with 1/3 bag miniature marshmallows and bake at 400° for 15 more minutes.

Holidays were always fun when we were small. We all looked forward to going to Grandma's because we knew we would get sweet potatoes prepared from her special recipe. They even looked festive with the addition of the colors of the cherries and pineapple. We still have them on special occasions because Mom makes them, too!

Stacey Messman
Lincoln, Nebraska

113

Midge received this recipe from Kitty Tilton, a superb cook, who lived next door to us for five or six years. Her husband Bill was the handiest man I ever knew, with the exception of my brother Paul.

Loren M. Carlson
My Brother
Vermillion, South Dakota

This has been a favorite of mine for years. Mother served it one time when we were visiting in Grand Island, Nebraska. From then on, I have made it many times—for the American Association of University Women's Antiques and Collectibles group, AAUW Cuisine group, and for church potlucks, as well as for family.

The ingredients are very easy to transport. I bring the ingredients with us and make it in our condo when we go skiing in Angel Fire, New Mexico.

Kathryn Thomssen Ritterbush
Albuquerque, New Mexico

Chicken Breast Roll-ups

Bone about 4 chicken breasts, Cut in half and push the flesh into a sort of "ball." Wrap 1/2 slice of bacon around each ball. Put 1/2 slice of dried beef under the bacon, making 8 servings. Place in 7 X 11 greased pan. May freeze for up to three weeks. Unfreezes rapidly. When ready to serve, mix a can of cream of chicken soup with 1/2 carton of sour cream and pour over chicken breasts. Bake for 3 hours at 275°. Baste about three times.

Mother Thomssen's Chicken Supreme

1 cup elbow macaroni, uncooked
1 cup diced chicken or 1 can of white chicken
1 can of cream of chicken soup
2 hard-boiled eggs, diced
1 1/3 diced pimento
1 1/2 cup chicken broth
1 2-ounce can mushrooms
1 onion minced
1/4 pound American cheese, cubed

Mix together and put in 9 X 13 inch pan. Refrigerate overnight. Allow to sit at room temperature for 1 hours before baking. Sprinkle with buttered bread crumbs and bake uncovered 1 hour at 350°.

Oven Orange Chicken

2 pounds of cut-up chicken
1/4 cup of green pepper   2 ounces of onion
1/4 cup undiluted orange juice 1/4 cup water
1/4 cup ketchup   2 tablespoons soy sauce
2 tablespoons flour   1/2 teaspoon salt
1/2 teaspoon garlic powder   1/2 teaspoon dry mustard
1/4 teaspoon pepper   2 medium oranges, optional

Place chicken in 2 quart baking dish. Sprinkle with peppers and onion. Combine remaining ingredients, except oranges, and mix until smooth. Coat chicken with mixture and bake, covered, for 1 hour at 350°. Place orange slices on for garnish. Serves 4.

Since having my heart surgery in 1989, I have lived on a diet of mostly poultry and fish. Consequently, Midge is always looking for a recipe that will meet the combined test of being dietetically correct as well as being tasty. This recipe comes from Inez Oleson; she and her husband, Quentin, have been part of our dancing/dining group for a long time.

Loren M. Carlson
My Brother
Vermillion, South Dakota

Clarice: I enjoy serving a similar orange chicken recipe that Eunice Cade adapted from Bryan Hospital's heart healthy recipes. You may want to try both versions.

Bryan Hospital's Orange Chicken

6 boneless chicken breasts   1/4 cup margarine   2 tablespoons flour
1/4 teaspoon dry mustard 1/4 teaspoon cinnamon   1/4 teaspoon ginger
2 tablespoons sugar 1 1/2 cups orange juice

Brown chicken in margarine. Remove and add flour and seasonings to the skillet to make a paste. Then add orange juice. Let the mixture boil until it thickens, although the sauce will be soupy. Add the chicken and cook for 45 minutes on medium to low heat, basting occasionally. You may also bake this in the oven. You may place the prepared chicken and orange sauce in a baking dish and put in the refrigerator. When ready to serve, warm in the oven. It's even better the next day. Eunice serves this with wild rice.

This is another of the recipes which has many additions or corrections. Usually, the chicken breasts were boned, but not always. There were times when we didn't use the orange juice, sugar, and honey, but just put about half of the juice from the peaches on the chicken for that baking. We could use more juice if needed and we might eat half of the peaches separately, with breakfast cereal for example. We might use molasses instead of brown sugar. We could omit the sweet potatoes and onion, and just cook chicken. I think the change I preferred was to omit those vegetables and to substitute a can of pineapple chunks for the peaches. I still cook that today.

All of Mom's recipes were just general guides. They were intended to be changed with whatever else the pantry had available. I think she believed that a good cook didn't need a recipe so much as he/she needed an imagination. I remember I made an Orange Pie once; it could have used more sugar and maybe some sort of thickener, but we ate it with spoons. That recipe is not written anywhere!

I think my mother-in-law's recipes were similar. My husband wanted me to cook some things that I'd never heard of that his mother had made. Some I could find, or knew, such as the Baked Omelet, and German Chocolate Cake. But

Peach Chicken

Heat oven to 375°. Place two whole chicken breasts in a baking pan.

Arrange around the chicken 1 1/2 pounds sweet potatoes, peeled and sliced, and 1 onion, peeled and sliced. Add salt and pepper. Bake 30 minutes, covered.

Mix in small bowl—
    1 tablespoon orange juice
    1/2 cup brown sugar
    3 tablespoons honey

Drizzle over chicken and vegetables. Bake 30 minutes uncovered. Add one 16 ounce can sliced peaches drained. Bake 30 minutes, uncovered, baste occasionally.

nobody could help me with Onion Pie. After my Orange Pie debacle I was not about to try an Onion Pie without guidance from somewhere, and I couldn't find any at all. Until one day in a waiting room, I picked up a magazine on cooking. I'd been there a while and was pretty bored, so I read and read. And I found Onion Pie! I read the recipe, and realized it was in an article on Quiches. I asked to borrow the magazine, went home and made Doug a real Onion Pie. He thought I was brilliant to figure that out; I never told him that I was just bored and lucky.

That story and Mom's ideas of adding and correcting should convince people that it is a very good idea to read a cookbook often. You just don't know when it might make you brilliant!

Amy Franklin
Lincoln, Nebraska

Oven Beef Stew

2 pounds beef chuck cut in 1 1/2 inch cubes
3 stalks celery, cut in 2 1/2 diagonal pieces
2 medium onions, cut in eighths
4 medium carrots, cut in half crosswise and lengthwise

Layer beef, onion, celery, and carrots in a 2 1/2 quart casserole or small roaster.

Mix in a small bowl:

1 12-ounce can tomato juice	1 tablespoon sugar
1/2 teaspoon basil	1/4 teaspoon pepper
1/4 cup quick-cooking tapioca	1 tablespoon salt.

Spread this mixture over the top. Cover and cook in a slow oven 300° for 3-3 1/2 hours. During the last hour, add 2 large potatoes, cut in 1 1/2 inch cubes. Stir occasionally. This stew does not require browning of meat. To serve 50 people, multiply the recipe by 8.

Clarice: Violet is an active and efficient community volunteer. She repairs and launders baby clothes that are contributed to the church's mission closet. She replaces broken zippers on baby sleepers and missing buttons and tears on other baby children's clothing that discount stores cannot sell. Along with small, soft flannel quilts she has made, these baby clothes are given to needy mothers in the community. Violet is a role model of sharing for her own six young adult grandchildren.

I have been using this recipe for several years to feed large groups of people at church and other functions. I have made it for the Senior Fellowship group, traveling college choirs, the homeless shelter, my family, etc. Everyone loves it because it is different and easy to prepare. It is good made ahead of time and reheated.

Violet Neshiem Carlson
My Sister-in-law
Williamsport, Maryland

Pioneer Onion Pie

Make enough rich crust for a 2-crust pie. Fill the bottom crust with sliced raw onions. Season with salt and pepper. Fill up crust with cream and milk. Cover with top crust and bake in a moderate oven.

From the recipes of Mrs. I.W. Tulley,
submitted by her granddaughter,
Eleanor Wolf,
Red Cloud, Nebraska

Clarice: Amy said she found a recipe for Onion Pie; I found this pioneer version in the Nebraska Centennial Cookbook *(1967).*

117

There was a time in my youth when we ate whatever we grew on the farm and didn't worry about what it was doing to our bodies. My Dad, who lived to be 89, did everything wrong. He liked his beefsteak fried hard, in lard. And then, as a final treat, would savor the inch of fat around the edge.

"One good thing won't spoil another," he reasoned as he poured thick cream on everything from apple pie to goulash to fresh sliced tomatoes with sugar—a treat I must eat when everyone else has left the table.

But now, we are calorie and cholesterol conscious and we cringe at the very thought of fat, so my method of fixing steak is far different from my mother's method. Since modern technology has made me even busier than my mother, I rely on this quick-and-easy-to prepare-recipe.

Chrys Daniel
My "Adopted Sister"
Wentworth, South Dakota

Barbecued Steak

1 cup ketchup
1/2 cup water
1/4 cup vinegar
2 tablespoons brown sugar
1 1/2 tablespoons Worcestershire sauce
1 tablespoon dry mustard
Salt and pepper to taste
Onion and green pepper rings to taste
1 to 2 pounds of round steak

Combine first six ingredients in a pan and bring to a boil, and simmer gently for 5 minutes. Pour hot sauce over round steak, pepper and onion rings if desired. Cover and bake for 1 1/2 to 2 hours in a 350° oven. Put on platter and serve sauce in a pitcher. For company or a crowd, multiply the recipe.

Clarice: Chrys and her husband Bill were each named Eminent Homemaker and Eminent Farmer in South Dakota in different years. As a prominent cattlefeeder, Bill has served on the Cattlemen's Beef Board and the Board of Directors for the National Cattlemen's Association. So it is understandable that beef has always been a mainstay on their menus. Chrys is always developing new ways to serve beef to her family and friends.

Mom's Barbeque

1 pound of cubed beef (lean round steak)
1 pound of cubed pork (lean pork steak)
5 stalks of diced celery   4 diced carrots
1 cup water   Salt to taste

Combine ingredients in pressure cooker and cook 30 minutes. Drain and mash with a hand mixer.

Add 1 can chili con carne with beans. Add 1 small bottle of ketchup. Mix and serve on buns.

After my sister and I left home, we never bothered to make Mom's barbeque as neither of us had a pressure cooker. Each time we went home for a visit, we expected Mom to serve her delicious barbeque. And, of course, being the wonderful mother and cook she is, she always came through. Our children have also become very fond of Mom's barbeque. Well, I suppose Mom finally got tired of my sister and me asking how to make her barbeque, so for Christmas, she provided us both with a pressure cooker. Inside the box was her secret recipe and this darling poem—

In the box is a book for you to read,
Study it well and you will succeed.
Here's the recipe, here's the pot,
Now, get busy and make barbeque, a lot!
Make no mistake,
It's easy to make.
It freezes well and very handy,
Kids really like it better than candy.
I got such a good deal on the cost,
Just had to buy the pot or get lost.
Now, you can make Mom's barbeque
Then, sit down with family and enjoy it, too!

Judy Brundege
Lincoln, Nebraska

Memories of the Early 1900s

This is the Craig house on our farm in South Fork township, near Taylorville, Illinois where we lived in a two-story brick house with ten rooms and an interesting cupola on the roof. We had a great view of the country in every direction.

Each Saturday, Grandma Achenbach (ah ken bak) made her special recipe of noodles and had them all cut and dried ready for soup. Mother and Aunt Ethel brought the chickens so the main entrée for our large family dinner was generous bowls of chicken noodle soup.

Our grandparents lived in Taylorville in a large house which had a butler's pantry off the kitchen with a pass-through window into the dining room. We grandchildren took advantage of this convenience to pass things back and forth to each other.

Lillian Slaughter
Lincoln, Nebraska

Clarice: Lillian is a long-time organist. At 90+ years, she is a regular church and Sunday School attender even though our forty-year old congregation moved to a new location, much farther from her home.

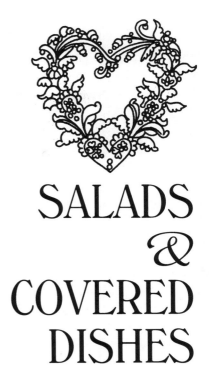

SALADS
&
COVERED
DISHES

*It is chance that makes
brothers and sisters, but
heart that makes friends.*

Boomers Need to Stay Tied to Grandma

I'm a "Boomer"—the last tie to Grandma's apron and the kitchen traditions that were a part of Grandma's home. As I worked on Clarice's manuscript, many thoughts filled my mind. How will my children remember the fading memories of my grandparents that I cling to through mind and matter? Even some of the things that I cherish from when I was growing up are foreign to my own kids and definitely strange to my grandkids.

I remember my mom wearing aprons, but they weren't always like the ones that Grandma wore—the long aprons with a bib and ties in the back. They provided pockets for handkerchiefs, were handles for hot dishes, and baskets for picking beans. With the absence of aprons have come new ways to spend time in the kitchen—quick and easy.

Life has changed since Grandma was around. She would be shocked at the packaged mixes and the canned goods that stock our cupboards. I cooked macaroni and cheese when I knew our granddaughters were coming to dinner. They didn't like it because it wasn't out of a box. I still spend summers canning vegetables (and now freezing some) but "fresh greenbeans aren't as good as the ones out of a can," one granddaughter told me.

I'm a holdout for some of the ways our grandparents lived and, especially, cooked. I love making an angelfood cake from scratch. I make biscuits and cinnamon rolls and dinner rolls from scratch. The sad thing is that my kids don't know how to make these delectable foods. Why should they, I always make them!

I'm convinced that being a "Boomer" brings with it special obligations to preserve those ways that were simpler and kinder to our souls. Many women are working today, so spending time fixing food like Grandma made is pretty much out of the question. Even though our children are grown and have families of their own, I find making a meal after a long day at work isn't done the way I "used to do it." I use the microwave, the quick-frozen meats, the boxed pastas and rices. I do it out of necessity. I tell myself it tastes good and the nutrition is there. As much as I want to be like Grandma and prepare meals that bring back the "old ways," I just can't do it.

One of my favorite memories of our trips to Iowa to visit my dad's parents was the black raspberry pie that Grandma baked. It was always delicious. My grandpa had a fruit farm and always had fresh strawberries for cereal and fresh raspberries for pie. In the fall there were peaches and pears and apples.

I still bake pies, but many of the women my age have never tried. My husband is one of the lucky ones. I buy a bushel of apples and a bushel of peaches in season and I bake pies and freeze them so he has pie for his lunches. He always teases that he could probably sell them at work.

My mom found the cookbook that belonged to her grandmother dating back to 1905. There's a certain sadness in the stained and yellowed pages. Reading the printed recipes remind us that people really did cook without microwaves and convection ovens and they didn't have refrigerators or freezers to store the leftovers. Making a fruit salad in 1905 would have gone something like this:

Fruit Salad

Dissolve one box gelatin in one pint cold water for a half day, then add one pint boiling water and juice of three lemons and four oranges, sugar to taste. Then stir into this halves and slices of fruit previously prepared. Set away on ice in a mold.

My grandmother prepared a special treat for her children. She made marshmallows. The recipe was handwritten and stuck between the pages of my great-grandma's cookbook. When I mentioned the recipe to friends, they laughed and said, "Don't they come in packages ready-made?" You might want to try this recipe with your grandkids.

Marshmallows

1 envelope Knox Gelatin
2 cups (1 pt.) sugar
Few grains salt. Flavoring.

Soak gelatin in 10 tablespoons of cold water.

Boil sugar in 10 tablespoons of water until it threads. Pour syrup over gelatin. Let stand until partially cooled. Add salt and flavoring and beat until white and stiff. Chopped nuts may be added.

Just picture Grandma in her apron with her wire whisk beating a bowl of sugar and gelatin to make the marshmallows that we buy in assorted sizes and colors today. No electric mixer; just a strong arm and a commitment to her family.

It's pretty easy in our "boomer world" to lose sight of the "good old days." Personally, I feel we have an obligation to remember the traditions that got us to where we are. It probably isn't ever going to be the same with our frenzied lifestyles; but as we enjoy our modern technology, we can teach some of the tradition and the sense of responsibility toward our families to future generations. If we don't, who will?

—Linda Dageforde

I remember having this salad at Grandma Orr's when I was staying at their house on my 11th birthday. My birthday is June 13th, the day before Flag Day, so the red, white, and blue salad was appropriate. And I got to sign my name to the Red Plate and eat off it, because it was my birthday. Grandpa and I played with a lot of little green army men. We would shoot each other's men with rubber bands. They had a lot of books that we always read before bedtime. We went to the top of the Capitol building and even met Governor Kay Orr, although we're not related. The East Campus ice cream store was always a great place to stop for a treat.

Matthew Orr
My Grandson
Columbus, Ohio

Red, White, And Blue Salad

2 boxes raspberry Jell-O,
   or 1 box of red and 1 box blueberry Jell-O
3 cups hot water   1 envelope plain gelatin
1/2 cup cold water
1 cup coffee cream or evaporated milk
1 cup sugar   1 teaspoon vanilla
8 ounces cream cheese   1/2 cup nuts
1 #2 can blueberries

First layer: Dissolve 1 box of raspberry gelatin in 1 cup hot water. Add blueberries and juice included. Pour in 9 X 13 inch baking dish or large glass bowl and chill.

Second layer: Dissolve plain gelatin in 1/2 cup cold water. Heat cream and sugar without boiling, then mix into gelatin mixture. Add vanilla, cream cheese and nuts. When cheese mixture is cool, and the blueberry raspberry layer is firm, pour the cheese mixture onto the first layer.

Third layer: Dissolve one box of raspberry gelatin in 2 cups hot water. Cool and add to firmly set second layer.

Clarice: I love making this salad and serving it. Except I tried not to serve it in the dining room on the carpet when the grandkids were very small, because the blueberries can stain tablecloths and carpet. My sister-in-law, Midge Carlson also sent this recipe; she says it never fails to get attention with its patriotic colors.

"Green Stuff"

1 28-ounce can pears
1 3-ounce package lemon Jell-O
1 8-ounce packages cream cheese
1 16-ounce tub Cool Whip
Few drops of green food coloring

Drain pears, saving one cup of the liquid. Heat pear juice to boiling. Dissolve Jell-O in hot juice. Blend drained pears and cream cheese together in a blender. (It helps if cream cheese is slightly softened.) Slowly blend cooled Jell-O into blended pear mixture. Add green food coloring to mixture and blend until smooth. Cool well and fold in the Cool Whip. Chill until set.

My Aunt Becky first began making this salad for holiday gatherings. I soon took over the responsibility of making it and we now have it nearly every Thanksgiving and Christmas. Originally, the salad was named Blended Pear Salad, but our family somehow took to calling it Green Stuff and the name has stuck ever since. The original recipe calls for only 5 drops of food coloring, but I have found that much more is needed to truly capture the title "Green Stuff."

Emilie Parrott
My Granddaughter
Omaha, Nebraska

Clarice: This is one of the fundamental components of our Nebraska family dinners. Green Stuff works for Christmas—with red maraschino cherries—and for Easter—'cause it's green. Its mild cream cheese fruity flavor suits all ages. You can also use sugar-free, low-calorie ingredients to fit your family needs. It's great with turkey, chicken, ham, roast beef, Emilie's Lasagna, and, as Claire suggests, it's essential with her Enchiladas.

Seventy Years of Cranberry Salad

As a small child, probably in the late 1920s, I remember sitting in the kitchen of Mrs. Effie McPerson, who was a neighbor lady, along with my mother. We were making a cranberry salad for the Riverside neighborhood holiday party. They whipped large bowls of whipped cream, chopped cranberries and apples. It was my job to pick the nutmeats out of the cracked walnut shells.

Sometime during the 1960s, I attended a church circle meeting. All female members of the church were assigned to a circle. I was a little uncomfortable being in the home of the two hostesses since the home where we met was dark and dreary with all the blinds closed tight. But, they served this delicious dessert. After a few bites it seemed very familiar to me. It took some courage on my part to go out to the kitchen and remark about their very good dessert, but I asked if they would share their recipe with me. They gave me this recipe.

Now, more than 40 years later, this salad recipe has evolved into a popular dessert. The only ingredient to change is that, in the 1960s, whipped cream was often replaced with a packaged dry topping mixed with milk and then whipped. Now in the 1990s, a pre-whipped frozen non-dairy topping is usually substituted for the whipped cream.

I think you can find this recipe in modern recipe books under the name of Cranberry Fluff.

1 package of fresh cranberries, chopped
1 apple   1 cup sugar
Marshmallows   Nuts
Real whipped cream, or 1 package of Dream Whip or 1 carton of frozen whipped topping

Mix all together and serve in a glass dish that shows off the pretty color.

Jean Harper
Lincoln, Nebraska

Cranberry Salad

1 cup ground cranberries
1 cup sugar
1 3-ounce package lemon Jell-O
1 cup hot water
1 cup pineapple syrup
1 cup crushed pineappple, drained
1/2 cup chopped walnuts
1 cup chopped celery

Grind cranberries and cover with sugar while preparing the Jell-O. (Frozen cranberries grind best.) Dissolve Jell-O in hot water. Add pineapple syrup and chill until partially set. Add cranberries, pineapple, walnuts, and celery.

Holidays just aren't the same without Mom's cranberry salad. I can't remember when or where this tradition started, but it goes well with turkey and dressing as well as other favorite meals.

Linda Dageforde

Applesauce Jell-O Salad

1 small box red Jell-O
1 cup boiling water
1 1/2 cup applesauce
Dissolve Jell-O in boiling water and let set in refrigerator until firm before serving.

My two grandchildren are very easy to please. This applesauce salad always makes Lisa and Tyler happy.

Hazel Hendrix
Lincoln, Nebraska

Mom's Potato Salad

3 potatoes (I prefer red)
4 hard boiled eggs (always one more egg than potatoes)
Chopped onion (1/4 to 1/2 cup)
Mayonnaise and salad dressing (prefer equal parts)
1 teaspoon yellow prepared mustard
Dash of Worcestershire sauce
Pinch of sugar
Splash of vinegar

DON'T OVERCOOK THE POTATOES. Peel them, cut them in half, boil until a fork can penetrate without difficulty. Set off burner, pour water off—they continue to cook even though out of water.

Cut potatoes into smaller pieces, mix in hard boiled eggs, and add mayonnaise/salad dressing mixture. Key point: You can always add more, but start with 1/4 cup each. Add onion and balance of ingredients. Taste and add additional mayo/dressing if too dry.

It is best to allow potato salad to sit in refrigerator for an hour or two before serving.

When I met Kay she was already a good cook EXCEPT no one, including Kay, made potato salad like my Mom. SO—I told Kay before we could marry, she had to learn how to make it like my Mom. She did—and soon we got married.

However, when she became State Treasurer and Governor she no longer was cooking. SO—it then became necessary for me to learn how. I did and still love to prepare (and eat) potato salad.

William D. Orr
Nebraska's First Gentleman
1986-1990
Lincoln, Nebraska

Clarice: We are not related to Bill and Kay Orr, but I have some good stories about those folks who think we are.

One of my favorite memories is driving 200 miles to visit my aunt and uncle on their farm. My aunt so enjoyed having us come visit them. She always enjoyed sharing their new baby kittens and pet lambs; they got to come into the kitchen to say "hello" to us. She would have us help make a salad for the next day. Every time I make this salad I think of the happy times with her.

Ione Hieter
Lincoln, Nebraska

Layered Lettuce Salad

1 head of lettuce (torn in pieces)
10 ounces of frozen peas   3/4 cup celery
Green pepper (cut up)   8 strips bacon (crisp fried)
1/2 cup chopped onion   2 cups Miracle Whip
2 tablespoons sugar   Grated cheese

Layer ingredients in 9 X 13 inch pan. Mix sugar with Miracle Whip and spread over vegetables. Sprinkle with grated cheese. Let set overnight before serving.

Clarice: Cuzzin Elaine, a retired nurse, continues to be a gentle and compassionate caregiver among her network of friends. She often is asked basic medical advice and drives friends to the doctors or to chemotherapy, still remembering her own bouts with cancer.

Soda Cracker Salad

1/2 cup chopped onion
1 cup celery (chopped)
3 or 4 hard boiled eggs
1 small can shrimp
1 cup mayonnaise or less
1/4 cup ketchup
15 to 20 broken soda crackers just before serving.

I usually add some red pepper to the salad mix to make it a bit spicy.

Elaine Stack
A Rosenquist Cousin
Great Falls, Montana

Grandma Beechner's Salmon Salad

1 can salmon—take off skin and remove large bones
1 cup chopped celery
3 hard-boiled eggs
1/4 teaspoon salt
Dash of black pepper
Juice of 1 lemon, optional
To extend the recipe, crush a few soda crackers and add.

Boiled salad dressing

3 eggs	4 tablespoons flour
1/2 teaspoon dry mustard	1/2 teaspoon salt
1 cup sugar	3/4 cup vinegar
1 1/4 cups water	

Mix dry ingredients. Beat eggs and add to dry ingredients. Add water, mix well. Heat and add vinegar slowly. Cook until thick, stirring constantly. This makes three cups. It takes about a cup for the salmon salad.

Every Friday night, the Beechners had salmon salad, fried potatoes, green peas, and applesauce. This was the Methodist minister's family in which my husband grew up.

Frances Beechner
Lincoln, Nebraska

Clarice: Frances enjoys memories spent with the family of her sister-in- law, Mary Beechner, the daughter of Nebraska's pioneer author Bess Streeter Aldrich.

Oriental Salad (Chicken or Tuna)

1 cup tuna, drained,
    or 1 cup chopped, cooked chicken
1 5-ounce can sliced water chestnuts
1 cup frozen peas (do not cook)
1 cup sliced celery
1/2 cup sliced green onions
Place in bowl and add dressing of:
    3/4 cup mayonnaise, 1 tablespoon lemon juice,
    1/4 teaspoon curry powder (can omit curry),
    1/4 teaspoon garlic powder,
    and 2 teaspoons soy sauce.

Let stand in refrigerator overnight.

Just before serving, add 1 can crisp Chinese noodles and 1/2 cup slivered almonds. Serve on lettuce.

This is a recipe served by a California cousin that I have used a lot for ladies' luncheons.

Gladys Woods
Lincoln, Nebraska

Clarice: The only cabbage salad Cousin Alyce and I ever tasted when we were growing up was cole slaw. Alyce and I were the closest in age of my Carlson Cousins. As children, we frequently stayed overnight in each other's homes. She told me where babies came from. We explored the haymows and corncribs and climbed to the top of the sheds and dreamed dreams.

Oriental Chicken Salad
Serves 6

1 head cabbage
1/2 cup slivered almonds
4 chicken breasts, cooked
2 packages Ramen noodles (Oriental flavor)

8 scallions
1/2 cup sesame seeds

Cut up cabbage and scallions. Toast sesame seeds and almonds in 1 tablespoon margarine in pan. Crush noodles and put on just before serving.

Dressing: 2 packages seasoning from Ramen noodles, 1 cup oil, 1/2 cup Seasoned Rice vinegar, 3 tablespoons sugar

Put on just before serving.

Alyce Knutson

Growing up on the farm in South Dakota in the 1930s, the only green salads that my mother and Alyce's mother, Aunt Minnie, served were spring garden lettuce made with a vinegar and sugar dressing or a little milk or cream mixed with vinegar and sugar. The early gardens also provided green onions and radishes that we crunched after generously dipping them in salt. We did not know about mandarin oranges and would not have considered using fresh navel oranges with lettuce, celery, and onions.

Mandarin Salad
Serves 6

1/2 cup sliced almonds
3 tablespoons sugar
1/2 head romaine lettuce
1 cup chopped celery
2 whole green onions, chopped
1 11-ounce can mandarin oranges, drained

Dressing:

1/2 teaspoon salt
1/4 cup vegetable oil
2 tablespoons vinegar
Dash of Tabasco sauce

Dash of pepper
1 tablespoon sugar

In a small pan over medium heat, cook almonds and sugar, stirring constantly until almonds are coated and sugar dissolved. Cool. Mix all dressing ingredients and chill. Mix lettuces, celery, and onions. Just before serving, add almonds and oranges. Toss with the dressing.

Alyce Knutson
A Carlson Cousin
Lakewood, Colorado

Grandma Gladys Carlson's Scalloped Corn

1 can whole kernel corn   1 can creamed corn
1/2 cup condensed milk   2 eggs
1 sleeve of soda crackers crushed
     (add more if it appears runny)
Add to taste: garlic powder, onion powder, chives (about 1/2 teaspoon each), plus salt and pepper

Mix well and pour into 3-quart casserole (preferably with green exterior with a pink long-stemmed rose on a white interior). Cube 2 tablespoons of butter on top. Bake about 45 minutes or until light brown and firm.

This scalloped corn recipe was Grandma Carlson's (Gladys) and was a favorite of our family when we all went home to visit. I started by trying to follow Grandma's verbal recipe and, over the years, have embellished a bit what she told me. She didn't have a written recipe either. It is now a staple for our major holidays and must always be served in the same casserole (one we received as a wedding present). One year I changed the recipe and tried one I had sampled and thought was great. I was almost exiled from the family, including extended family, and have had to re-promise every year before each holiday meal that I am using Grandma's and my recipe and have the green casserole ready.

Donna C. Carlson
A Carlson Cousin
New Brighton, Minnesota

Aunt 'Manda's Scalloped Corn

1 can cream style corn   1 cup milk
1 cup cream or half and half   2 eggs
1/2 teaspoon salt   1 teaspoon sugar
2 tablespoons flour, heaping   2 tablespoons butter

Beat eggs, add corn and dry ingredients. May measure milk and cream into the corn can and add to first mixture. Pour into greased casserole. Bake at 350° one hour or more until set in the center.

Evelyn Pierson
A Carlson Cousin
Ethan, South Dakota

Clarice: This was one of the favorites we enjoyed at the Carlson Family Reunions.

As an incentive to get our first Wilkins Cousins Reunion off to a good start, we solicited recipes from the many family members and compiled them in a WILKINS FAMILY DELECTABLE DISHES COOKBOOK. The various family members did all the work, compiling it with illustrations by our own 10-year-old artist, and using a computer program to get uniformity. A son-in-law provided the bindery necessary and we gave the book to each person who came and sent in a recipe. We had over 100 people there and it was the beginning of more fun reunions—without the work of doing a cookbook.

This recipe is from that family cookbook. It has been my stand-by to take to Keenagers at church for many years. I never have to take home leftovers.

Muriel Wilkins
Lincoln, Nebraska

Clarice: I'm pleased that my cousins have been sharing some of the NEW foods in interesting ways. I'm sure our Grandma Ida Carlson and Grandma Anna Rosenquist never ate artichoke hearts, and I wonder about broccoli! However, I applaud my cousins for trying these combinations of food.

California Blend Casserole

2 16-ounce bags of California Blend Vegetables
1 can cream of celery soup, undiluted
8-ounce jar of Cheez Whiz
1 can fried onion rings

Cook vegetables until half done. Drain WELL and put in buttered casserole. Mix soup and cheese. Pour over vegetables. Bake 350° for 30 minutes or until bubbly. Spread onion rings on top and bake for the last 5 minutes. Can be fixed the night before except for the onion rings.

Sometimes I add a few tablespoons of milk to the soup mixture.

Broccoli Artichoke Casserole
Serves 6

1 12-ounce can of artichoke hearts (packed in water, not oil)
1 8-ounce package of cream cheese, softened
1 stick melted butter
3 cups steamed broccoli

Grease casserole and quarter artichokes and layer on the bottom. Sprinkle with garlic salt. Mix cream cheese and butter. Add broccoli to cream cheese and butter. Top with crushed wheat thin crackers. Bake at 350° for 30 minutes.

Alyce Knutson
A Carlson Cousin
Lakewood, Colorado

132

Mom's Better than Stroganoff

1 1/2 pounds hamburger, browned

Add 1 can of chicken with rice soup, 1 can of cream of chicken soup, and 1 can of cream of mushroom soup.

Add 1 cup of diced celery

1 medium onion diced, or 2 1/2 teaspoons of dried onions
1 tablespoon of soy sauce, 2 if you like
1 cup of water
1 teaspoon of salt
1 cup of uncooked rice, not Minute
Bake 1/2 hour covered or 3/4 hour uncovered at 375º.

Pat Kjelland brought this to us when Mom came home from the hospital in Pierre after a bout with pneumonia over 30 years ago. She has used it hundred of times for casseroles for potlucks, funerals, etc. One time when she was president of Faculty Women, she made this for a family who had just had a new baby. When they were about to return the Crock-Pot, the lid got broken. Months later, Bernie the husband, found a lid that matched perfectly. The folks still have it. This is the most popular casserole dish in Vermillion, South Dakota; I can vouch for that. Almost everyone in Mom's bridge and church circle groups have glommed on to this one!!! And now, I'm making it.

Cathy Carlson Gray
My Niece
St. Louis Park, Minnesota

Broccoli was new to the United States in 1928. A New Yorker cartoon by Carl Rose, with a caption by E.B. White, has a child looking disdainfully at a dish of broccoli and saying, "I say it's spinach and I say to hell with it."
—from the *Lincoln Journal-Star*, May 26, 1999

I was quite young when we visited Grandpa and Grandma Rosenquist and sat around their dining room table. All I can remember is how Grandpa used to put his morning Postum in a saucer and blow on it before he drank it. I always wanted to do the same thing, but I was told that I had to wait until I was older!

Carol Anne Keyser Hodge
Arizona

Clarice: Carol Anne lived in or on the edge of the Black Hills of South Dakota for most of her life. Often our family vacations were spent visiting them— I saw Mt. Rushmore before it was finished. (See a snapshot of Pa and me at Mt. Rushmore at the beginning of Grandkids' Favorites.) Later, she moved to Montana, outside of Missoula, another lovely place to vacation. Now that they are retired, they are in Arizona.

Elaine Stack and Carol Anne both sent this recipe. The only difference is that Elaine adds 1 cup ketchup. When two cousins recommend the same recipe, it must be good.

One Pot Dinner

1/2 to 1 pound of ground beef
Several slices to 1/2 pound bacon, in small pieces
1 cup of chopped onion
2 31-ounce cans of pork and beans
1 1-pound can kidney beans—drained
1 1-pound can butter beans—drained
1/4 cup brown sugar
1 tablespoon liquid smoke
3 tablespoons white vinegar
1 teaspoon salt
Dash of pepper

Brown ground beef, bacon, and onion together and drain off the fat. Put this in a slow cooker, then add the rest of the ingredients in order. Mix well, cover, and cook on low for 8 to 9 hours or on high for 4 hours. This can also be done on top of the stove. It's even better the second day after all flavors have blended. My kids and all my guests like it.

If you can't feed a hundred people then just feed one.
—Mother Teresa

Midge's Lasagna

10 cooked lasagna strips (to cover pan twice)
1/2 pound of ground lean pork
1 pound of ground beef chuck
1 medium chopped onion   2 cloves of garlic crushed
2 tablespoons of olive oil   1 can (28-ounces) tomatoes
2 cans (6-ounces each) tomato paste
1/2 cup water   1 teaspoon salt
1/2 teaspoon basil leaves   1/2 cup oregano leaves
1/4 teaspoon crushed red pepper
1/4 cup chopped parsley
1 pound ricotta or cottage cheese
1/2 pound sliced mozzarella cheese and Parmesan cheese

Sauté meat with onion, garlic in oil until lightly browned. Add tomato paste, water, salt, basil, oregano, red pepper, and parsley. Simmer covered for 1 hour. Meanwhile, cook lasagna about 8 minutes. Drain and place in 13 X 9 X 2 1/4 roasting pan. Pour in 1/3 of the meat sauce. Cover with lasagna, dollops of ricotta, and Parmesan cheese. Repeat layers until all ingredients are used. Put mozzarella slices on top. Bake at 375 for 25 minutes. Serves 8.

Pasta Primavera

Sauté the following in 2 teaspoons oil:

1/2 cup diced red and/or green pepper
2 cloves minced garlic   1/4 cup diced onion
1/2 cup zucchini   1/2 cup broccoli flowerets
1 cup diced plum tomatoes

Add 1 cup cooked spaghetti noodles and 2 ounces of cooked red kidney beans.

Cook covered for about 10 minutes. Serve covered with 3/4 pound grated mozzarella cheese.

Elaine Stack
A Rosenquist Cousin
Great Falls, Montana

I don't ever remember my mother making lasagna. But her pasta dishes (macaroni and cheese, spaghetti, and noodles) were always one of my great expectations. Midge has a lasagna recipe that beats any I have ever tasted in any Italian restaurant. And we have been to Italy and cruised the Costa Line, an Italian steamship, so we have been exposed to some of the best!

Loren M. Carlson
My Brother
Vermillion, South Dakota

Clarice: My sister-in-law Midge really is a great cook; I've enjoyed many meals at their table. Midge and Loren are also a great dance team. They look for cruises that include a lot of dancing. At family weddings, Loren may be the oldest Carlson attending, but they are the last ones to leave the dance floor. After his heart surgery, he chose dancing as his main exercise, since he can only golf in the summer.

This is a favorite of our family's which I have made hundreds of times.

Marge Young
Lincoln, Nebraska

Clarice: Marge's husband, Lyle, was one of my bosses for the 20 years that I worked in the office of the dean of UNL's College of Engineering and Technology. I knew Marge as a good cook who sent goodies to the office get-togethers.

Mother was well known for this delicious casserole. Her friends always hoped she would bring it to their quilting potluck luncheons or her Sunday School Coworkers Class dinners. She also made wonderful macaroni and cheese and a great soufflé. She was a wonderful cook and we'll always remember her rye bread. She made delicious pies. My husband Dick's favorite was gooseberry as well as many other kinds. I have her recipe box and going through it brings back many wonderful memories.

Nadyne Bauer
Lincoln, Nebraska

Ground Beef/Rice Casserole

1 pound lean ground beef, browned
Add:
   1 1/2 cups rice
   1 1/2 cups chopped celery
   1/2 cup chopped onion...or more
   1 can cream of mushroom soup
   1 soup can of water...more if needed

Cook over low heat until rice is done. Season with salt, pepper, and soy sauce to taste. Serve over dried Chinese noodles and more soy sauce to taste. Or spoon casserole mixture on plates and top with Chinese noodles.

Lois Pentico's Cabbage Cheese Casserole

Cook until thick and add cheese to make a cheese sauce.

4 tablespoons butter	2 tablespoons flour
2 cups milk	2 cups cheddar cheese

Mix and add to cheese sauce.

   Cook 6 ounces of noodles and drain
   4 cups raw cabbage

Put buttered crumbs on top.

Clarice: For more than 40 years, along with Nadyne and Lois, her mother, and other Demeter Extension members, I learned homemaking tips right along with the value of the friendships of women.

ALL-AMERICAN PIES

I have learned that cooking is not just a necessity—it's a philosopy. It's a way of life. It's the only way to get a pie. Food can save the world.

—Chuck Kosterman
Knight Ridder Newspapers

Picture Perfect Apple Pie

The most important part is the crust. Don't ever use a commercial one. They aren't fit to eat and most people don't eat the crust when it has been purchased. Use either a glass or tin pie tin, and the crockery ones are ok, but never, ever use an aluminum one.

Then, depending on the depth of the pie tin, use 1 1/2 cups to 1 3/4 cup flour for a double crust pie.

With pastry blender cut in 2/3 cup fat. Lard is fine. I use Crisco and 2 tablespoons of butter, for good taste.

The next step is most important. This is the "pinch test." Pinch the dough together. If it stays pinched, there is enough fat, but chance is that it needs more, which I add a bit at a time until the pinch stays pinched. (Different flours take different amounts.)

Now the water. Take 1/4 cup water from refrigerator. Add 1/2 teaspoon cider vinegar. Add this and then water 1 tablespoon at a time. With a fork, blend it in until you can form dough into two balls. I use my hands as I have cold hands. Or you can put it in wax paper and form it into two balls.

Now, roll one ball out on a floured cloth or board. I roll it into a thin circle. If the circle has jagged edges, patch the edge by cutting dough pieces and put on with a finger dipped in water. Fold in half and fit in pie pan. Sprinkle 1 tablespoon flour in the bottom and add 1/4 cup sugar.

Peel and slice 5 or 6 large apples. McIntosh are best. Don't use Delicious as they are for eating fresh and have no flavor in baking. Put 1/2 cup sugar on apples and sprinkle generously with 1/2 teaspoon nutmeg and 1 teaspoon cinnamon.

The top crust is its crowning glory. Roll the other dough ball into a circle. Aim for a thin crust. Cut a pretty design, only a few cuts completely through the dough. I use my mother's design. I was going to originate my own, but my mother would have felt bad if I hadn't used hers. Fold the top and place on the bottom filled crust and flute the edge. Now it is sealed so it won't leak juices.

To put on the finishing touches, with a spoon and your fingers spread a thin layer of cream on the crust. Sprinkle with sugar.

THE RESULT IS A THING OF BEAUTY. Serve cold with a slice of cheese. My late husband, John Younger, used to say,

"Apple pie without the cheese
is like a kiss without the squeeze."

Beryl Younger
Brookings, South Dakota

Wonderful Fresh Peach Pie

This pie takes an already baked crust. The secret of this kind of crust is adhering the crust to the pie pan. After the crust is in the pan and fluted, prick the crust with a fork dipped in flour in each flute and over the sides and bottom.

Filling: Combine 4 1/2 tablespoons cornstarch and 1 cup sugar. Add 2 cups water gradually. Cook, stirring constantly until thick. Add one 6-ounce can of frozen orange concentrate and 1 teaspoon vanilla. Cool.

Cover the bottom of the pie shell with a layer of the filling. (This is to prevent sogginess.) Peel and slice 5 or 6 peaches into the shell. Pour on rest of the filling. Let set 1 hour. Then refrigerate.

Serve with real whipped cream. (The additives in frozen whipped topping are not good for you.)

In my lifetime, I've been considered a good cook, especially pies. I have thought of publishing my own recipes, but it is too late now. I would have included my mother's recipe for bars dating back to our Montana Homestead Days. Also a Plum Pudding from my English grandmother and a liver recipe called Yorkshire Ducks, which takes the lining of a cow's stomach, so it could only be made at butchering time.

Beryl Younger
Brookings, South Dakota

Clarice: I have eaten Beryl's Picture Perfect Apple Pie and I remember the cheese as the exquisite touch! Her husband, John Younger, was a giant in the development of leadership training for rural young people through the Cooperative Extension Service. Beryl and John's legacy continues on in many South Dakota families.

139

Mother was an excellent cook and could make a pie crust that would melt in our mouths. It looked so easy when she put the ingredients together. Being the youngest, I spent little time at the old cook stove. I remember asking mother about her pie crust and she gave me the above ingredients but no exact measurements. She said, "Put in enough flour to make it feel right when you roll it in your hands." FINE. I knew my crust would be just like mother's. WRONG.

When I was first married, we lived in an apartment in the little town of Hay Springs. The church was planning a special dinner and asked the ladies for food contributions. I bravely said that I would bring a pie. The day before the event, I started putting ingredients together for an "out of this world" pie. All went well until I tried rolling the dough in my hands. The first batch stuck to my fingers; the second was so dry it fell apart; the third was no better. With three sad little piles of dough on the counter, I called for the landlady's help. I never told anyone about the fiasco nor did I offer to ever make pie again.

Bertha Mae Jackman
Lincoln, Nebraska

Mother's Pie Crust

Pie crust for 9-inch two-crust pie

2 cups white flour
2/3 cup plus 1 tablespoon shortening
1 teaspoon salt
4 to 5 tablespoons cold water

Place flour and salt in bowl. Using two table knives, cut in the shortening, working until crumbly. Add water a small amount at a time. Mix with a fork until well blended. Work with floured hands and make a ball, adding more flour or water if needed. Divide and shape on floured board. Flatten the first ball of dough, sprinkle with flour and roll out with rolling pin; criss-cross the rolling until desired size—2 inches larger than inverted pie pan. Fold crust in half and ease into pie pan, gently pushing the dough to conform to the pan. Add the filling.

Roll out the top crust the same as bottom. Carefully place on top of filling. Trim the crusts so that there is enough to fold the top edge over and under the lower crust. Seal edge using the thumb to make a fluted design. Prick top of crust with fork and bake as directed.

Clarice: These two ladies, Beryl and Bertha Mae, have never met. However, I cherish the fact that each one took the time to share the details, special tips, and stories about making pie crust. Many people nowadays have NEVER tasted an authentic homemade pie. You are in for a real treat if you follow their instructions.

Pie Crust Recipe of the Pie Queen of Hanson County

3 cups sifted flour

1/4 teaspoon baking powder

2 teaspoons sugar

1 1/2 teaspoons salt

Combine the ingredients in the sifter and sift into a large bowl.

Cut 1 cup lard into the flour mixture with a pastry blender.

Beat 1 egg with 5 tablespoons cold water.

Stir into above mixture. Combine lightly and roll on floured board. Can be used for single or double crust pies. Tender and flaky.

My mom was the Grand Champion pie baker of Hanson County in 1942. According to the old news clipping, the contest was held at the Corn Palace in Mitchell, South Dakota, and required the use of lard as shortening but any filling could be used. Mom's entry had a cherry filling. Sponsored by a farm paper, the purpose of the contest was "to promote the use of lard and help maintain a fair price on hogs." The editor of the paper reported that one merchant, in a South Dakota town where a contest had been conducted, claimed that the sale of lard in his store had jumped 400 percent after the contest.

Evelyn Pierson
A Carlson Cousin
Ethan, South Dakota

Clarice: Evelyn's mother was my Aunt 'Manda. I can report that Evelyn is carrying on her mother's great cooking and baking traditions.

141

Aunt 'Manda's Chocolate Cream Pie

1/2 cup sugar
3 tablespoons flour
2 cups milk
1 square unsweetened chocolate
2 eggs separated
Butter the size of a walnut
1 teaspoon vanilla for filling

In a kettle, mix sugar and flour. Add milk and chocolate. Place over low heat and stir as chocolate melts. Beat egg yolks and add a little of hot mixture as you add to cooking ingredients. When thick and cooked, remove from heat. Add butter and vanilla. Pour into baked pastry.

Beat 2 egg whites until foamy, adding 4 tablespoons of sugar and 1/2 teaspoon vanilla. Spread over chocolate filling. Lightly brown the meringue in 350° oven.

Evelyn Pierson
A Carlson Cousin
Ethan, South Dakota

Life is not a bowl of cherries.
It's a bunch of raisins.
Raisin' heck, raisin' kids,
and raisin' money.

My mom made the best sour cream raisin pie in the world. Pa often preferred it to our traditional angel food cake for his birthday. There are several sour cream raisin pie recipes that follow in this book, (even more than the anecdotal "Mother's Apple Pie.") I'm sure each one is "delicious and delectable" …for each had "Mother's special touch."

Clarice Carlson Orr

My Mom's Sour Cream Raisin Pie

Boil together 1 cup raisins and 1/3 cup water until the raisins are plump. Add 1 cup sour cream and 2 tablespoons of lemon juice, or vinegar if lemon juice is not available.

Then add:

2/3 cup sugar	1 teaspoon cinnamon

Pinch of salt
3 egg yolks—keep the whites separate
2 tablespoons of cornstarch dissolved in a bit of water

Cook until thick and pour into a baked pastry shell. Beat the 3 remaining egg whites until foamy and add 1/4 teaspoon cream of tartar, 6 tablespoons sugar, and 1 teaspoon vanilla. Beat until the meringue holds stiff peaks. Bake at 350° until the meringue is slightly browned.

142

Betty's Mom's Sour Cream Raisin Pie Made With Sweet Cream

1 cup whipping cream
1 cup raisins, may be ground
1/2 cup sugar
1 teaspoon cinnamon
1/4 teaspoon nutmeg
1/4 teaspoon cloves
1 whole egg and 2 egg yolks

Boil all together until thick. Pour into a baked pie shell and top with meringue. Brown the meringue in a hot oven, watching carefully.

Clarice: When Betty and I were little girls, we often went home with each other after Sunday School. I had my first and only ride in a rumble seat in her brother Lee's new red Ford Roadster on the way home from church. I remember that Betty's mom ground the raisins for her pies, and that just wasn't quite the same as my mom's! But, that didn't spoil the good times we always had.

This is from my Mom's recipe box. Instead of using cultured sour cream, which doesn't work for this, I just use whipping cream. I guess it should be called sweet cream pie. I don't put vinegar in the sweet cream to sour it because I don't care for the taste of the vinegar. My mother always ground the raisins. When I started cooking, I hated washing the grinder, so I didn't make it for many years. Then I discovered it was pretty good with whole raisins; so I have made it that way ever since. It's a favorite of Britt's; he asks for it instead of cake for his birthday.

Betty Gulberg Bruner
A Shirt-tail Relative
Mitchell, South Dakota

My Mother's "Mean" Sweet Cream Raisin Pie

1 cup raisins	3/4 cup sugar
4 tablespoons flour	2 eggs, separated
1 cup cream	3/4 cup milk
Pinch of salt	

Stew raisins, drain. Add sugar and flour and add milk and cream. Cook until slightly thickened. Pour small amount over well-beaten egg yolks. Add salt and cook until thick. Pour into baked pie shell and cover with meringue. Brown in a hot oven.

Meringue: Add a pinch of salt to egg whites and beat until foamy. Add sugar slowly, 6 tablespoons to 3 egg whites.

My mother could make a "mean" raisin pie with sweet cream. That's another of her recipes I have had trouble duplicating. I still have the recipe that was scribbled off many years ago on a piece of scrap paper. I like to look in my recipe box and see her handwriting on several of my recipe cards.

Joyce Tyrrel
My Heart Transplant Friend
Lincoln, Nebraska

143

My grandmother, Ruth McPherson Moslander, died when I was only eight years old, but I have many fond memories of her. She was a "larger-than-life" woman, mostly due to her gregarious nature, can-do attitude, and unwavering faith. She had a basketful of talents…breaking horses, teaching school, farming, entertaining small grandchildren with simple ordinary tasks…but I remember her in front of her old stove in my grandparents Quonset house more than anything. She would whisk, sift, beat, and voila! A tasty concoction appeared in a whipstitch! Of course, this was always done while humming along to the tunes on The Arthur Godfrey Show.

My grandma's sour cream raisin pie is, in my opinion, one of her most terrific creations and one I still make on occasion. I've written it exactly the way she did…some exact and some inexact measurements. As I think about it, that characterizes Grandma's life; the security and comfort gleaned from faith, family and hard work coupled with spontaneity and a zest for laughter. Grandma, I hope I am some of you.

Kim Behrens
Lincoln, Nebraska

Grandma Moslander's Sour Cream Raisin Pie

1 baked pie crust	1 cup sugar
1 cup sour cream	2 egg yolks
2 tablespoons of flour	Pinch of salt
1 cup raisins	1 cup nuts
Butter the size of a nut	Cinnamon to taste

Cook raisins, in water enough to cover, until plump. Add remaining ingredients and cook until thick. Pour into pie shell, make meringue with the remaining egg whites and brown slightly.

Dora Wright's Sour Cream Raisin Pie

Make a graham cracker crust or regular pie crust.

Filling:

4 tablespoons cornstarch	1/2 teaspoon cloves
1 cup sour cream	1 cup sugar
3 egg yolks	1 cup raisins

Cook until thick. Cool slightly and pour in baked pie shell. Make a meringue of 3 egg whites and 1/3 cup sugar. Cover the pie with the meringue and bake at 425° 5 to 7 minutes.

Dora Wright was my grandmother.

Doris Freeman
Lincoln, Nebraska

Chocolate Sundae Pie

1 baked pie shell

Mix together in top of double boiler:

    1 cup evaporated milk   1/2 cup water
    1/4 teaspoon nutmeg

Beat until very light:

    3 egg yolks
    1/2 cup sugar
    1/4 teaspoon salt

Pour hot milk over egg mixture. Return to double boiler and cook until the texture of thick cream. Remove from heat. Add: 1 tablespoon gelatin soaked in 3 tablespoons cold water and 1 teaspoon vanilla. Cool.

When ready to set: Beat 3 egg whites until light and stiff. Fold into chilled filling; pour into pie shell and refrigerate. When set, cover with 1 cup sweetened whipped cream. Top with 1/4 cup grated bitter baking chocolate.

A close second to date pudding was another traditional family-favorite called chocolate sundae pie. We sometimes had this on Christmas and often upon other special occasions, especially when guests were present. Mother's pie crust was unfailingly flaky, and the cool, smooth, yet light texture of the filling evokes memories of perfect pleasure. I made this special pie many times when I entertained in later years, but I have never encountered it anywhere outside our family. Try it—it could well become special to your family also.

Sid Hahn Culver
Lincoln, Nebraska

Forgiveness is giving up the Hope you can change the Past.

I've loved pumpkin pie for as long as I can remember. If there was ever a choice, I always picked a piece of pumpkin pie. Grandma Geyer's pumpkin pie was always so good that Mom wanted to know how she made it. Grandma told her it was "just the recipe off the Libby's pumpkin can." So Mom started making the same recipe. Or so she thought. It was never quite the same as Grandma's. But Grandma always insisted that it was Libby's.

One time when my sister, Karen, was visiting, Grandma started to make her pumpkin pie. Karen took note, and what she found was that, although it was based on the Libby's recipe, Grandma had added a few twists of her own. The result...one great pumpkin pie. Both of my grandmothers were great cooks and they both tinkered with recipes. This one we were lucky enough to catch and write down. And now my mom, my sisters, and I will be able to pass this on, along with our memories of a wonderful lady.

Mary Senne
Lincoln, Nebraska

Libby's Pumpkin Pie
(with a little added tinkering)

3 eggs, lightly beaten
1 cup brown sugar
2 teaspoons cinnamon
2 tablespoons molasses
1 12-ounce can evaporated milk
1 9inch unbaked pie crust

1 16-ounce can pumpkin
1/2 teaspoon salt
1 teaspoon ginger

Combine ingredients, pour into unbaked pie crust. Bake at 425° for 15 minutes. Reduce temperature to 350° and bake an additional 40-50 minutes or until knife inserted about 2 inches from the edge comes out clean. Cool, garnish with whipped topping, and serve.

Aunt Dora's Butterscotch Pie

1 cup brown sugar	2 tablespoons butter
2 tablespoons cream	2 tablespoons flour
1 cup milk	2 egg yolks
	(reserve whites for meringue)

1 8 or 9 inch baked pie crust

In heavy saucepan, slowly bring to boil the brown sugar, butter, and cream. Make a thickening of the flour, milk and egg yolks. Stir a small amount of the hot mixture into this. Mix well, then add the rest of the hot mixture and cook until thick. Keep stirring to keep from scorching or getting lumpy. Pour warm mixture into baked crust and top with your favorite meringue.

Rhubarb Custard Pie

Pour boiling water over 2 cups chopped rhubarb. Let set for five minutes. Drain off water then mix rhubarb with 1 cup sugar, yolks of 3 eggs, 1 tablespoon butter, 1 tablespoon flour, and 1 cup cream. Bake in unbaked pie crust at 350° for 45 minutes or insert knife to see if custard is done.

Top with egg whites beaten into a meringue, return to oven and bake until golden brown.

How could anyone forget when rhubarb season came around? We had rhubarb pudding, rhubarb jelly, rhubarb upside down cake, and a host of other foods Mother could think of. I'm sure these recipes came over with the boat, along with my Grandmother. I remember the rhubarb days well, because it was during the Dirty Thirties when we appreciated any type of food available to us. We were among the fortunate who lived on the farm and grew much of our food.

Delta Schmidt
Lincoln, Nebraska

This recipe is short and simple, but the enjoyment and love of it has continued for many years at our "Annual 3-S Brayer Family Picnic." (My four sons named it that since we always met the Second Sunday of September.) My mother's sister, Dora, never failed to bring her Butterscotch Pie. As years went by, it seemed that each year someone else would decide that was their favorite pie. Now, many years after Aunt Dora, and her daughter Myrtle—who kept the tradition of making this pie for the picnic—have been called from our midst, Christine, Aunt Dora's granddaughter, pleases our taste buds each year. The only change is that now it's become "tradition" to take your piece of pie when you get your main course of food. Otherwise, chances are you may be waiting until next year for that favorite piece of Aunt Dora's Butterscotch Pie!

Darleen Richard
Lincoln, Nebraska

Clarice: Delta was the first friend to welcome me to Lincoln way back in 1956 when we moved from Brookings, South Dakota. We've watched our families grow up and leave the nest.

147

This recipe and the Chocolate Cheese Pie (below) go back to the 1940s when Dream Whip and Eagle Brand sweetened condensed milk became available. Its smooth texture was unlike anything I had tasted before. This is an updated version using low fat, low sugar ingredients.

Marge Young
Lincoln, Nebraska

Springtime Lime or Lemon Dessert or Pie (low fat, low sugar)

Crust: 1 1/2 cups crushed graham crackers, 1/2 cup melted Imperial margarine, 2 packets Equal or sugar substitute

Combine these ingredients well, and firmly pat into a 9 inch pie plate. Reserving some to sprinkle on top of the pie.

Filling: Beat one package of Dream Whip according to directions or use one 8-ounce carton of Cool Whip. Set aside.

Using an electric mixer, mix the following together until smooth: 3 ounces low fat cream cheese or Neufchâtel with 2 tablespoons of milk. Add 1 can low fat Eagle Brand sweetened condensed milk, 1/2 cup lime or lemon juice, zest of either one lime or lemon. Then add the prepared Dream Whip and few drops of green coloring to the lime filling.

Spread over the crust and sprinkle the remaining graham crumbs on the top. Refrigerate several hours. Serves 8.

This very rich dessert may be cut into 6-8 servings. The filling may also be spooned into sherbet dishes (no crust) and served with an extra dollop of whipped topping or a maraschino cherry on top of each one.

Marge Young
Lincoln, Nebraska

Chocolate Cheese Pie (low fat, low sugar)

Crust: 1 1/2 cups crushed graham crackers, 1/4 cup melted Imperial margarine, 2 packets Equal or sugar substitute

Combine these ingredients well, and firmly pat into a 9 inch pie plate, reserving some to sprinkle on top of the pie.

Filling: Prepare Dream Whip as directed on package. Set aside. An 8-ounce carton of frozen whipped topping may be used instead.

Melt 6 ounces of chocolate chips in microwave. Add 3 ounces of low fat cream cheese, softened. May add 3 packets of Equal (optional). Blend 1/2 cup of this mixture into the prepared Dream Whip, then fold in the remainder and spoon into the crust.

DESSERTS
FOR CLUB
& LADIES
AIDE

*God could not be everywhere
so he created Grandmothers.*

—an old Yiddish saying

Momma and the Club Ladies

Each month, the women in our neighborhood took a "day off" from laundry, cooking, gardening, and sewing to go to Club—the Social Hour Club. This dozen or so ladies met in each others homes—mostly for socialization and womanly support. I treasure the pink and white friendship quilt the club members made for Mom, and I like to read the faded names on the flower-embroidered squares—Ann Tyler, Sengne Gulberg, Emma Alsene, and Lana Carlson—were a few. Momma also went to Ladies Aide where there were devotions and a Bible lesson before the business of the day—when the women of the church planned picnics, dinners, or missionary efforts.

Getting ready for Club or Ladies Aide at our house meant that Momma embarked on a huge house cleaning project. She washed the kitchen curtains and the windows and got a new oilcloth for the kitchen table. When I was old enough, I painted the kitchen table and the chairs. My penny loafers got spattered so I painted them blue and white, too. Sometimes Momma would persuade Pa that we needed a new linoleum in the kitchen or the dining room. I still remember the clean, shiny smell of the new floorcovering, the new oilcloth, and fresh furniture wax.

Deciding what to have for refreshments was usually a committee responsibility. After one committee meeting, Momma was annoyed that "Alice" had insisted on "plain old red Jell-O" for dessert. Even afterwards at home, whenever we had red Jell-O, Pa would pat Momma on the knee and tease her with Alice's words, "You know, there's nothing nicer than a nice dish of red Jell-O."

Often, two or three ladies would help with lunch and bring their favorite kinds of cakes. There would be sour cream chocolate with brown sugar icing topped with nuts, white cake with sticky seven-minute frosting, marble cake with fudgey chocolate icing, and an occasional burnt sugar cake—all baked in 9 X 13 glass or aluminum pans. Sometimes, there was a tall angel food or sponge cake with powdered sugar frosting.

Clarice Carlson Orr

150

Aunt 'Manda's Angel Food

12 large, cold eggs. Separate the yolks from the whites.

1 cup cake flour plus 2 tablespoons
    (sift in flour sifter before measuring)
1/4 teaspoon salt
1 teaspoon vanilla
1 1/2 cups white sugar
1 teaspoon cream of tartar

Directions: Sift flour and salt together 7 or 8 times. Sift the sugar 7 or 8 times.

Put the egg whites in a large enamel or glass bowl and beat with a wire whisk beater until half beaten; then add cream of tartar. Finish beating until the egg whites are stiff. Add the sugar, folding in a small amount at a time with the whisk beater until all is added.

Fold in the flour a small amount at a time with a large mixing spoon. Add vanilla. Pour into an ungreased angel food tube pan. Bake 1 hour at 350°. Invert the pan to cool.

This cake was very high and delicious. Remember, it was baked in an old-time cookstove, where cobs and wood were the fuel. To keep the temperature even, one cob was added at a time. These were called pigpen cobs as the pigs were fed whole ears of corn, and only the corn cobs remained to be picked up by the children for fuel. This cake was served at Hank's and my wedding supper on December 4, 1940.

Evelyn Pierson
A Carlson Cousin
Ethan, South Dakota

Clarice: I asked my cousin Evelyn about the "legend" my folks used to tell of her mother's (my Aunt 'Manda's) angel food cake being crushed with a silver knife at the school social by an inexperienced cake cutter. She didn't remember the situation, but since her angel food has such a delicate texture, it could very well have happened. And maybe my mother knew the true story.

Being at peace with yourself is a direct result of finding peace with God.
—Olin Miller

My childhood was sprinkled liberally with scrumptious Angel Food cakes. It was my Mom's special recipe that no one else in my large extended family, nor my extended neighborhood, ever made quite in the same "drop-dead-melt-in-your-mouth" way as my mother's. My own special version had a Kewpie-doll in the center hole and Mom would decorate it so it looked like Kewpie was going to a great ball with the cake being a beautiful skirt.

It took around a dozen eggs, at exactly the right temperature, separated carefully to keep every speck of yolk out; and then an aerobic exercise not seen in kitchens today—hand beating, beating and beating until the egg whites stood up in perfect peaks. Then came the delicate art of folding the other ingredients in carefully, so as not to collapse the many little air pockets that had been created by the beating, beating, beating process.

Whenever I eat an average angel food cake made from a mix, I am reminded of a very motherly message: **Things in our life that go beyond average take time, patience, and the special caring of an artful creator.**

Have you ever eaten clouds? I have, and an 89-year-old angel in my life, whom I call Mom, made them.

Angel Food "Cloud" Cake

1 1/8 cups sifted cake flour
3/4 cup sugar
1/2 teaspoon salt
1 1/2 teaspoon cream of tartar
1 teaspoon vanilla
1 1/2 cups egg whites
1 cup sugar
1 teaspoon almond extract

Sift flour and the 3/4 cup sugar together. Put room temperature egg whites and salt in large bowl and beat until foamy. Add cream of tartar and continue beating until there are firm peaks, but do not over beat. Sprinkle the one cup of sugar in while beating the egg whites. Beat only until sugar is blended. Add vanilla and almond extract. Sprinkle in flour and the 3/4 cup sugar mixture evenly and fold in carefully.

Pour into 10" tube pan.

Bake at 375° for 30-35 minutes until the top is golden brown.

Eat and enjoy your heavenly experience!

Deanna Baxter Eversoll
Lincoln, Nebraska

Clarice: It is interesting that two angel food cake recipes are similar, yet the details reveal the special techniques that each lady deemed important. Their exquisite taste is worth all the trouble—especially if someone else has done all the work!

Homemade Ice Cream

8 ounces egg substitute
2 cups sugar
1 1/2 pints cream
5 cups milk
3 teaspoons vanilla

Beat egg substitute and sugar. Beat in cream and vanilla. Pour milk into ice cream freezer can and add egg mixture. Using the ice and salt around the filled can, freeze the ice cream as directed.

H omemade ice cream is a staple on Christmas and July 4th in our family. The egg substitute keeps it safe.

Claire Altoff
Minnesota Extension Service
Breckinridge, Minnesota

Clarice: Claire introduced me to the educational program, "Who Gets Grandma's Yellow Pie Plate?" This program helps folks decide how to distribute family keepsakes.

Viennese Sacher-Torte

Heat together in a double boiler:

1/8 liter of oil (about 3/8 of a cup)
1 3-ounce bar of sweet cooking chocolate

In another bowl beat together:

3 egg yolks
1 cup sugar

Add:

1 cup flour
1 teaspoon of baking powder
3 tablespoons of rum
The melted chocolate with oil

Fold in carefully, the 3 beaten egg whites

Pour batter into a spring-form pan lined with greased vellum or waxed paper. Bake the cake for 40 minutes in a medium oven.

When the cake is cold, cut it horizontally into three layers.

Spread the top of two layers with apricot jam—about one jar. Place the layers on top of one another. Cover the cake with another melted bar of sweet chocolate mixed with 2 ounces of butter or margarine. Decorate it with blanched almonds.

T his recipe, Sacher-Torte, is from Austria. The famous Sacher invented it, when he was the cook for Furst Metternich in 1832. Later on, he started the Hotel Sacher and restaurant in Vienna, which remains very famous. You can still buy this cake there.

Rena Bolza-Schünemann
Würzburg, Germany

Clarice: Rena is a special lady to my daughter Becky's family. My son-in-law, Nick, was an exchange student in Germany in 1969 and Rena was his host-mother. Thirty years later, Nick and Becky's daughter, Claire, was an exchange student and lived with Nick's host-brother's family. Claire enjoyed many happy times with Rena. I am grateful to Rena for "grandmothering" Claire during her stay. I also appreciate the effort she made to translate this recipe from German to English.

Celebrating My New Heart Strawberry Cake

The BIG DAY, when I officially got my new heart was October 30, 1989. I went back to work at the University of Nebraska-Lincoln in December 1990 and may retire soon. I celebrate my Heart Birthday each year by bringing this strawberry cake to the office for everybody to enjoy.

While I was waiting for my heart that summer, I waited, impatiently at home, for my beeper to go off telling me this was the day. Keeping a journal on my new computer helped me pass the time and I sometimes baked something to entice my kids to come over.

On July 9, 1989, I wrote, "While I was baking cookies, I looked at my recipe and noticed it is about worn out. I thought I should probably make a new card and my immediate reaction was that this one would probably last as long as I do." I went on to say, "Examining that thought makes me realize I really don't think I have a very positive attitude about being fortunate enough to get a heart transplant. It's kind of like going to church—when you go on a regular basis and receive encouragement and enthusiasm, you stay excited about what you believe in. I had lots of enthusiasm when I talked to people in the hospital and when I repeated my information to

1 package white cake mix
1 package strawberry Jell-O
1/2 package frozen strawberries
4 eggs
1/2 cup salad oil
1/2 cup water

Mix thoroughly, bake according to directions on cake box.

Frosting: 1/2 stick margarine, 1 pound box powdered sugar; Use other part of the 1/2 of box of frozen strawberries as liquid for proper consistency of frosting.

This is a pretty simple recipe, but it's a beautiful pink cake and frosting, and really tastes like strawberries. It's very moist and the folks at work always clean it up. The frosting never needs all the strawberries left from the 1/2 box so I just eat what's left myself!

my friends after I came home. Now I rarely talk to people about it."

I got up on Sunday morning, the 29th, and baked a pumpkin pie in hopes of luring the kids over for pie later in the day. I'll always remember joking with Glen that "I sure hope I get this pie out of the oven before Nancy calls from the hospital." Of course, I did get it baked, but Nancy did call about 4 hours later and I was on my way to the hospital for my long awaited transplant, after I called Clarice and asked her to pray.

The best part was that I never got any of that pie. But I had my new heart and was doing fine at 2:30 A.M. and my family all went home to celebrate with that pumpkin pie. Just the mention of pumpkin pie after all this time, still brings to mind that very special occasion.

Joyce Tyrrel
Lincoln, Nebraska

Clarice: That BIG DAY was a time for reJoycing. Thank you, Joyce for sharing thoughts from your heart.

Edna Carlson's Sour Cream Chocolate Cake

1 cup sugar
2 heaping tablespoons of cocoa
2 cups cake flour (scant)
1 cup sour cream
2 eggs
1 teaspoon soda dissolved in a little hot water
vanilla
pinch of salt.

Mix dry ingredients. I think Mom sifted this if she had time and if it was for a special occasion. Add sour cream, eggs, soda, vanilla, and salt. Beat well. Bake in 9 X 13 pan at 350° for 45 minutes or until the clean end of a broom straw comes out clean from the center of the cake.

Dakota Farmer Red Devil's Food

1 cup sugar
1 cup sour cream
1/2 cup cocoa dissolved in 2 1/2 cups hot water
3 eggs
1 teaspoon soda
1 teaspoon vanilla
1 1/2 cup flour

I found both of these recipes in Mom's handwriting on recipe cards. I think the first sour cream cake was her favorite quick recipe. She mixed it all up quickly, without having to look at the recipe. She varied the frosting with the event or what she might have on hand. For a group of ladies, it might be a sugar and water syrup beaten into egg whites (with a rotary egg beater in a double boiler) for seven minutes with nutmeats or coconut sprinkled on top. Or for the men who were working out in the field, she might cook butter, cream, and brown sugar for a penuche frosting. For a quick supper dessert, powdered sugar, a walnut-size piece of butter, cocoa, and a little milk made a good lick-the-spoon icing.

Clarice Carlson Orr

As a child, I learned early to enjoy chocolate!

As my September 3rd birthday approached, I made my plans on how to celebrate. Usually it meant I had permission to invite my best pal, Elaine, for supper and overnight.

All this was accented by my annual special request—my Mom's Sour Cream Chocolate Cake. "No frosting, please, just some butter!" We were permitted not only to have it for dessert, but for a bedtime snack.

My Mom enjoyed fulfilling my birthday request, as mothers do whenever they can please their child. She continued fulfilling my request well into my adult years—a special, sweet memory of my special, sweet mother, Eunice Edwards Bintz.

Ruth Bintz Knight
Sun City, Arizona

The 1930s Sour Cream Chocolate Cake

1 stick butter
2 cups sugar
2 eggs
1/4 teaspoon vanilla
2 squares melted unsweetened chocolate
2 teaspoons baking soda
1 cup sour cream
1 cup sifted cake flour
1 cup sifted regular flour
1 teaspoon salt.

Cream butter and sugar. Add one ingredient at a time: salt, eggs, vanilla, and chocolate. Mix soda and sour cream together. Add to mixture. Add flour. Bake in well-greased 9 X 13 cake pan at 350° for 45 minutes to 1 hour, or until cake comes away from the sides of the pan.

Clarice: After many moves and many years, it's good to reconnect with my friend, Ruth. It was a nice surprise to learn that her mother made sour cream chocolate cakes, too.

Coffee Chocolate Cake

1/2 cup cocoa	1 cup boiling coffee
1/2 cup shortening	2 cups sugar
3 eggs	1 teaspoon vanilla
3/4 teaspoon salt	2 1/2 cups flour
2 teaspoons soda	1 cup sour milk or buttermilk

This favorite chocolate cake was served many, many times to my children at Sunday dinners and after school snacks. It is so-o-o-o tasty.

Myrtle Monia
Lincoln, Nebraska

Mix cocoa and coffee together and cool. Cream shortening and sugar until light and fluffy. Beat well and add vanilla. Sift flour, salt, and soda. Add flour mixture and milk alternately to creamed mixture. Beat until smooth. Blend in cocoa mixture. Bake in two 9 inch greased and floured pans at 350° for 30 minutes. Makes a large layer cake. Frost as desired.

Grandma Covey's Spice Cake

Mix all together in one large bowl:

2 eggs	2 cups of sugar

1 cup of lard (scant, it says in the old cookbook)
I now use 1 cup of Crisco.

1 1/2 cups buttermilk	1 big teaspoon soda
1 teaspoon cinnamon	1 teaspoon nutmeg

1 cup raisins, and I also put in some cut dates

Dissolve the soda in milk and add 3 cups flour and 1/2 teaspoon baking powder. Mix well and bake in a large sheet pan, the next larger than 9 X 13 or two smaller ones. Generously sprinkle sugar all over the cake before baking, then no frosting is needed as it forms a little sweet crust on top and it carries well as there is no messy frosting. My husband enjoyed it many years in his lunches.

Mother Hilda Hansen's Spice Cake

Boil one cup raisins in 1 cup water

1 cup white sugar	1/2 cup brown sugar
1/2 cup lard (scant)	3 eggs beaten

Mix the raisin water with 1 teaspoon soda, 2 teaspoons cinnamon, 1/2 teaspoon cloves, 3/4 teaspoon allspice, and 3/4 teaspoon nutmeg and 1 teaspoon baking powder and mix with all the other ingredients along with enough flour to make the batter right. Bake in 9 X 13 pan at 350° for 45 minutes or until top doesn't remain depressed when touched with your finger.

In place of the lard, I use 2/3 cup shortening, 2 cups flour, 2 teaspoons baking powder. Also you may soften the raisins in 1 cup of applesauce instead of the water. Everyone in our big family loved this spice cake.

Maxine Nickel
A Carlson Cousin
Fulton, South Dakota

I started baking this cake when I was very young and now I am 96 years old. My Grandma was born April 7, 1849, in Ireland and died in 1917. She was Isabelle Corning Covey and I was named after her. She moved to Canada, then New York State when young, and married Albert Covey and moved to Lincoln. They lived a couple blocks from where I grew up. When I was a girl, about 7 to 12, I spent a lot of time playing games with her and enjoying a piece of her spice cake and a glass of milk.

Isabelle Lampshire
Lincoln, Nebraska

Clarice: I knew that when I went to Isabelle's for club, we were in for a treat. She often baked a scrumptious cherry pie. Although she is 96+ years old, Isabelle remains an eager, enthusiastic fan of Nebraska Cornhusker Football and Basketball.

Clarice: Hilda was my father's oldest sister and I really didn't get to know her very well. I'm glad that now I see my Hansen cousins once in awhile... That's one of the values of having regular family reunions.

157

I don't remember much about Mother's cooking in my childhood. Since we lived on an isolated ranch in Wyoming, I left home at 13 to go to high school and was only home for summers and occasional weekends. I do remember Mother's kitchen when I was married and going home to visit. Mother had eight children; I was second oldest and she always worked after they moved to town.

Sundays were family days. When we went home, everybody who could came for Sunday dinner. It was a houseful and we ate anywhere we could find a spot to put down a plate as there were always 15 or 20 there. In the summer we moved to the backyard, which was Mother's pride and joy. Dad loved to mow the lawn and Mother had flowers everywhere—in pots on the garage wall, around the vegetable garden, and in beds by the house. In summer, before she went to work, you could always find her in the garden, barefoot, with a coffee cup in her hand. She was a true "mother"—she mothered everyone and had such a cheerful disposition.

Mother also taught Sunday School for many years, so Sunday dinners were a real production. She loved to do fried chicken, or a big beef roast, and fresh yeast rolls came hot out of the oven. When she was rushed, this Oatmeal Cake was a favorite.

I don't remember having a favorite dish I asked for—she didn't use many recipes anyway. What I remember was the warmth of the family, the laughter, the visiting in the kitchen as we washed the dishes, the time to have a second dessert and cup of coffee late in the afternoon and talk to my sisters. It was HOME and we could have eaten biscuits and bacon and eggs and had a wonderful time.

Gladys Woods
Lincoln, Nebraska

Mother's Oatmeal Cake

1 cup oatmeal	1 cup boiling water
1/2 cup butter	1 cup white sugar
1 cup brown sugar	2 eggs
1 teaspoon vanilla	1 1/3 cups flour
1/2 teaspoon salt	1 teaspoon soda
1 1/2 teaspoons cinnamon	1/2 cup chopped walnuts or pecans

Pour boiling water over oatmeal. Let stand 20 minutes. Cream butter, sugars, eggs, and vanilla. Add oatmeal mixture and dry ingredients. Stir in nuts. Bake at 350° for 35-40 minutes in 9 X 13 pan. While still warm, top with mixture of 3/4 stick butter, 3/4 cup brown sugar, 1/2 cup nuts, 1 cup shredded coconut and enough milk so it can be spread. Place under broiler until bubbly and brown.

Betty's Prune Cake

Cream together: 1 cup sugar + 1/2 cup butter + 2 eggs

Add alternately: 2 cups flour + 1 teaspoon nutmeg + 1 teaspoon cinnamon + 1/4 teaspoon cloves and 1/2 teaspoon salt

With: 3/4 cup sour cream + 1 teaspoon baking soda + 1 teaspoon vanilla

Put 1 cup chopped prunes in cup and add enough hot water to fill the cup. Let set a few minutes in the cup. Stir prunes into batter.

Pour into 2 greased and floured 9 inch round cake pans. Bake at 350° for 25-30 minutes until cake is just done to the touch. Don't over bake.

Filling: 1/2 cup raisins + 1 egg + 1/2 cup sour cream + 1/2 cup sugar + 2 tablespoons flour. Cook until thickened. Put between layers and top with 7-minute frosting.

Aunt Clara Knefelkamp's German Apple Cake

Mix and let stand:

    2 cups chopped or shredded raw apple
    1 cup sugar

Sift together: 1 cup flour + 1 teaspoon soda + 1 teaspoon salt + 1 teaspoon cinnamon

Stir in 1 egg, 1/4 cup salad oil, and 1/2 cup nuts. Mix all together and pour into 8 inch cake pan. Bake at 350° for 30 minutes.

Marge Thomssen
Lincoln, Nebraska

Brother Bill and I rode horses to country school, District #19 in Hall County, Nebraska. It was his job, being the older brother, to put the horses away in the barn, take the saddles off and feed them when we got home from school each day.

This one particular day, in about 1946, I came into the kitchen where our sister Ellen was making a prune cake. Knowing that Bill really liked prunes, she tried to hide them before he came in from the barn. He came stomping in and grabbed for the package of prunes. Prunes flew everywhere in the kitchen. Both of them scrambled for the prunes. Bill grabbed the ones from the floor and began stuffing them in his mouth. Included with some of the prunes was a little something that had dropped off his boots when he stomped into the kitchen from the barn.

He spit and swore, and swore and spit some more. Poor Bill doesn't like prunes anymore.

This story has been a family favorite of all my siblings and our children. For his birthday recently, I sent him a prune cake and thanked him for providing us so much fun through the years of telling the Bill and the Prunes Story.

Marge Thomssen
Lincoln, Nebraska

This cake has always been my very favorite. My mother made it when I was small. It had a caramel frosting, too. I tried and tried to learn how to make it myself, but I always burned the sugar! Mom said that anybody could do it, that it was very simple and easy. I tried and tried—and failed and failed! It was the best cake I ever ate, and if anyone knows how to do that Caramel, please tell me and I'll try again!

I think Mom quit baking it during WW II because sugar was rationed, and also because I wasted so much sugar in my futile efforts to learn to cook!

Amy Franklin
Lincoln, Nebraska

Burnt Sugar Layer Cake

To make caramel, brown 1 cup sugar then add ½ cup hot water.

1. Beat together the following ingredients for 5 minutes (this recipe was before electric mixers, so it meant to beat by hand.)
1 1/2 cup sugar
1/2 cup butter
2 egg yolks
1 cup water
2 cups flour
2. Then add:
2 tablespoons caramel
(from the prepared caramelized sugar)
1 teaspoon vanilla
2 teaspoons baking powder
1/2 cup flour
3. Then add:
2 well-beaten egg whites

Pour into cake pans and bake.

Mom used a lot of fruit cocktail in Jell-O and I know this recipe for Fruit Cocktail Cake was a wonderful innovative way to combine canned fruit and a pudding/cake. It's a little like applesauce cake. One of the best things about it is that it doesn't have any fat or shortening and it still tastes good.

Clarice Carlson Orr

Fruit Cocktail Cake

1 cup sugar
1 egg
1 teaspoon vanilla
1 cup flour sifted with 1/2 teaspoon salt
and 1/2 teaspoon soda.
1 #2 can of fruit cocktail well drained

Beat the sugar and egg together until light and fluffy. Add the other ingredients. Put in greased 12 X 7 pan. Sprinkle with a little brown sugar and a few nutmeats. Bake at 350° for 35 minutes.

Farina Torte

Beat 6 egg yolks and add 2 cups sugar.

Mix the following and add to the egg/sugar mixture:

- 3/4 cup farina
- 2 tablespoons flour
- 1/4 cup bread crumbs
- 2 teaspoons baking powder

Add 1 cup nuts and fold in 6 egg whites, stiffly beaten.

Pour batter into cake pan lined with wax paper. Bake 40 minutes at 350°. Turn out on a rack and remove wax paper while cake is hot. When cool, break into pieces (about 1 inch) and arrange on platter with whipped cream and maraschino cherries. Mound up like a cake. Takes about 1 quart of whipping cream. Allow to stand in refrigerator at least 2 hours. Serves 16.

In the early 1950s, I was an extension specialist at Cornell University. I had a friend whose parents came from Norway and lived in Jamestown, NY. Whenever I had meetings in that area of New York state, I stayed with my friend's mother. She always served this dessert. It is wonderful.

Marie E. Knickrehm
Lincoln, Nebraska

My friend Jackie Sykes gave me this recipe many years ago. My father and mother, Bill and Esther Thomssen, find this cake one of the best. I asked my mother what she wanted for her 90th birthday and she replied, "Make your great Bundt cake."

I made it in Albuquerque, New Mexico, and took it to Grand Island, Nebraska, carrying it on a Fostoria cake platter. WOW! The smell of fresh baked cake on the airplane. Mother liked this cake so much she asked me to send her one through the mail and include the recipe so she could make it. I knew she didn't have a Bundt pan so I bought one for her. I made the cake in my own pan. Then I frosted it like usual, cooled it and put it in her gift Bundt pan and sent it through the mail. It traveled safely. At Christmas time I sent one to my dad. I wrapped it in several layers of foil. It too, traveled great. It freezes well, too. Yum! Yum!

Kathryn Ritterbush
Albuquerque, New Mexico

Bundt Pan Cake

1 box yellow cake mix	1 small vanilla pudding mix
1/4 cup flour	1 1/4 cup water
1/3 cup oil	4 whole eggs

If you live in a high altitude, as I do in New Mexico, be sure to use those directions for the cake mix or the cake will fall. Beat until light, then add 1 teaspoon butter extract and 1 teaspoon vanilla.

Put Crisco all over the bottom of the Bundt pan and flour well.

Make a mixture of 2/3 cup finely chopped pecans, 4 tablespoons sugar and 1 teaspoon cinnamon. Put 1/4 of batter over some chopped pecans and spoon more of the pecan/sugar mixture over the batter. Keep the mixture out of the center or sides. Do 4 layers using all and end up with batter on the top.

Bake 375° for 1/2 hour then at 350° for 20 minutes or until inserted toothpick is clean. After it's been out of the oven for 10 minutes, invert on a glass platter.

Make a glaze of 1/2 teaspoon butter extract, 1/2 teaspoon vanilla, 1 cup powdered sugar, and 3 tablespoons of hot milk. I scald it in the microwave. Dribble this up and down the warm cake. (This glaze works well on angel food cake, too.)

Necessary Apple Cake

4 cups of raw cubed apples

Mix the following:

    1/2 cup brown sugar
    1 1/2 cups white sugar
    1/2 cup salad oil
    2 eggs beaten
    1 teaspoon of vanilla
    2 cups flour
    1/4 teaspoon salt
    2 teaspoons soda
    2 teaspoons cinnamon
    1 cup nutmeats, chopped
    1/4 cup of milk

Put all together and add apples and mix. Bake for 40-45 minutes at 350°.

Opal's Date Cake – 1974

    1 cup chopped dates
    1 1/2 cups boiling water poured over dates
    2 1/2 teaspoon soda

Allow to cool.

Blend the following and add to date mixture:

    3/4 cup shortening
    1 cup sugar
    2 egg yolks or 1 egg, beaten

Sift 1 3/4 cup flour, 3/4 teaspoon soda and dash of salt

Add to date mixture and beat. Spread in 9 X 13 inch pan. Over top, sprinkle 6 ounces chocolate chips + 1/4 cup white sugar + chopped walnuts. No need for frosting later. Bake at 350° about 35 minutes.

Marge Thomssen
Lincoln, Nebraska

We moved to Vermillion in 1968 although we had been here numerous times while Midge and I were attending the University. We bought our home at 229 Catalina and one of our first landscaping projects was to plant a dwarf apple tree in our back yard. We bought it at Gurney's in Yankton. There was something wrong with that tree. It wasn't a dwarf. Instead, it became a large shade tree and has borne apples with great gusto. That is why the apple cake recipe is a necessity at our house. Midge's notes say that this is Ethel Larson's, but we aren't really sure who Ethel was. The cake needs no introduction.

Loren M. Carlson
My Brother
Vermillion, South Dakota

In Lincoln, Nebraska on football Saturdays, wherever you look—the streets, the stadium, the restaurants—you see RED. Everyone wears red even though they aren't going to the big game. This red buttermilk cake with its rough and tumble texture capped with a thick creamy topping is perfect for tail-gate parties or after-the-game snacks or buffet.

One year, my daughter, Becky, gave a 4-H demonstration at the Lancaster County Fair on how to make a Big Red Cake. We all got very tired of eating all those practice cakes. Becky still doesn't like red cake.

Clarice Carlson Orr

Go Big Red Cake

1 cup plus 1 tablespoon margarine
1 1/2 cups sugar
1 teaspoon salt
2 eggs, well beaten
1 tablespoon vinegar
2 tablespoons cocoa
1 ounce red food coloring
1 teaspoon soda
1 tablespoon water
1 teaspoon vanilla
2 1/2 cups flour
1 cup plus 1 tablespoon buttermilk

Cream margarine and sugar and salt. Add eggs and beat well. Add vinegar and mix. Make a paste of cocoa and food coloring and add. Dissolve soda in water and add that and vanilla. Add, alternately, flour and buttermilk. Bake at 350° in a loaf pan.

Frosting:

3 heaping tablespoons flour   1 cup milk
1 cup butter   1 teaspoon vanilla
1 cup powdered sugar
    (another recipe says use half granulated sugar)

Combine flour and milk in double boiler. Cover, cook, and cool. Cream butter until fluffy and gradually add sugar. Combine with heated mixture. Add vanilla. Frost and refrigerate cake.

My daughter Lori likes this recipe because it can be made without milk. If you are concerned about using fresh egg whites, you can purchase pasteurized or powdered egg whites.

Joan Martin
A Rosenquist Cousin
Concord, California

Fluffy Butter Cream Frosting

4 cups powdered sugar   1/4 cup egg whites .
1 teaspoon vanilla   1/8 teaspoon salt
1 tablespoon water
1/3 cup soft margarine or Crisco

Blend and beat at high speed for 5 minutes. Will frost two 8 or 9 inch layers.

Pineapple Granny Cake

1 20-ounce can pineapple with juice

2 eggs	1 1/2 cups sugar
2 cups flour	1 teaspoon soda
1 teaspoon salt	1 teaspoon baking powder

Topping mix:

3/4 cup Pet milk	1/2 cup sugar
3/4 cup butter	1 teaspoon vanilla
1 cup chopped nuts	

Mix all ingredients for cake, put in greased 9 X 13 X 2 inch pan. Sprinkle with 1/2 cup brown sugar. Bake 40 minutes in 350° oven.

Mix first four ingredients of topping together and boil, add chopped nuts, and pour over hot cake. Serve warm or cold.

Gary's Cake

1 package of yellow cake mix

1/2 cup oil	4 eggs

11-ounce can mandarin oranges with juice

Mix together for three minutes and pour into a greased and floured 9 X 13 cake pan. Bake 30-35 minutes at 350°. Cool.

Frosting: 8-ounces Cool Whip, 1 large can crushed pineapple with juice, 1 package instant vanilla pudding

Mix and spread over the cake. Refrigerate. Can be made the day before serving.

Clarice: Gary's always a frontrunner in the Carlson Open, but I didn't know he was a winner in the kitchen!

Each year I add a recipe of the year in my cooking files, so in 1999, this is that recipe. The grandkids like it without the nuts on top. I leave them in big pieces so they are easily removed.

Gayle E. Harmon
Mesa, AZ

Gary's cake came about when Gary announced one evening that he needed to take a dessert for work the next morning. I suggested that he go to the grocery story and buy a cake since I was on my way to show homes to a client. He was standing in the cake aisle when the mother of our daughter's friend came by. He told her his dilemma and she told him to buy three or four items and go home and call her for the recipe. He did; made the cake; baked it in an aluminum bakery pan I had saved and took it to work the next morning. The cake met with rave reviews—no one believed that he had made it! When he convinced them he did, everyone wanted the recipe for "Gary's Cake." He is the only one in the family who makes it, but we all love it. We like it especially for Easter or any summer event. (Some people know this as Hawaiian Cake.)

Donna C. Carlson
A Carlson Cousin
New Brighton, Minnesota

A friend at work gave me this recipe in the 1970s and I liked it. About this time, Nebraskans wanted to know everything about then Cornhusker Coach Tom Osborne. Recipe books of that time claimed the Cocoa Cola Cake was his favorite. Since Osborne had bypass heart surgery about ten years ago, he has changed his eating habits and may not eat much Cocoa Cola Cake anymore. However, this Cocoa Cola Cake is still a favorite with many.

Clarice Carlson Orr

This easy-to-put-together dessert is a popular dessert at salad luncheons for women's groups.

Emily Hayden
Lincoln, Nebraska

Clarice: Isn't it great to be able to make a great dessert without using a mixing bowl? What would Emily's great-grandmother think of that?

Cocoa Cola Cake

2 cups flour	2 cups sugar
1/2 cup butter or margarine	1/2 cup vegetable shortening
3 tablespoons cocoa	1 cup Coca Cola
1/2 cup buttermilk	1 teaspoon baking soda
2 eggs, beaten	1 teaspoon vanilla

1 1/2 cups miniature marshmallows, optional

Frosting:

1/2 cup margarine
3 tablespoons cocoa
6 tablespoons Coca Cola
1 pound powdered sugar
1 teaspoon vanilla
1 cup vanilla
1 cup walnuts

Combine flour and sugar and set aside. In a saucepan, mix margarine, shortening, cocoa and cola. Bring to boiling; pour over the flour and sugar mixture. Stir by hand until well mixed. Add buttermilk, soda, beaten eggs, vanilla, and miniature marshmallows. Stir by hand until well-mixed. Turn into greased and floured 9 X 13 inch pan. Bake at 350° 35-40 minutes or until cake tests done.

Frost while warm. To make frosting: Combine margarine, cocoa and Coke in a saucepan and bring to boiling. Beat in powdered sugar, vanilla and walnuts.

Dump Cake

1 13-ounce can crushed pineapple
1 can cherry pie filling
One yellow cake mix, two layer size
1/2 to 1 cup chopped nuts
1 1/2 sticks margarine

Dump crushed pineapple, juice and all, into a greased 9 X 13 inch pan. Dump cherry pie filling on top. Dump cake mix over top and spread evenly. Dump nuts on top of cake mix. Slice margarine in to pats and distribute evenly over cake mix. Bake at 350° for about 50 minutes.

Frozen Chocolate Peanut Butter Pie

1 cup heavy cream
1 Oreo Cookie pie crust
1 8-ounce package cream cheese, softened
1 cup powdered sugar
3/4 cup peanut butter

In a medium bowl, beat cream cheese, powdered sugar, and peanut butter with an electric mixer on medium speed until well blended and fluffy, 1 to 2 minutes. Whip 1 cup cream until stiff; beat half of whipped cream into peanut butter mixture until well mixed, then fold in remaining whipped cream.

Spread filling evenly over crust. Freeze. After 1/2 hour wrap tightly and store in freezer. Transfer pie to refrigerator 1 hour before serving. Cut into wedges to serve.

This is probably the richest dessert you can make. Our family has had this at The Garden Café many times and loved it. So when I found this recipe, I really surprised them by making it myself. You see, I'm not much of a cook, but this is so good and it is so easy, anybody can make it.

Carrie Parrott
My Granddaughter
Omaha, Nebraska

Clarice: Carrie has been involved in doing so many other things well, I guess she's never taken time to learn to cook or bake. She's a fast-paced college student who had a semester in Paris and then traipsed all over Europe before coming home.

Caramel Pecan Cheesecake

18 squares graham crackers, crushed
1/4 cup sugar   1/3 cup melted margarine

Put 1/2 cup chopped pecans on top and bake in 9 inch pie plate or springform pan for 10 minutes at 350°.

2 8-ounce packages cream cheese
1/2 cup brown sugar   2 teaspoons vanilla
2 eggs
1/4 cup caramel ice cream topping
Pecan halves

Blend cream cheese, vanilla, and eggs. Put over crust. Put halved pecans on top to decorate.

Bake at 325° for 40-45 minutes. Put caramel on just before serving.

This is a new recipe I took to a potluck recently that everyone liked.

Alyce Knutson
A Carlson Cousin
Lakewood, Colorado

Grandma asked me to pick and pit enough cherries for a shortcake. I pitted about 2 cups while Grandma made the shortcake.

Frances Beechner
Lincoln, Nebraska

Clarice: Frances enjoys reminiscing about family dinners with Bess Streeter Aldrich, one of Nebraska's favorite pioneer authors. Mary, the daughter of Mrs. Aldrich, and Frances married the Beechner brothers.

Quick Cherry Shortcake

Mix 2 beaten eggs, 1 cup flour, 1 cup sugar, and 1 teaspoon baking powder. Put in 2 greased pie pans. Spread 1 cup drained cherries on top. Bake in moderate oven 15-20 minutes.

Make a sauce of 1 more cup of cherries and add sugar to taste and 1 tablespoon cornstarch for a syrup to serve over shortcake.

Aunt Reathel's Ice Box Cake was a trademark recipe for my family. When I was growing up, I always thought she fixed fancy recipes. This was the one to serve at "club," or if company was coming, or to take to a potluck. It just wasn't served at an everyday meal. The recipe had been given to my aunt by a neighbor.

I have never seen this recipe in any cookbook. It is unusual in that it doesn't use any milk products. Substitutions can be strawberry Jell-O and strawberries, or orange Jell-O and oranges.

Marge Rider
Lincoln, Nebraska

Aunt Reathel's Ice Box Cake

1/2 pound crushed vanilla wafers

1/3 cup oleo mixed with 2/3 of the crushed wafers. Pat into glass dish and chill in the refrigerator. Set aside the other 1/3 of vanilla wafers for topping.

4 egg yolks, well beaten
1/2 cup sugar
1 small or medium can of crushed pineapple

Cook until thick. Add 1 box lemon Jell-O. Let cool.

Add 4 beaten egg whites with 1/2 cup sugar added. Fold into custard. Pour into vanilla wafer crust. Sprinkle the reserved 1/3 cup of crumbs over the top. Let chill overnight or 4-5 hours.

Clarice: Since this has no milk, this may be good for folks who have a problem with dairy products. Marge and I talked about the safety factor of using the uncooked egg whites. However, the egg whites are folded into the hot custard which probably solves that problem. Marge said they never had any problem when this was served to the family.

Peach Jell-O Supreme

1 1/2 cups Ritz crackers, crushed
1/2 cup margarine
4 tablespoons sugar
2 boxes peach or orange Jell-O
2 medium cans sliced peaches
1 package cream cheese
1 scant cup sugar
1 large container Cool Whip (12 ounces)

Mix crackers, margarine, and 4 tablespoons of sugar together and press into a 9 X 13 inch pan. Bake 10 minutes at 350°. While baking and cooling, mix 2 boxes of Jell-O with 2 cups boiling water plus juice from peaches. Chill until slightly congealed. Mix the cream cheese with the cup of sugar and fold in Cool Whip. Spread over crust. Lay peaches over this mixture and pour congealed Jell-O over the peaches. Chill several hours and serve.

Keep this recipe handy; your guests will love it. I made it again recently and it really is good! It can also be made with strawberry Jell-O and frozen strawberries.

Betty Bruner
A Shirt-tail Relative
Mitchell, South Dakota

Grandma Rawson's Salad (or Hershey Almond Dessert)

28 regular marshmallows	2/3 cup milk, heated
1 cup cream whipped	3 Hershey Almond bars
1 teaspoon vanilla	Graham cracker crumbs

Dissolve marshmallows in hot milk in a double boiler and cool. Fold in whipped cream and vanilla. Cover the bottom of 7 X 11 pan with crumbs. Pour mixture over the crumbs and sprinkle more crumbs on top. Cut in squares and garnish with whipped cream and a maraschino cherry.

To modernize the recipe: Melt marshmallows and milk in microwave. Use a frozen whipped topping. Since the candy bars are smaller than they used to be, use 1 or 2 more.

Grandma would usually offer to bring a salad when they were coming for a meal. Almost always she would bring the Hershey Almond dessert. The kids were delighted as this salad wasn't vegetables or fruit. So, occasionally we still have Grandma Rawson's Salad, only now we really use it for dessert.

Ruby Bacon
Lincoln, Nebraska

169

About My "Clarice" Dishes on the Cover

I'm not an avid antique hunter although I sometimes snoop around those musty nooks and crannies. A few years ago, I was browsing through the stalls of an antique shop with friends noting "My mom used to have one of those," or "What do you suppose this is for?" or "Who would have ever thought this little plate would be worth something someday?"

A nest of pretty blue and white flowery dishes, in an open cardboard box, piqued my interest. Some of the plates and cups were crackled and brown, but that only gave them character. A scrap of paper on the dishes had the price $75 crossed through and the sale price $50 for 49 pieces was written below.

Curious, I turned over a dinner plate; a cobalt blue scroll and flower design encircled the description.

It was odd, yet amazing to see my name Clarice linked to Royal Staffordshire Dinnerware. "You've got to buy them, Clarice; they've got your name on them, " Chrys urged. I thought of my grandchildren and great-grandchildren to come and, loving a bargain, my resistance went out the window.

I've since learned that Clarice Cliff designed this pattern, Charlotte, which is not typical of her work. Her vivid hand-painted Art Deco ceramics are highly sought after, while my dinnerware has "little value in the collectors' market." However, that makes additional dinnerware at china replacement companies more available and less costly for me!

Through an antique china service, I have replaced cracked dinner plates and cups. I'm not sorry my investment has increased as well as the inventory. Who knows how many descendants there will be!

HOLIDAY
TREATS

Grandparents are for telling
you what it used to be like,
but not too much.

—Charlie Shedd

Holiday Treats

Holidays are when we gather like chicks under the wings of a mother hen to connect with our dear ones from across the country and from the past. These most meaningful and significant family times are when we remember the stories, the silly rituals, the traditions, the customs; but most of all we remember the foods.

We search our memories for all the recipes that Mother and Grandmother taught us as we seek to recreate the warm and tender feelings we remember. But, more than filling our stomachs and nurturing our bodies that day, it becomes our obligation and trust to hand down the legacy of love that our foremothers and forefathers bequeathed to us.

Grandma's Ways on Holidays

These loving memories of Vivian Hoff Thomas were expressed by three generations of descendants, while the Robertson family was celebrating Christmas in 1998, and recorded by her daughter, Jacqueline Thomas Robertson.

"Vivian would tell me to add more milk to the dressing!" said her son-in-law.

"I think Grandma would like my new method of doing sweet potatoes," her granddaughter offered.

"Our whole family insisted on following ALL the holiday traditions again this year, including the menus. Grandma would be proud, don't you think?" Her grandson, granddaughter-in-law, and three teenage great-grandchildren agreed.

"Each of the dishes we're preparing are the result of Grandma's encouragement, criticism, and influence...except now we're trying to use less fat...even though she thought food had no taste without a lot of butter and salt!" remembered her grandson.

"I wish our daughters and I could have known your Mom better, Jackie," said her granddaughter-in-law.

"We all can almost hear Grandma Thomas say she 'got a good do' on fudge, popcorn balls, or certain dishes...We can almost hear her say 'It's not JUST right.'"

We feel her spirit as we continue our journeys and know that deep inside she'd be proud of her family. No one EVER doubted her love and loyalty!

"Maybe, just maybe, I bought the right kind of rolls this year to make Swedish rusks," I thought. It seemed like every holiday season, I'd try and fail. I was often in a hurry and picked up dinner rolls, potato rolls, or whatever looked similar, and hoped. Mama would say something like, "We'll make the best of it, but, next year, Jacqueline, remember to get day old tea rolls!" My thought and her response have become a memory that makes those who understood smile now, especially remembering that I was in my 50s and she in her 80s when this scene was repeated year after year. Prior to that time, she made rusks "on her own."

My maternal grandmother came to Nebraska from Sweden and brought this recipe "in her head." I've only seen it written in my mother's hand (not my grandmother's) in an effort to help me. I think my mother wanted to make the rusks correctly to measure up to her mother's expectations. For whatever reasons, getting a good "do"is still a challenge. However, I noticed that good batches and those judged to be poor disappear at about the same rate!

A friend said, "This is nothing but dry toast." And to him it is. For me, it's a special tradition...

making and eating them help me remember... before I was 5...the smell of food and cigarette smoke, the laughter, the talk, the feel of a family gathered for the holidays. As the youngest, I was assured that I belonged, as some adult would take me on his/her lap to help me dunk my rusk in their creamed and sugared coffee.

Having rusks at Christmastime is a continuing part of our children's Christmases, so it's an established tradition. It has become a part of the season for friends, too, who remember Mom's directions. My husband has become the "expert" in slicing the rolls with an electric knife. Of course, we all tease him by saying that they are too small or too big so they won't bake evenly. In that tradition, too, we're carrying on where Mom left off...

Swedish Rusks

This is the recipe exactly as my mother wrote it for me when she was 75 years old.

"Buy TEA ROLLS! Day old!

I slice them by the thickness I want the rusk (not only by the thickness of the tea roll).

Then, I have a bowl of sugar ready. (I also add a dash of salt to the sugar)

I take one row at a time and Butter generously.

Then, dip Hard in sugar and salt mixture.

Separate, put them on cookie sheets (I see that about same amount goes on each)

Put in oven NOT OVER 350° one pan at a time.

It takes app 30 min to brown top AND bottom

When all are done, I shut off oven and

Then, put back in oven to DRY. Oven shut off

If it seems too hot, leave door open a min., then, close."

The Christmas Stollen recipe comes from Irene Pfeiffer in Seward. We became friends at Concordia during Summer Sessions. She taught at St. John's in Seward and I taught at Beaver Crossing. Irene passed away in 1975. I started making the recipe in 1958 when our daughters thought we should establish some Christmas traditions. I have made it every year since. It is a family favorite. No one in the family likes candied fruit; this has the fruit, but not candied.

Arlene Ficken
Milford, Nebraska

Christmas Stollen

2 cups lukewarm milk	3 cakes compressed yeast
1 teaspoon sugar	

Combine milk, yeast, and sugar and set in warm place until yeast floats. Add 3 cups flour. Mix and put in a warm place until light.

Mix separately:

1 cup butter or oleo	4 egg yolks
1/2 teaspoon salt	

Combine both mixtures and add enough flour to make a firm dough. Work on floured board until dough ceases to stick to hands. Let rise until dough is double in bulk, then place on board. Roll to about 1 inch thick and sprinkle with: 3/4 cup raisins, 3/4 maraschino cherries, 1 cup chopped walnuts, 3/4 cup chopped dates. Work fruit and nuts into dough. Cover. Let rise one hour, or until double in bulk. Put into 4 single loaf pans, small size. Let rise about one hour. Brush top of loaf with a little milk. Bake at 350° for 45 minutes.

Ice with powdered sugar icing: 1 cup powdered sugar, 1 lemon, rind and juice, 1/4 teaspoon crushed cardamom seeds.

A good thing to remember
And a better thing to do
To work with the constuction gang
And not with the wrecking crew.

Hoska

2 packages of yeast
1 cup milk
1/4 cup shortening
1 teaspoon grated
    lemon rind
4 1/2 to 5 cups sifted flour
1/2 cup blanched chopped almonds
1/2 teaspoon anise seeds

1/4 cup lukewarm water
1/2 cup sugar
2 teaspoons salt
1/8 teaspoon mace
2 eggs or 4 egg yolks

1 package of citron

Soften yeast in lukewarm water. Scald milk. Add sugar, shortening, yeast, lemon rind, mace, eggs, and mix well. Add raisins, citron, nutmeats, and anise. Add flour to make a soft dough. Turn out on lightly floured board and knead until satiny. Place in greased bowl, cover and let rise until doubled in bulk. Punch down. Divide dough in half. Divide one of the halves into three large portions and three smaller ones. Roll each portion into a long roll. Braid the large rolls loosely and place in a greased loaf pan. Braid the three smaller rolls and place on top of the large braid. Do the same to the other half. Cover and let rise until double in bulk. Bake 35-40 minutes in 375° oven. Before baking, I push whole almonds into the bread. You can also brush with beaten egg white and sprinkle with poppy seed. The bread is good plain or toasted.

The recipe I am sharing is one my mother made every Christmas. She made Hoska, a Czech Christmas bread. I am sure she made at least two loaves as one would never last in a family of four children with three of them being boys.

As I got older and realized I would not have my mother around forever, I asked her to teach me how to make hoska and kolaches. I have tried several different kolache recipes over the years, but always use the same hoska recipe. With my lifestyle, I do very little baking, but at Christmastime, in honor of my mother, I make the time to bake hoska and kolaches. I share those five dozen of kolaches and two loaves of hoska with family and friends.

Rose Marie Tondl
Lincoln, Nebraska

*In 1948, the first cake mix, a single-layer cake,
and the now-standard devil's food cake
from Betty Crocker and Pillsbury came out.
The first Pillsbury Bake-Off Contest
took place at New York's Waldorf-Astoria Hotel
in 1949 as the Grand National Baking and Recipe Contest.
The grand prize was $50,000.*

Christmas Dinner wouldn't be the same without Grandma Conley's "Red Apples!" They were always a family favorite, so through the years as we made our own traditions, the Red Apples had to be in place on the table or else it wasn't a real Christmas dinner. Now, my daughter always helps or prepares them herself for our Christmas dinner. She has also introduced them to her husband's family for their Thanksgiving celebration! They are not fancy, just simply delicious (unlike the ones out of the jar) and a great addition to any festive occasion!

Susan Macy
Lincoln, Nebraska

Grandma's Red Apples

Make a syrup of 2 cups sugar and 1 cup water in a large skillet. Add 1/3 cup cinnamon candies (red hots) and a few drops of red food coloring. Stir and bring to a boil. Add 6-10 (number that will fit in the pan) peeled, cored and quartered apples (Jonathan or Golden Delicious) to the syrup mixture. Simmer until apples are tender. Remove to another container and refrigerate until serving time. Spoon into a serving bowl that will enhance the red color and enjoy!

Jeweled Cranberries

1 package of cranberries   1 cup of sugar
1 1/4 cups water

Put all in a glass or enamel cake dish. Stir until sugar is dissolved. Put in 350° oven and bake 1 hour. Do not stir. Cool.

Spoon the cranberries into a pretty glass bowl turning the cranberries over. The result is that the cranberries are like rubies with luscious juice. Try this and you will never cook cranberries any other way.

Beryl Younger
Brookings, South Dakota

Clarice: Besides being a great cook and baker of pies, Beryl has a special knack for preparing a feast for your eyes.

You take this little cranberry and stew him.
He makes just as good applesauce as prunes.
—An old Norwegian neighbor lady

Swedish Cookies

1/2 cup butter   1/2 cup margarine
1/3 cup whipping cream 2 cups flour

Mix and roll as paper thin as possible. Dip both sides in granulated sugar. Use a small dainty cookie cutter. Bake at 350° until very light brown. Watch carefully.

Filling:
 1/4 cup butter
 1 egg yolk
 1 3/4 cup powdered sugar
 1 teaspoon vanilla
 Tint filling if desired.

The trick is rolling them very thin. Putting the filling between two cookies is tricky, too. If the cookies are thoroughly cool, the breakage is not so great. You can top each cookie sandwich with a rosebud of the filling to make a dainty party cookie. They freeze well.

Swedish Spritz Cookies

Thoroughly cream 1 1/2 cups butter or margarine and 1 cup sugar. Add 1 egg, 1 teaspoon vanilla, and 1/2 teaspoon almond extract. Beat well. (We use real butter and extra almond extract.)

Sift 4 cups all-purpose flour with 1 teaspoon baking powder. Add to creamed mixture; mix till smooth. Do not chill. Force dough through cooky press forming various shapes onto ungreased cooky sheet. Sprinkle with candy decorations. Bake in hot oven, 400°, about 8 to 10 minutes. Cool.

I love Grandma's spritz cookies at Christmas. We make them every year. It's fun to squeeze the dough out of the machine and put on the sprinkles. The best part is eating them and sneaking them off the tray when Grandma isn't looking!

Kelsey Schmitt, Age 8
Publisher's Granddaughter
Crete, Nebraska

I got this recipe from a Norwegian friend in Iowa. I make them every Christmas along with many other kinds. They are very tedious and time consuming to make, but they melt in your mouth. Everyone who eats them can't believe someone would take the time to make them. That's why I only make them once a year! Family and friends look forward to them every Christmas.

Violet Nesheim Carlson
My Sister-in-law
Williamsport, Maryland

Clarice: Violet has always been the best cook! During World War II, because of gas and tire rationing, four of us country girls lived together in town—Mitchell, South Dakota—during the school week. We always knew that Violet could fix our cooking and baking boo-boos, such as when our cream sauce was lumpy and when we burned the tea rolls.

Publisher's note: My daughters and I have developed a family tradition of baking Christmas cookies on the day after Thanksgiving each year. We usually have a Husker game to watch while we mix and roll and squeeze and bake. Our granddaughters have grown up with this family tradition that we hope they will continue.

My mother used to make this dough and we made cookies for Christmas with it. She would make all colors of frosting and we had lots of fun decorating them. I make them now for special occasions and people just love them!! I don't know if my mom got this passed-down recipe from her mom or not. My grandma was not sure when I asked her about it. I guess she has made so many sugar cookies over the years that all the recipes run together.

Dawn Billings Voreis
Mansfield, Texas

Cookie Cutter Sugar Cookies

Mix 2 cups sugar, 1 cup shortening, 2 eggs, 2 teaspoons vanilla, and 1/2 teaspoon salt

Mix together: 2 cups flour, 3 teaspoons baking powder, 1 teaspoon soda

Add flour mixture to creamed mixture with 1 cup milk. Add more flour until easy to handle (about 5 1/2 cups flour altogether). Roll out on a floured surface and cut into shapes.

Bake at 370° for 6 minutes. (Do not overbake) Top with frosting if desired. Freeze well—you can frost later.

Clarice: I learned from Dawn how much she valued her grandmother's prayers. Her grandmother had seven grandchildren and each grandchild was the focus of her prayers one day of the week. Dawn said, "If I can hold out until Friday, I can make it through anything. 'Cuz on Fridays my grandmother prays for me."

Clarice: The next five recipes for Pfeffernuesse are all different, yet similar. I find it interesting that those who submitted the differing recipes have the same passion and warmth for their mothers and grandmothers who passed on this delightful Christmas tradition.

Lena Kay's Old Fashioned Pfeffernuesse

1 cup white sugar	1/2 cup oleo
2 eggs	1 1/2 cups molasses
1/4 teaspoon nutmeg	1 teaspoon cinnamon
1/2 teaspoon cloves	2 teaspoons soda
1/2 teaspoon anise extract	chopped almonds
flour to make as stiff as bread	

Make long rolls the size of a nickel, slice and bake at 350°.

Clarice: Dorothy and I worked together for nearly twenty years in UNL's office of the Dean of Engineering and Technology. We also were both born and raised in South Dakota.

Every Christmas, mother would mix up the hard, spicy cookies. Since there was no heat in the upstairs, I recall the many rows of dough that were placed on breadboards, covered with tea towels and put upstairs to chill before baking. When company came to play cards, there were always bowls of peppernuts on the tables. The hard cookies were a great snack while playing cards as they took a long time to soften in your mouth and you never got your fingers messy!

Dorothy Kay Abbott
Lincoln, Nebraska

Pfeffernuesse

Take 3 cups sorghum, 2 cups sugar, 1 cup butter, 4 eggs, 1/4 lb. shelled almonds chopped fine, 1 teaspoon each of fennel, anise, and coriander (ground), 1/2 teaspoon each nutmeg and pepper, 2 teaspoons cinnamon, 1 teaspoon cloves, 4 level teaspoons soda, and flour to make a dough as stiff as bread.

If sorghum cannot be had, use 2 cups very mild molasses and 1 cup honey. Use a moderate hot oven as they scorch easily if not watched closely.

German Pfeffernuesse are very appropriate for Christmas. Can be made several weeks before as they will keep well when put in a tight container. The fennel, anise, and coriander can be bought at a drug store and grind it in a coffee mill as needed. One-half ounce of each is enough to buy. This is overnight cookie dough. If kept cool, it may be kept 2-3 days before baking without harm. To bake, take bits of dough and roll between your hands to the size of a quarter and place on cookie sheet far apart so they don't meet when baked. (Doesn't this sound like a mother?)

This recipe for German cookies is one that my mother, Cecelia Metzger, made every year at Christmas time for as long as I can remember. She still makes them. The German people were "dunkers." They dunk cookies and kuchen in their coffee. This is a very good dunkin' cookie because it is so hard it does not fall apart in hot coffee.

Karen Pooley
A Carlson Cousin
Mitchell, South Dakota

179

My grandmother, Elizabeth Nispel, Plymouth, Nebraska, always made Pfeffernuesse at Christmas. The recipe was brought to Nebraska by Germans born in the Hessen Province who immigrated to Ontario, Canada in the 1860s before coming to Jefferson County, Nebraska in the 1880s. I always make at least a double batch and share with my 79-year-old aunt. It wouldn't be Christmas without Pfeffernuesse. Today the tradition continues as I am grandma, baking Pfeffernuesse for my grandchildren Josh, Kaitlyn, and Elizabeth. They call them "Grandma's cookies."

Sheila Green
Lincoln, Nebraska

Pfeffernuesse

1/2 cup fat (or butter)
1/2 cup milk
2 cups white sugar
4 cups flour, divided
1/2 cup dates
1/2 cup nuts
1/2 cup sugared citrus peel
1/2 teaspoon cinnamon
1/4 teaspoon nutmeg
1 rounded tablespoon anise seed
2 eggs
1 1/2 teaspoons baking soda
       dissolved in 1 tablespoon cold water.

In the evening, cook together until all is dissolved: fat, milk, and sugar. Remove from the stove, cool, then add 2 cups flour. Stir until it makes a smooth paste. Add remaining 2 cups of flour. Transfer to a large mixing bowl and set overnight in a cool corner of the kitchen. Do not refrigerate. In the morning, the mixture should be solid enough to dent with a finger. While it warms up near the stove, combine dates, nuts, citrus peel, cinnamon, nutmeg and anise seed. Grind together with a food grinder. Add to the first mixture. Stir well and add eggs. Add baking soda dissolved in water and two remaining cups of water. Mix well and chill dough overnight in refrigerator. In the morning, take small chunks of dough and roll into long "snakes" 1/2 inch in diameter. Cut into 1/2 inch sections. Place on ungreased cookie sheets, slightly flatten each with your thumb. Keeping the bulk of the dough cold will help reduce stickiness. Bake at 350° for 5-8 minutes, depending upon size and crispness desired. Cool, store in tightly covered tins. They are best if aged a month with a few fresh apple slices.

Pepper Nuts

5 1/3 cups syrup (dark Karo)
1 cup shortening
1 teaspoon cinnamon
2 teaspoons cardamom (powder)
1 teaspoon nutmeg
2 teaspoons pepper
4 cups sugar
1 1/3 cup milk
1 teaspoon cloves (scant)
2 teaspoons star anise (powder)
3/4 teaspoon allspice
1 teaspoon salt
1 tablespoon + 1 1/2 teaspoons baking powder
Flour to make dough very stiff, about 6 1/2 lbs.

Melt shortening and syrup; add sugar and spices. Add milk and flour, using hands at the end. (Amount of flour may vary with brand.) Bake a few, if they flatten at all, add more flour.

To shape; take a small ball of dough and roll between palm of hand and cutting board until it becomes a long roll like a pencil, 1/2 inch in diameter. Cut off a 6 inch length, lay on greased cookie sheet, cut off 1/2 inch slices, moving longer piece as you cut off pepper nut slice.

Bake at 400° until lightly browned, approximately 10 minutes. Yield about 8 pounds.

NOTE: Let the dough sit at least a week before baking as this blends the spices. May be made a little at a time; the dough doesn't need to be refrigerated.

Clarice: Bev is a lucky grandmother of eight, including two sets of twins!

Christmas is coming! Are there any pepper nuts left? Mother Hillman would make them in the fall, put them in a pillowcase, and then hang them up in a closet. By the holidays they were usually gone. Little elves seem to have become hungry. She probably would have been disappointed if some had remained.

Our family started this tradition of pepper nuts every Christmas, but we were fortunate if they were baked before the special day. Art and I, with the help of our four daughters, would gather around the kitchen table to roll out the pepper nuts. The dough had been made days ago to mellow. We would all have our jobs. Someone would roll out the dough in the shape of a pencil; someone would cut the pieces; and the rest would put them on the cookie sheets. My job was baking them (until the girls were older). Then the pepper nuts were removed from the oven and placed on the counter to cool. Sometimes a few vanished as we worked. When the girls were babies, they were given a large cookie, made from the dough, to use as a teether. The girls still ask "When are the pepper nuts ready?" The grandchildren now do the same as their mothers!

Be sure to let the pepper nut melt a little in your mouth before chewing.

Bev Hillman
Lincoln, Nebraska

181

For the first twelve years of my life, my Mother's best friend and family shared Thanksgiving with us, usually at our home. The gathering was filled with tradition. My Father and Ed always sat at the dining room table and ate oysters on the half-shell prior to the meal on Thanksgiving Day…yuck…while Mother and Irene prepared the meal. While our family was small, just my sister and me, the Allens had five children so it made for a lively time when they all came.

Phillip, their youngest, was closest to my age so we spent time together. One of the better traditions of the gathering, in my opinion, was the chocolate cookies that my mother always made. The recipe was handed down to her from a Mrs. Hilliard evidently, since that is what is on her recipe card; but I don't know who that is or what the relationship was. The important part is that, since the cookies need to be kept in a cold place, but not the refrigerator, she would make them several days in advance, place them on waxed paper in Miller & Paine dress boxes, and store them in the attic.

Mrs. Hilliard's Chocolate Ice Box Cookies

Melt over hot water:

> 1 pound sweet chocolate
> 3 squares bitter chocolate

Mix together thoroughly:

> 1 cup nuts chopped
> 2 cups Rice Krispies
> 1 cup "cocoanut" cut up (I left in the incorrect spelling of coconut as on Mother's recipe for flavor!)
> 3 cups corn flakes

Pour chocolate over above ingredients and mix—then drop by spoon on wax paper, form in shape desired, and let set. Keep in a cool place but not in refrigerator.

Phillip and I eventually got it down to a science; when we would sneak up to the attic and snitch a couple, we moved them around on the waxed paper a little so that it didn't look like any were gone. It became my favorite tradition. I'm sure that Mother realized what we were doing, but she never said anything. Mother always made plenty of food so no one was deprived of cookies either. They were just special to me since they were the "forbidden fruit" as well as being delicious. Mother was an excellent cook and didn't always use recipes, but this particular one she had written down, thank goodness. I now make them for my family and the cookies are considered a treat for all of us.

Susan Campbell
Ashland, Nebraska

Grandma Shirley's Fruit Cake

1 cup dates
1 cup raisins
1/2 cup chopped dried apricots
1/2 cup chopped dried prunes
1/2 cup chopped dried apples
1/2 cup applesauce
1/2 cup sour pie cherries
1/2 teaspoon salt
1/3 cup crushed pineapple
1 cup chopped pecans
1 cup sugar
1/2 cup Crisco
1/2 cup apricot brandy
1/2 cup apple juice

Bring all the above ingredients to a boil in a large saucepan. Simmer 30 minutes. Cool to room temperature. Add 2 1/3 cups flour sifted with 1/2 teaspoon baking powder, 1 teaspoon soda, 1 teaspoon cinnamon, 1/4 teaspoon cloves, 1/4 teaspoon nutmeg.

Mix well. Bake in two 8 1/2 X 4 1/2 loaf pans at 325° for about 1 1/2 hours. Put a pan of hot water on lower rack. Make a foil tent over pans first hour, then remove. When a toothpick comes out clean, cake is done. The time always seems to vary.

This fruitcake recipe goes back to the 1930s—The Depression Years. My mother, Olive Grayce Noakes, made this cake every year for Christmas. It was called Depression Fruitcake. She put all kinds of leftover jams and jellies plus raisins, dates, nuts, and applesauce in it.

I first made the cake in 1949, the first Christmas after I was married. It turned out so badly and was so heavy, I had to throw it away. Fortunately, I had better luck as time went on. I have modified the recipe over the years and now add dried apricots, prunes, dried apples, pie cherries, crushed pineapple, apple juice, pecans, and apricot brandy.

I make 10 to 15 cakes every year starting in October and give them for Christmas gifts. The cakes are quite expensive to make, but I get a lot of pleasure doing it.

Grandma Shirley Bruns
Beatrice, Nebraska

What would the Christmas feast be without at least one sinfully rich tasting dessert? In my family, Mother's baked date pudding was the unanimous choice to conclude our holiday meal. Just a small serving was needed to insure that long sigh of contentment, despite grown-up declarations of already full stomachs and, "I shouldn't... but...well, maybe just a bit." We children had always saved enough room for Date Pudding.

Sidney H. Culver
Lincoln, Nebraska

There are some people you just feel God is directing—even when they are not proclaimed Christians. So it was with my mother, Faye Malick Mathews. My mother served love through food. Her greatest joy was cooking for family and friends.

Every holiday was an excuse to join family in Hastings, Nebraska for a "gourmet" feast. We didn't use the word gourmet in those days, but laced all with real country butter and cream. Isn't that "gourmet?"

The two memorable foods at our family gatherings were Grandma's turkey and noodles and my mother's Date Pudding Cake served with real Whipped Cream. The cake recipe is easy and still tastes delicious.

In Cozad, Nebraska, Mother was known for her food, too. Travelers on

Baked Date Pudding

2 cups chopped dates	1 1/2 cups sugar
1 cup broken nut meats	1 teaspoon vanilla
1/8 teaspoon salt	1/2 cup flour
2 teaspoons baking powder	4 egg yolks, beaten
4 egg whites, beaten	

Beat egg yolks. Add dates, sugar, salt, nuts, flour sifted with baking powder, and vanilla. Mix in beaten egg whites. Smooth the mixture over the bottom (buttered) of a heavy skillet. (Ours was an iron skillet.) Set the skillet over a pan of water and bake at 350º for 35 minutes. Serve with whipped cream. (The water is essential to keeping the pudding soft and moist; it should not be dry.)

Hiway 30 stopped at her cafe for large meals and homemade pie. Perhaps you ate at Malick's Cafe and Station in the late 1930s and early 1940s. If so, you know that with the food she shared a welcome. Customers weren't just customers, but friends. People felt at home.

Bonnie Malick Mulder
Lincoln, Nebraska

Date Pudding Cake

1 package of dates (10 to 16 ounces)	
1 cup boiling water	1 teaspoon soda
1 cup sugar	1 egg
4 tablespoons butter	1 3/4 cups flour
1/2 cup milk	
1 cup chopped walnuts or pecans	

(Reduce the amount of liquid slightly if you use less than 16 ounces of dates.) Dissolve soda in water and pour over stoned dates. Let stand until cold. Add sugar. Beat in egg and melted butter, flour and nuts. Put in 9 X 13 pan sprayed with Pam. Bake for 25 to 30 minutes at 350º. Serve with whipped cream or Cool Whip, or plain.

Grandma's English Plum Pudding

3 eggs	1 teaspoon soda
1 teaspoon cinnamon	1 teaspoon ginger
1 teaspoon nutmeg	1 teaspoon salt
1 cup sour milk	3 cups sugar
1 pound raisins	1 pound currants
1 quart or 1 pound suet, ground	

Enough flour to make stiff (6 1/3 cups is usually right amount)

Mix all ingredients well. Scald pudding rag, wring out and sprinkle with flour. Put pudding in center of cloth and tie tightly with a string. Put in large kettle of boiling water to cover the entire pudding and boil (simmer) 6 to 7 hours. (Add boiling water if needed to retain water covering pudding.) Use a weighted plate to hold pudding below the water line. Take out of boiling water and let cool awhile before you remove the pudding rag. This will let the pudding firm up to hold its shape.

This is the Thanksgiving or Christmas treat that was made by my grandmother Maude Goodall Staats. The origin of the recipe is not known. My mother tells of the many times that the two would get together and make two puddings at a time. It's always a food that is mentioned during the holiday time, however very few of the younger generation like the taste. Our family makes one each year, passing around the "honor" of making it so the younger ones do not forget how it was done.

Herschel Staats
Lincoln, Nebraska

Norwegian Holiday Bread

Heat 1/2 cup butter and 1/2 cup milk to melt butter. Cool to lukewarm. Soften 1 package dry yeast in 1/2 cup warm water. Sitr in 1/4 cup sugar, 1 teaspoon salt, 1 cup raisins, 1/2 cup chopped candied fruit, 1/2 cup blanched almonds,1 slightly beaten egg (reserve 1 tablespoon for brushing loaves) and the milk mixture. Gradually add 3 1/2 to 4 cups sifted flour to form a stiff dough, beating well after each addition.

Let rise in warm place (85°) until double (1 to 1 1/2 hours).

Turn out on floured surface. Toss lightly until coated with flour and not sticky. Shape. Cover and let rise until double, about 1 hour. Brush with egg and bake at 350° for 30 to 35 minutes.

Christmas mornings just aren't the same without Mom's Holiday Bread. She still makes it every Christmas in her old Butternut coffee cans saved just for baking. When I left home and started my own family, Mom still gave us a loaf of bread for Christmas morning which we enjoyed with a glass of Orange Julius. Now that my daughters are gone, we still try and and keep the tradition when we all get together.

We often see the coffee cans at antique stores selling for five to ten dollars but none are worth more than the ones that hold the Norwegian Holiday Bread!

Linda Dageforde

Money was scarce in our household when I was a child. Mother often said if fifty cents were left at week's end, it was a goal reached. Our home was comfortable, but we had few items beyond the necessities. The food we enjoyed was the same—tasty and nutritious— but nothing fancy.

At the Christmas season, though, Mother always made a holiday treat—a steamed pudding—served with a hard sauce. Whether this was a delicacy brought from England by my great-grandfather, I'm not sure.

I can remember Mother always made the pudding in taller and larger sized cans (juice or coffee cans), but I can't recall how she covered the cans—if at all. What I can remember is the excitement of watching the finished puddings being lifted, steaming, from the cooker.

Christmas was finally here!

Ruth Cromer
Lincoln, Nebraska

Christmas Steamed Pudding

4 cups flour	2 cups ground suet
1 cup sugar	2 teaspoons baking powder
1 teaspoon baking soda	1 teaspoon cinnamon
1/2 teaspoon nutmeg	1/2 teaspoon allspice
1 cup raisins	

1 cup currants (plumped in water and drained). If currants aren't available, use additional raisins.

Mix ingredients in a large bowl. Dissolve 1 teaspoon soda in a smaller bowl in 1 cup buttermilk and add 2 well-beaten eggs. Combine buttermilk mixture and dry ingredients. Place in a pan that accommodates containers for the stiff batter. Fill containers no more than 3/4 full. Place filled containers in large pan with boiling water. Steam for 3 hours. Serve with hard sauce or whipped cream.

Hard sauce: 3 tablespoons sugar, butter the size of an egg, 1 tablespoon cornstarch, and flavor to taste. (Mother used vanilla.) Pour on boiling water to thickness desired. Stir until smooth and thickened.

Grandchildren are God's reward for growing old.

186

Suet Pudding

1 cup ground suet   1/2 cup molasses
2 eggs

Dissolve 1 teaspoon soda in the sour milk

2 cups flour   1 teaspoon nutmeg
2/3 cup brown sugar   1 cup sour milk
1 cup raisins   1 teaspoon cloves

Steam 1 1/2 hours.

White sauce for suet pudding:

  1 1/2 cups water
  2/3 cup sugar
  2 tablespoons corn starch
  1 tablespoon butter
  1 teaspoon lemon flavoring
  a little nutmeg

This is an old English recipe. We always had it for Christmas dinner. My grandmother, who was English, made it. She was the only one I ever knew who made it. It is yummy.

Helen Witters
Lincoln, Nebraska

Merry Thoughts

Using your favorite recipe, make enough pastry for a double crust pie (good, short pastry). Roll it about 1/8 inch thick and using a 2-2 1/2 inch cutter cut the pastry into rounds. Put the rounds into the bottoms of muffin tins, add one tablespoon (no more!) mincemeat (to which you have added a little bit of brandy for zip) and cover with another round of pastry, moistening the edges with water or milk and using a fork to press the top crust onto the bottom. Then poke the fork through the top of each tart 1 or 2 times. Bake at 425° for 12-15 minutes or until golden. Sprinkle with sugar when done.

My father was British, and my mother Canadian, but her mother was British, so I grew up on afternoon tea and flaming plum pudding at Christmas. Merry Thoughts is a favorite holiday recipe.

Many people don't really like mince pie. Mincemeat is rich and potent, and a slice of mince pie is often overwhelming. The British love mincemeat, but they never eat it in quantity, because they make Merry Thoughts which are quite small—mince pie at its best.

So even if you think you don't really care for mincemeat, give it one more try with Merry Thoughts.

Pippa White
Lincoln, Nebraska

My dad came from a family of eleven children. Most of them and their families would gather at someone's house for Christmas dinner. One of my favorite dishes to appear at these wonderful potluck dinners was my Aunt Frieda's Nut Pudding. Of course, she used all the fresh-from-the-farm ingredients—fresh eggs, whole milk, and real whipped cream. Now we're all so "fat" conscious that I have a slimmer version that I prepare for my family. It's still a family favorite!

Arbutus Hanson
A Carlson Cousin
Custer, South Dakota

Aunt Frieda's Nut Pudding

1 envelope unflavored gelatin soaked in 1/4 cup cold water

Combine the following ingredients; heat, but DO NOT BOIL

    1 3/4 cups sugar   2 1/2 cups milk
    3 eggs, slightly beaten

Cool slightly; add small amount of warm milk mixture to gelatin until gelatin is completely dissolved. Cool, but before it sets, add 1 cup whipping cream, whipped, 1 teaspoon salt, 1 teaspoon vanilla, 1 cup chopped walnuts. Chill until ready to serve. Serves about 12 to 15.

Today's Slimmer Nut Pudding

2 envelopes unflavored gelatin soaked in 1/2 cup cold water.

Combine the following ingredients; heat, but DO NOT BOIL.

    1 cup sugar   2 1/2 cups 1% milk
    3 eggs slightly beaten

Cool slightly; add small amount of warm milk mixture to gelatin and stir until gelatin is completely dissolved. Cool, but before it sets, add 1 teaspoon vanilla, 1 cup chopped walnuts, and 1 (8 ounce) carton of Cool Whip. Chill until ready to serve. May garnish with red and green maraschino cherries or walnut halves. Serves 12 to15.

Just stand aside and watch yourself go by,
think of yourself as "she" instead of "I."
—Strickland Gillilan

Doug's Fourth of July Cherry Pie

3 cups sour, pitted, fresh cherries, drained
1 cup drained juice
2 1/2 tablespoon quick cooking tapioca
1/2 cup sugar
1/4 teaspoon salt
1 teaspoon butter, melted
1 teaspoon almond flavoring
Red food coloring
Pastry for 8 inch, double crust pie

If there is not enough juice to make a full cup, add water. Add tapioca, sugar, salt, butter, flavoring, and food coloring. Mix and let stand 15 minutes. Blend in the cherries. Pour filling into unbaked pie shell. Cover with strips of pastry in lattice fashion. Bake at 425° for 15 minutes. Reduce heat to 375° for 45 minutes.

For close to twenty years, Doug has been making cherry pies. He has perfected his lattice top crust, and knows just the right amount of sugar and almond flavoring to add. His best pies are made for the Fourth of July. Annually, Doug secretly stops in Nebraska City to buy the cherries. Because the cherries depend on ideal growing conditions, the trip to Nebraska City is made in faith that there will be cherries! If we're lucky, Doug buys a supply to freeze for the year's supply of cherry pie. These pies have traveled to Doug's aunt and uncle's cabin near Ashland and to the Seward Fourth of July celebrations. Of course, the pie is better with soft-serve ice cream.

Cyndi Orr Parrott
My Daughter
Omaha, Nebraska

Clarice: What a treat it is to savor my son-in-law's special cherry pie! We may also get cherry pies (along with another of Doug's favorites, pumpkin pie) at Thanksgiving and Christmas, but they aren't quite as good as those made fresh off the trees.

A popular tradition in the small town that my husband and I first lived in was to go downtown to the local tavern on New year's morning. Not for leftover beer or anything else from the night before. But to wish each other a Happy New Year over a plate of steaming Hoppin' John.

After the owner of the tavern retired, my father-in-law began serving it up out of their kitchen. Word caught on quickly, as in later years, they served many folks—family and friends. Such a wonderful, tasty tradition. I have no idea what culture presents this dish, or why the name!

Sandy Wright
Seward, Nebraska

Hoppin' John
(New Year's Brunch)

6 pieces of bacon
1 medium onion
1 cup black-eyed peas
1 cup cooked rice

1. Fry up bacon
2. Dice onion and brown in bacon grease
3. Mix in rice and black-eyed peas (with juice)
4. Heat until mixture is warm

Serves 4.

Serve with lots of good wishes for a Happy New Year.

When God closes a door,
He opens a window.

MUNCHIES & BACKYARD BONUSES

According to the laws of aerodynamics, the bumblebee can't fly, but nobody told the bumblebee.

Munchies

When one sits down to ponder family—memories—and food, it is amazing how interconnected those things can be. When I think of my Grandma Unger...I remember wonderful, warm-spirited Christmas Eves when she brought out all her baked goodies. My favorites were her wreath cookies that must have taken HOURS to make—and mere minutes for her grandchildren to devour!! Grandma Beggs wasn't much for elaborate cooking, but she loved to play "Jesus Wants Me for a Sunbeam" on the piano. And since it was the only song she knew, we heard it a lot!

I asked my 13-year-old daughter, Molly, what foods she most associated with her grandmothers. Molly's Swedish grandmother, Grandma Oberg, is known far and wide for her tremendously delicious Swedish rye bread, though Molly hasn't actually helped in the preparation of it. As far as her Grandma Applebee (my mother), the big family food tradition is her Shrimp Dip. For the past 15 years or so, her children and grandchildren always look forward to that Shrimp Dip at each of our get-togethers. We can't get enough of it! The only problem is that sometimes we don't know when to quit eating it—and since it's served as an appetizer, we often don't have much room left for the main course!

Molly says her all-time favorite childhood memory is when Grandma Applebee had what she called Grandma Day at her house. One Saturday each month, ten of her grandchildren would all converge on the house for an entire day of fun with each other—and fun with her. Though many of the grandchildren are now close to being grown up, Grandma Day will always be remembered as an extra special time for them.

Cathy Blythe
KFOR Morning Show Radio Host
Lincoln, Nebraska

Grandma's Shrimp Dip

Blend with a mixer on medium speed until smooth in consistency:

One 8-ounce package of cream cheese, softened

1/4 cup mayonnaise   2 tablespoons chopped onion
2 tablespoons ketchup

Add a 4 1/2-ounce can of broken shrimp, drained and mix dip at low speed.

Can serve with crackers, chips, or veggies. However, our personal family favorite is this dip served with Bugles.

Clarice: Cathy and co-host Scott Young give news and information to the folks in the Lincoln area along with their morning radio banter. Cathy also renders a service with her call-in program, Problems and Solutions. Her mother, Grandma Applebee, is famous in her own right, having played the organ many, many years at Lee's popular chicken restaurant. She continues to delight audiences with her piano performances in the community.

Guacamole Puerto Rican Style

3 large ripe avocados
1 medium yellow onion, minced
1 tablespoon vinegar
1/4 cup fresh lemon juice
1 jalapeno pepper, minced
1 tablespoon chili powder
1 large tomato, coarsely chopped
1/2 cup extra-sharp grated cheddar cheese

Mash avocado, mix in lemon juice to prevent discoloration. Mix in all other ingredients. Serve with Plantain chips or tortilla chips. Serves 4 to 6.

John D. Orr III
My Grandson
Columbus, Ohio

Clarice: Grandson John and his wife, Tanya, were awarded a trip to Puerto Rico when he was named Rookie Bank Manager of the Year. The postcard they sent me included this "Free Caribbean Recipe," and John's message, "Here's your recipe from John and Tanya. Ha Ha." I didn't let them off the hook quite that easily.

Dried Beef Dip

3 ounces of dried beef cut into pieces
2 3-ounce packages of cream cheese
1/4 cup milk
1/4 cup finely chopped onion
2 tablespoons chopped green pepper
1/4 teaspoon pepper
1 cup sour cream

Blend milk and cheese. Add remaining ingredients and mix. Bake at 400° for 20 minutes until bubbly. Serve with crackers or small bread rounds.

This recipe came from a co-worker who always brought tasty snacks to work.

Clarice Carlson Orr

193

These are two of my VERY favorite recipes from Saudi Arabia. Riyadh has such a pull for me—I miss the way of life and my taste buds were working overtime as I chose two of my favorite recipes to share. Whenever I prepare these, I can just close my eyes and hear the unique sound of the Arabic market place with open sacks of multi-colored and shaped spices. What wonderful scents float in the air there. And the smell of the flat pita bread coming out of a brick oven on a wooden paddle… fresh coffee beans roasting…the hustle and bustle of the market place…there's something that will always call to me.

These two recipes are great for informal get-togethers, appetizers or snacks. Or the tabouli can be a regular salad for a meal. Slightly warm your pita bread in the oven; tear off small strips or bite-size squares and "make a tent" over some of the tabouli or eggplant and pick up a mouthful that way—Arabic style!

Letha Rowley
Mitchell, South Dakota

A FRIEND IS ONE
TO WHOM ONE MAY POUR
OUT ALL THE CONTENTS
OF ONE'S HEART,
CHAFF AND GRAIN TOGETHER
KNOWING THAT THE
GENTLEST OF HANDS
WILL TAKE AND SIFT IT,
KEEP WHAT IS WORTH KEEPING
AND WITH A BREATH OF KINDNESS
BLOW THE REST AWAY.

—ARABIAN PROVERB

Eggplant-Sesame Dip

(This is called Baba Ghannouj in many books, but it is in error. Baba Ghannouj is the raw eggplant appetizer; Motabel is the cooked eggplant dish that is given here.)

1 large eggplant
1/2 cup sesame seed paste (tahini paste).
    Can be purchased in health food store
    or special foods sections in grocery stores.
2 tablespoons vegetable oil
Juice of 2 lemons (6 tablespoons)
2 garlic cloves, cut in halves
Salt and freshly ground white pepper to taste
Chopped parsley or pomegranate seeds, if desired
Bit of cumin, if desired

Preheat oven to 400°. Use a fork to pierce eggplant in several places. Place pierced eggplant on oven rack and bake 1 hour or until soft. If using microwave oven, bake pierced eggplant at full power (high) 5 minutes or until soft. Cool. Peel. Dice pulp into a blender or food processor. Add sesame seed paste, oil, lemon juice, garlic, salt and pepper. Process until mixture is smooth and pale, but thick and not liquefied.

Spoon into a serving bowl; garnish with parsley or pomegranate seeds or a little cumin, if desired. Serve with warm pita bread.

Tabbouleh (Tabouli)

3 1/4 ounces of fine burghul
    (bulgur—crushed wheat)
3 medium-sized fresh, ripe tomatoes,
    finely chopped
3/4 ounce finely chopped parsley,
    preferably flat-leafed parsley
4 ounces finely chopped onions
4 tablespoons fresh lemon juice
1/2 teaspoon salt
4 tablespoons olive oil.
1 1/2 tablespoon finely cut fresh mint
    or 2 1/2 teaspoon dried, crumbled mint

Place bulgur in a bowl or pan and add enough cold water to completely cover the bulgur. Let stand approximately 10 minutes. Drain in sieve or colander that is lined with double thickness of dampened cheesecloth. Wrap bulgur in cheesecloth and squeeze until very dry. Drop bulgur in a deep bowl. Add tomatoes, parsley, onion, lemon juice and salt. Toss gently but thoroughly together with a fork.

Just before serving, stir in olive oil and mint. Taste for seasoning. Heap in a bowl alone or on lettuce leaves. You just have to keep tasting it to get the flavor you like. Some like more lemon juice and olive oil, etc. You can put a little garlic powder in it, too, if you like.

Serves 4-6 with warmed pita (Arabic) bread.

Letha Rowley
Mitchell, South Dakota

Clarice: I got reacquainted with Letha at our 50th high school reunion and I learned about her exciting Civil Service career. For ten years she worked for Medical Directors in hospitals in Riyadh, Saudi Arabia. Letha said, "This was the absolute highlight of my life." Now retired, she enjoys living in our hometown. "There's just an 'at home' feeling and Life is good," she says.

People think that I got this recipe from my very Italian mother-in-law, but really it came from the *Los Angeles Times*. I've been making it for twenty years, and it still seems new. Phil and Mike really like them. These Puffs make a nice different addition to our Christmas Open House. Enjoy.

Cheryle Orr Paglialonga
My Daughter
Atascadero, California

Italian Cheese Puffs

1 cup water
1/2 cup butter or margarine
1/2 cup plus 2 tablespoons flour
1/2 cup Italian-style bread crumbs
1/4 teaspoon salt
1/4 teaspoon black pepper
3 eggs
1 (16-ounce) package shredded mozzarella cheese
Grated Parmesan cheese

In a medium saucepan, bring water and butter to the boiling point. Remove from heat. Stir in flour, breadcrumbs, salt and pepper, all at once. Cook and stir over low heat for 1 minute. The mixture comes together as in a ball, like cream puffs. Place mixture in the large bowl of an electric mixer. Add eggs one at a time, beating well after each addition. Beat until mixture is smooth. Beat in mozzarella cheese. Drop mixture by teaspoons or pipe through a pastry bag fitted with a large star tube onto ungreased baking pans. Sprinkle tops with grated Parmesan cheese. Bake at 375° until golden and puffed, about 15 minutes. Serve hot.

You can cool the puffs on wire racks, freeze wrap and freeze until ready to reheat and serve. To reheat, place frozen cheese puffs on baking sheets and bake at 375° until hot, about 10 minutes. Makes about 3 dozen cheese puffs.

The real voyage of discovery consists
not in seeking new landscapes
but in having new eyes.

—Marcel Proust

Backyard Bonuses

Carolina Pulled Pork

5 pounds boneless pork butt (shoulder) although I use
    boneless pork when I can get it on sale
4 tablespoons salt
2 tablespoons paprika
3 tablespoons black pepper
4 teaspoons cayenne
1/2 cup bourbon (I use Jim Beam)
2 tablespoon molasses
1 1/2 cups cider vinegar
1 cup water
2-4 chopped chipotle (Since I've never figured out what
    chopotle pepper is, I chop up some jalapenos.)
1 tablespoon crushed red pepper
Hardwood hickory chips, soaked in water for an hour

Combine 2 tablespoons salt, paprika, 2 tablespoons black
pepper, and 2 teaspoons cayenne. Rub on all surfaces of
pork. Refrigerate, covered, up to 24 hours (Ha, who prepares
that far ahead? I sprinkle it on just before I start the grill.)

Prepare grill with banked coals. Smoke pork (turning occasionally) away from coals with soaked hardwood chips,
adding charcoal to maintain medium-low temp (whatever
that is).

After about 3 hours, put pork in a pan with a cup+ of mixture
of 2 parts vinegar and 1 part water, and cover with foil. Cook
for another 2 hours or so (you'll probably need to add a couple of coals every 1/2 hour.)

In a saucepan, combine bourbon, molasses, 1 1/2 cups vinegar, 1 cup water, peppers, 2 tablespoons salt, 1 tablespoon
crushed red pepper, 1 tablespoon black pepper, and 2 teaspoon cayenne pepper. Simmer 5 minutes.

Boil any leftover basting sauce 5 minutes. Shred meat by
pulling apart and discarding fat. Add sauce. Serve on buns.
Coleslaw is good with it. Makes 12 servings for small eaters.

I ran across this recipe in our local *St. Louis Post Dispatch*, and every time I make it I'm reminded of my father, al-though for reasons he would probably never imagine. Number one, it uses whiskey, which I NEVER saw my father drink. If there was a bottle in the cabi-net, it was one that he found by the road-side (left by pheasant hunters) and he retrieved it to have for the lambs when they got sick. I never knew how this worked, but I know for a fact this is what my father thought. Number two, my fa-ther raised pigs, besides sheep. And I am reminded that one fall when he was sick, I was "in charge" of farming opera-tions. I made the "brilliant" decision to sell the hogs when they were bringing eleven cents a pound (this was in 1955). So much for my venture into farming. But, I like this Carolina pork recipe.

Keith Carlson
My Brother
St. Louis, Missouri

Clarice: I knew that Keith has been cook-ing since he retired, but I didn't know he went to all this trouble. I betcha it's good, tho'. I wonder if his experience selling the hogs at 11 cents a pound influenced his decision to become an economist for his lifelong career.

Ken's Grilled Chicken

Many of our meals are prepared on a grill. Ken assumed the role as the official chef at the grill within the first months of our marriage. The first barbecue was his own version of grilling chicken sprinkled with Lawry Salt. To this day it remains a favorite and one that has guests asking how he prepared the chicken.

London Broiled Beef Cubes

I usually buy a sirloin roast and cube it. Ken marinates the beef cubes overnight, then puts it on skewers and grills it.

London Broil Marinade: 1/2 teaspoon lemon peel, 2/3 cup lemon juice, 1/3 cup salad oil, 2 teaspoons salt, 1/2 teaspoon pepper, 1 teaspoon Lea & Perrins Worcestershire sauce, 1/2 teaspoon dry mustard, 2 chopped green onions with tops. Mix and marinate the beef cubes.

Marcia Carlson Rislov
A Carlson Cousin
Green Oaks, Illinois

Steak Roll

1 slice of round steak
1 small jar of kosher dill pickles
1 dozen slices of beef bacon

Lay the steak on a cutting board, put on a layer of thinly sliced dill pickles. Then top with a layer of beef bacon. Roll the steak, pickles, and bacon to the inside. Both the steak and the pickles must be thinly sliced, or it will not roll properly. Wrap the remaining bacon slices around the roll and tie it in several places with a heavy cord that you have soaked in water. It takes no further seasoning. Put a grill spit lengthwise through the roll and put on rotor of grill.

Cook until center of roll is done. When done, remove the spit and slice the roll as you serve it, just like slicing a banana. Two slices make a good serving, so one cut of round steak makes a meal for a large family.

About fifteen years ago, a friend of mine who was a backyard grill expert, told me a new way to grill a steak. He gave me the recipe for a steak roll. I had to try several times before being successful. First, the steak was cut too thickly and wouldn't roll. When I learned to get the steak specially cut, I found the kosher pickles were too thick. I then found it took a longer time to grill a roll of steak than it did a flat steak and the center sometimes was rare.

Success at last, and I submitted the recipe to a grilling contest sponsored by the natural gas company. It won me first prize and a gas grill.

Don Crosier
Lincoln, Nebraska

Tender Roasting Ears

Submerge freshly husked and cleaned corn in ICE COLD water. At cooking time, put on kettle and add enough water that will almost cover the corn. Add 2 rounded tablespoons of sugar and 3 tablespoons of vinegar. Bring to BOIL and then add ears of corn and cook (need not boil) only 5 minutes. Remove from heat. Put on cover and let stand 10 minutes. EAT and ENJOY. DO NOT ADD SALT while cooking as salt hardens the kernels.

Clarice: Tender Roasting Ears isn't prepared in the backyard, but it just seemed to go with the grilled recipes. This method really works, so I hope you'll try it.

In August of 1974, as a 4-H family, we hosted Himiko, a Japanese exchange student. The children's TV show, ZOOM came to televise our family. They filmed Himiko and me picking and shucking sweet corn. Another segment showed my brother Byron blessing the food—it took five times before the filmmakers were satisfied. Then they let us enjoy the sweet corn. Himiko loved it. She ate six ears of corn.

The next year, I went to Japan and spent 33 days at Himiko's home. While she was finishing a week away at school, I spent my time with Grandma Takasaw. The only English she knew was No. Two times she chased me out of the house with a broom because I forgot to take off my shoes and put on the slippers. I was so-o-o-o homesick that I wrote to Mom and begged her to come and get me. Then Himiko came home. I joined her, her mother, an actress, and her father, a pottery maker, on a tour of Japan. But I forgot to write anything more to Mom and she was frantic. Himiko tried to teach Grandma Takasaw how to fix sweet corn. She boiled it until no one could eat it.

Renae Hunt
Grand Island, Nebraska

199

High on my list of "precious" time is fishing for trout in Colorado with my son, Stephen. He is the fisherman in the family, but he is also the chief cook when it comes to preparing the trout for eating. This is his sure-fire way of making fresh trout the centerpiece for a delectable meal.

Gordon F. Culver
Lincoln, Nebraska

We grow old when regrets outnumber our dreams.
—Jimmy Carter

Delectable Trout

4 personally caught and dressed trout
    (approximately 12-14 ounces each)
Store-bought trout will substitute in a pinch!
1 bottle of Italian salad dressing

Marinate trout for at least one hour in the Italian salad dressing.

Place trout on hot, covered grill for exactly four minutes—not 4 and 1/2 !—before turning and cooking on the other side—also for not more than four minutes.

Remove trout from grill. Remove skeleton from each trout; place deboned trout on serving tray; and fight over who gets them at the dinner table. Enjoy! Serves four.

Wyoming Campfires

When our family was growing up we spent a lot of vacations in Wyoming. Then, the men could still get their limit of mountain trout. It you want a really good meal, have fresh caught trout, fried in a black iron skillet over a campfire. Have another skillet full of fried potatoes and onions. I drool thinking about it.

My grandmother didn't cook for us. She was still having children when my mother was raising a family, so we only got together for meals on holidays and then it was "everybody cook." Grandma Surrena was a true Grandmother as any of her 19 grandchildren would attest. She COOKED. I miss her every day; she gave us so much more than food, she gave all of us total love. She was awesome.

When I think of grandmothers, it isn't the cooking we remember so much as it is the family and the love and the acceptance.

Gladys Woods
Lincoln, Nebraska

THIS 'n THAT

Ice Cream, Candy, Beverages, & Pickles

A Simple Prayer

I want to thank you, Lord,
for being close to me so far this day.
With your help,
I haven't been impatient,
Lost my temper,
Been grumpy, judgmental,
Or envious of anyone.
But, I will be getting out of bed in a minute,
And I think I will really need your help then.
Amen.

Putting Food on the Table

When I think about the effort put into the food preparation, it blows my mind. Much of it started with the garden. It was hard to grow a garden in the drought years of the 1930s. We had no electricity so if it didn't rain, we had to carry water in buckets to the plants. A little low spot down by the windmill was the best place during those years. That's where the early produce—the lettuce, radishes, peas, onions, and tomatoes—could be watered.

Sometimes the sweet corn, green beans, and squash were planted on the edge of the field corn which wasn't always near the house. And Pa knew where the potatoes grew best. During the wet years, there was some fruit. The story was told that Grandpa August Carlson had some training at a nursery in Sweden and planted the apple and cherry trees, as well as the asparagus in the roadside ditches down by the mailbox.

On the homestead side of the gravel road, there were cottonwood trees in the fence row. We were told that Grandpa planted asparagus at the base of the trees. By the time I was growing up, most of the fast-growing cottonwoods had been cut down, or had fallen victim to the drought, wind, or lightning. But, the asparagus seemed to thrive around the rotting roots of those trees.

Early on spring mornings, Mom would head down the lane or send Pa down looking for the tender asparagus shoots. Unfortunately, the neighbors also knew of this great delicacy and assuming that the road ditch was public property, they helped themselves. So it was a battle of the asparagus every spring. Who would get to the asparagus first? I don't know if there was ever any face-to-face confrontation, but at our house every spring there was always plenty of table conversation about who could get there first!

The trouble with fresh garden produce is that it doesn't keep. Since we didn't have electricity (or freezer) until I was a teenager, I helped Mom can, pickle, and preserve many of the vegetables for winter. I helped pick and prepare the bushels of green beans, tomatoes, and big bags of sweet corn. I would go down to the cellar and bring up the empty Mason jars and wash them in hot water. It was kinda fun to sit beside Mom and snap beans or husk the corn. We had some very good visits at those times. I felt grown-up.

All the food we ate was prepared on the kitchen table; asparagus cut up, potatoes were peeled, corn silked, cabbage chopped for slaw. Apples were peeled, cherries pitted, the vegetables and fruit were canned. Bread was kneaded, pie crusts were rolled out, cakes were mixed and frosted. The table was covered with layers of newspapers when spring chickens were dressed there, fresh beef and pork was cut up, and sausage was ground.

Mom was a really good cook. Too good— she always wished she could wear a size 14. We ate a lot of eggs and potatoes because that's what we had on the farm. Enough potatoes were boiled for dinner to fry for supper to go with eggs. We had fried eggs, scrambled eggs, poached eggs, omelets with home canned chili sauce, boiled eggs, deviled eggs, egg sandwiches, egg salad, and potato salad with lots of eggs. I loved baked eggs; Mom put butter in muffin tins and broke an egg in each cup, sprinkled salt and pepper on it and poured a spoonful of cream on top and baked it in the oven.

On wash days, Mom often cooked a big pot of beans. We ate the broth over bread for our noon meal and for supper the beans were baked with a little bacon or ham. Usually we had scalloped potatoes with the beans, although sometimes it was baked macaroni and cheese. In the winter, when the cook stove purred all day long, oven meals often included rice pudding or custard. We had pie for everyday, too—chocolate, lemon, butterscotch—pudding pies made with milk and eggs that had heaping meringue on top. Oranges, apples, and bananas were our fresh fruit until late summer when Mom bought lugs of peaches, pears, and prune plums and then canned much of it for sauce.

When the grain was harvested, a dozen or so men on the threshing crew had to be fed. Always in July, the temperatures were high and the hot winds blew from the south. We had no airconditioning or electric fans. The round dining room table was stretched to its limit and covered with a long oilcloth. Neighbor ladies Gladys and Sengne came to help Mom fix the food. The platters were piled high with chicken that Mom had butchered and fried, or meatloaf, roast beef, or pork chops. There were bowls of mashed potatoes and at least one other vegetable besides the pickles, jelly, and jam to dress up the homemade bread and rolls. And always pies, often two or three kinds.

About 4 o'clock in the afternoon, Mom took lunch out to the field where the threshing machine (that looked like a dinosaur) was spewing out a strawstack. Mom and the ladies had ground up minced ham with pickles and added salad dressing for sandwiches. There was often a sour cream chocolate cake with brown sugar frosting plus oatmeal cookies for the men to nibble on with their choice of Watkins nectar, coffee, or iced tea. The young bundle haulers rested under the hayracks in the shade as they waited their turn to unload at the threshing machine.

Cooking for threshers was over for the year, but then it was time for school and Mom had to pack school lunches. And she kept on baking sour cream chocolate cakes and oatmeal cookies to fill our dinner pails.

203

Mom made Red Anise Candy in the middle of winter when there was a lot of snow on the ground. After a big snowstorm, my little brother Keith and I would trudge outside past the board fence at the end of the barnyard, out to the gravel pit to play in the snow. The pit filled up with snow and we would jump off the steep sides PLUMP into the soft snow. Sitting with our legs and bottoms surrounded by the fluffy stuff, it was like sitting in a big comfy chair. Then, we'd scramble out and up to the top, jump off the edge again and make another cushy throne. Other snowy days, we pulled our sleds up the hill to the schoolhouse and slid down the steep embankment made by the new road.

When the shadows grew long, our noses were running, and our cheeks were like roses, we stumbled home on our frozen feet. The lamplight and warm kitchen cookstove welcomed us home. On the oilcloth-covered table was the plate of Red Anise Candy, looking for all the world like broken pieces of blood-stained glass. I always marveled at the contrast of the crimson crystalline smoothness and the sharpness of the edges. And we could EAT this magical stuff that Mom had brewed out of sugar and water while we were outside playing.

Clarice Carlson Orr

Red Anise Candy

2 cups sugar
1/2 cup water
Few drops of anise oil

1/2 cup white syrup
Red food coloring

Cook and stir to very hard ball stage or when the syrup spins a thread, about 270°. Add red food coloring and a few drops of anise oil flavoring. Pour onto greased cookie sheet—one with raised edges. It is very hot, so be very careful. It will harden up quickly. When it is cool, break into pieces, like peanut brittle.

Snow Ice Cream

A dishpan full of newly fallen, sparkling clean, white snow
1 egg   1 cup sugar
2 teaspoons of vanilla

Beat the egg, sugar and the vanilla and stir into the snow. Eat immediately. If you try to freeze it, it will turn to ice.

I made this treat for my children when they were growing up. It was a fun treat to make and eat after the blizzard had passed and we were still inside. Now, pasteurized eggs provide the safety from salmonella. I wish we had known about snow ice cream when I was a girl; I remember a lot of drifts of white snow. However, we made more real ice cream in the winter time, since ice was accessible from the livestock water tanks.

Clarice Carlson Orr

Grandma Carr's Homemade Ice Cream
(Adapted for IFYE Host Family Weekend)

4 eggs	2 cups sugar
1/4 teaspoon salt	2 quarts milk
2 pints cream	1 tablespoon vanilla

Beat eggs well until light and lemon color. Slowly add sugar and salt, beat well again. In mean time, heat milk. Add some of the warm milk to egg mixture, to temper the eggs. Then add this back into heated milk and cook, stirring constantly until mixture slightly coats spoon. Remove from heat and allow to cool, then add vanilla and cream. Put in freezer can. Makes 1 gallon. In the larger container around the ice cream can use 1 part rock salt to 8 parts of ice.

The gradual heating of the eggs is necessary to insure a perfectly smooth custard. Check the custard by testing, it should be as thick as heavy cream.

For 5 gallons we used 16 eggs, 7 cups sugar, 8 quarts milk, 4 quarts cream, 1 teaspoon salt and 5 tablespoons vanilla.

Clarice: Ray and LaVerne Burke provided the sweetest highlight of IFYE Weekend for many years. As young adults from around the world and their Nebraska families gathered each September, it was terrific for young and old to see the process and taste the great American experience of Grandma Carr's Homemade Ice Cream.

The first Dairy Queen opened in Joliet, Illinois in 1940.

In 1955, we started going to IFYE Host Family Weekend at the Nebraska State 4-H Camp at Halsey, Nebraska. IFYE sounds like IFFY and stands for International 4-H Youth Exchange. All the families who previously and currently had IFYEs stay with them were invited to attend the camp with their exchangee. We hosted 8 young people from other countries. In 1974, Himiko came from Japan and ZOOM TV filmed our family. The next year our daughter Renae went to Japan. Then, in 1977, the Kids World TV group was here when we had Ozeki from Japan. That year, Renae was to demonstrate making 100% wheat bread, but she had broken both wrists so Ozeki had to make the bread. The other day I had another nice letter from Himiko.

It was probably in the 1960s that we started taking the five-gallon freezer to Halsey to make ice cream. We got the milk and cream from a neighbor and the eggs came from our boys' 4-H poultry project. Ray and I always planned to arrive at camp on Friday night. I would cook the custard that night and cool it overnight in the camp's big walk-in refrigerator. At least a half-dozen times, I had to make a double batch (10 gallons) when we had big crowds.

LaVerne Burke
Stromsburg, Nebraska

Homemade ice cream is a staple on Christmas and July 4th in our family. The egg substitute keeps it safe.

Claire Altoff
Breckinridge, Minnesota

Clarice: Claire introduced me to the Minnesota Extension Service's educational program, "Who Gets Grandma's Yellow Pie Plate?" This program helps folks decide how to distribute family keepsakes.

This is a favorite quick and easy dessert that our guests always enjoy.

Marcia Carlson Rislov
A Carlson Cousin
Green Oaks, Illinois

I first tasted this while visiting our friends, Harold and Esther Sampson. Later, I've found it a wonderful treat on a very hot day. My neighbor's grandson helped clean up my patio and he was impressed with this delightful refreshment. One of the reasons I like it is that I usually have all the ingredients on hand.

Clarice Carlson Orr

Homemade Ice Cream

8 ounces egg substitute
1 1/2 pints cream
3 teaspoons vanilla
2 cups sugar
5 cups milk

Beat egg substitute and sugar. Beat in cream and vanilla. Pour milk into ice cream freezer can and add egg mixture. Using the ice and salt around the filled can, freeze the ice cream as directed.

Brandy Ice

Mix 1/2 cup brandy and 1/4 cup crème de cacao with 1/2 gallon slightly softened vanilla ice cream. Blend with electric mixer and refreeze until ready to serve.

Orange Julius

1 (6 ounce) can frozen orange juice
1 cup milk
1/2 cup sugar
Ice cubes
1 cup water
1 tablespoon vanilla

Mix all together in a blender until foamy. It is so cold, you will get a headache.

Our Favorite Hot Cocoa

1/2 cup sugar
vanilla extract
4 cups milk

1/3 cup hot water
1/4 cup Hershey's Cocoa
Pinch of salt

Mix cocoa, sugar, water and salt in a saucepan. Stir constantly over medium heat until mixture boils. Cook and stir 2 minutes. Stir in milk and heat. DO NOT BOIL.

Remove from heat; add vanilla. Pour in cups and top with marshmallows, if desired.

Six servings.

While babysitting with our three grandchildren overnight, I decided to make some hot cocoa the old-fashioned way for them. As they are standing near the stove to watch, I am telling them we are making this hot cocoa from "scratch." Our three-year-old granddaughter, Stephanie, kept asking where the "itch" was. Finally, realizing what she was thinking, we all had a good laugh.

LaDonna Pankoke
Lincoln, Nebraska

Life is like a field of newly fallen snow;
where I choose to walk every step will show.
—Denis Waitley *from Priorities, 1999*

My Grandmother Peace's home in the Rio Grande Valley of Texas was a grandchild's paradise—palm trees, tropical plants, and citrus orchards outside, two floors of nooks and crannies to explore inside. It made a wonderful setting for endless hours of make-believe fun. Grandmother always made us feel so welcome and so special—not a small task considering there were 21 of us grandkids. One of my earliest memories is of that precious little lady in her cozy kitchen making vinegar taffy surrounded by children. Everyone was included, regardless of size. Guided by Grandmother's patient instructions, we would cover our hands with butter and begin to pull the hot candy and then pull some more, until it turned a rich, pearly white color. What fun to be part of that group effort, especially since the end result tasted so good.

Grandmother Peace's Vinegar Taffy

2 cups sugar
1/2 teaspoon vanilla
1 tablespoon oleo
1/2 cup boiling water
1 1/2 tablespoons vinegar

Boil together without stirring to 265° or until brittle when dropped into cold water. Turn onto greased platter. Pull until white and glossy. Cut into pieces.

Although Grandmother left this earth more than 25 years ago, I'm grateful for sweet memories of her love and many happy hours spent in her "House of Peace."

Karen Carr
Lincoln, Nebraska

Our family looks forward to caramels as a treat every Christmas.

Alyce Knutson
A Carlson Cousin
Lakewood, Colorado

Caramels

2 cups cream or Carnation milk
2 cups white sugar
1 cup butter
2 teaspoons vanilla
1 1/2 cups white syrup
1 1/2 cup chopped walnuts
1/4 teaspoon salt

Cook sugar, syrup, butter and 1 cup cream or milk until it boils. Add second cup of cream. Boil to hard ball stage (242°). Stir constantly. Add vanilla and nuts. Pour into buttered pan. Cut in squares and wrap in waxed paper when cool.

My Mother's Taffy

2 cups brown sugar	1 cup molasses
1 tablespoon vinegar	1/8 teaspoon salt
1 tablespoon butter	1 teaspoon vanilla

Combine sugar, molasses, vinegar, and salt in heavy saucepan. Cook to the hard ball stage (265°). Add butter and vanilla and pour on a buttered platter. When taffy is cool enough to handle, butter fingers and pull until light in color and slightly firm. Make a rope like string about the size of a nickel. Twist. Cut with scissors into one-inch pieces.

Some of the fun times we had growing up were when Mother would make taffy. What fun we had pulling and stretching it.

One Monday morning back in 1924, my mother had to go to Grandma's to do the family wash. I was five and it was part of my morning chores to do the breakfast dishes before I went to school. We always used P&G bar soap. I only had a small piece of soap this particular morning to do the dishes so I melted the small piece of soap and twisted it so it looked like taffy. When my nine-year-old brother Barney saw it, he grabbed it and stuck it in his mouth and started chewing it. He spit and sputtered and started crying that it wasn't taffy but soap. Grandpa was mowing hay by our house and heard the disturbance. He climbed the fence and started to scold me. I said I couldn't help it if he thought it was taffy.

Jaunita Duffek
Seward, Nebraska

Clarice: Sally is a great friend and, as my academic advisor, she guided me through the steps of getting my bachelor's and master's degrees in Gerontology and Grandparenting.

Caramel Crispix

1 17-ounce package of Crispix Cereal
12 ounces of dry roasted peanuts
1 can of mixed nuts   2 cups brown sugar
1/2 cup white Karo syrup   1 teaspoon baking soda
1 cup butter or margarine

Place cereal and nuts in a large brown paper bag. Mix butter, sugar and syrup in saucepan. Bring to a full boil for 1 1/2 minutes. Add soda until foamy.

Pour over cereal and nuts in paper bag and shake well. Fold over ends and microwave on high for 4 minutes, shaking bag every minute. Cool on waxed paper, separating mixture while it is cooling.

Sally VanZandt
Lincoln, Nebraska and Mesa, Arizona

When my brother was in the Army in 1943 during World War II, he was and stationed overseas in the North African, Sicilian, and Italian Campaigns. I sent him a "care package" of goodies for Christmas which included an unsliced roll of the date nut fudge along with pieces of conventional fudge and several types of cookies. He did not receive the box until the middle of February. He wrote to thank me for the goodies, but said that unfortunately everything was smashed into small bits except the roll of date nut fudge. That, he said, "was the best candy he had ever eaten."

Sarah Viola Gregory Cox
Raphine, Virginia

Date Nut Fudge

3 cups sugar   1 cup milk
1 1/2 cups chopped pecans   1 tablespoon butter
Dates, about a pound   1 teaspoon vanilla

Cook sugar and milk over medium heat, stirring constantly until a soft ball is formed, 236°. Add dates and butter and continue to cook over medium heat for 5 minutes; stir often.

Remove from heat and cool to lukewarm without stirring; add 1 cup of chopped nuts and 1 teaspoon vanilla, and beat until creamy. While fudge is cooling, immerse a clean dish towel in warm water, wring it out and refrigerate it to chill it. Now pour fudge onto the chilled and dampened dish towel, then roll it into a roll about 1 to 1 1/2 inches in diameter and about 12 inches in length. Place in refrigerator overnight. Then roll in the remaining 1/2 of chopped pecans and slice into 1/4 to 1/2 inch slices for serving.

Grapenuts Candy

Melt 1 12-ounce package of chocolate chips

Stir in 1 can sweetened condensed milk
and 1 teaspoon vanilla

Add 1 cup Grapenuts

Drop by teaspoonfuls on waxed paper. Chill in refrigerator.

Rudge's mom always made these at Christmas time. Since this was before Tupperware and Rubbermaid, she would store the candy in two- or three-pound coffee cans.

Dottie Vifquain
Lincoln, Nebraska

Earl W. Tupper invented resealable food containers in 1945.

Christmas Spiced Almonds

1 1/2 tablespoons unsalted butter
3/4 cup sugar
1 tablespoon ground coriander
3/4 teaspoon ground cloves
2 tablespoons ground cinnamon
3 egg whites
1 1/2 tablespoons grated orange zest
6 cups whole unblanched almonds.

Line 2 rimmed baking sheets with foil and butter foil generously. Combine sugar, coriander, cloves, and cinnamon in bowl and stir to mix. Place egg whites in mixing bowl and whisk until frothy. Add seasonings and mix again. Stir in orange zest. Add almonds and mix, stirring, until nuts are coated well. Transfer nuts to baking sheets and spread evenly. Bake on center shelf at 275° for 40 minutes, stirring every 10 minutes. Remove and cool 1 hour. Store in airtight container. Nuts can be made 3 weeks ahead. Makes 6 cups.

Dan was a teacher I worked with and he was an almond grower. In this part of the country, if you are a farmer, not a rancher, you either grow grapes or almonds. Dan grew almonds, so at Christmas time I bought almonds from him. When you buy 15 pounds of almonds, you had better have a good recipe in mind. Here is mine. I gave them away as presents for my boys' teachers and as hostess gifts.

Cheryle Paglialonga
My Daughter
Atascadero, California

Gram Kerr cooked basics well, but had a reputation for only using the HIGH setting on the stove, as she occasionally had burnt offerings on the table and a pan soaking in the sink. Her goal to cook fast led to a favorite family story. It is told she had a batch of applesauce in the pressure cooker, which blew up in her face. Scared and scalded, she ran around and around the kitchen with applesauce coating her glasses screaming, "I'm blind! I'm blind!"

When Gram came to visit we hoped for a batch of her sugar cookies. They were always crisp, round, sprinkled with white sugar, and carried in an old oatmeal box. At big dinners (nearly every Sunday) we counted on her delicious crescent rolls. They went fast with all twenty of us there.

Memories of Gram are more of life-lessons than recipes. She was a staunch Methodist and had no tolerance for smoking, drinking, or strong language. She routinely inspected our hands, fingernails, and elbows for proper cleanliness and reminded us often of proper manners. She demanded honesty and her life was a lesson in frugality. Washing her 1951 Pontiac was worth a nickel to each of us.

For a real treat at Christmas she would splurge and make Sugared Walnuts. They disappeared in a hurry, but that's OK, they are best fresh anyway!

Peg Hurrell
Lincoln, Nebraska

Sugared Walnuts

Boil to soft ball 240°: 1 cup sugar and 1/2 cup milk

Stir in 2 tablespoons margarine or butter and 1/4 teaspoon salt. Stir in 2 - 2 1/2 cups whole or broken walnuts—not chopped. This is quick and easy, a great addition to a buffet table or as a hostess gift.

Potato Candy

1/4 cup hot mashed potatoes
2 1/2 cups sifted confectioner's sugar
Dash of salt
1 1/3 cups flaked coconut
2 squares unsweetened chocolate, melted
1 teaspoon butter
1/2 teaspoon vanilla

Mix potatoes and butter in bowl; add sugar gradually and beat thoroughly. Add vanilla, salt and coconut. Pack in greased 8 X 8 inch pan and spread melted chocolate on top. Chill until chocolate is firm. Cut into squares.

Rose Marie Tondl
Lincoln, Nebraska

Clarice: Rose Marie's recipe was published in the Lincoln Journal Star. *There were a few other suggested variations. Grated orange or lemon peel could be added. Instead of coconut, you might add walnuts or pecans. My brother Paul made a similar fondant mixture without the coconut. He molded a small amount around a drained maraschino cherry. Then he dipped each piece in chocolate.*

Lemon Cheese
(A sweet spread to use like jam)

4 tablespoons butter
2 cups sugar
2 lemons (6 tablespoons juice and rind, finely grated)

Put ingredients in a double boiler to cook, stirring frequently.

Add 4 eggs which have been well beaten and keep stirring until it thicken. Cool. Store in the refrigerator. The mixture thickens a bit as it cools.

A fter each visit with my Grannie, she sent home a jar of lemon cheese which we all really liked. As we were leaving to go to our home, she gave the treat to my brother, Dick, saying "This is for you." My brother thought she meant it was just for him and he would not share it with our family. After that, she made sure she told us it was for all of us.

This is a recipe Grannie brought from England. It was a favorite for all of the family to use on fresh-baked scones, biscuits, or toast. I still love it, but don't make it often. When I lived in Florida, lemons were in plentiful supply so I did make it more often then.

Marilyn Gates
Lincoln, Nebraska

Sweetened Condensed Milk
(Quite Thick)

Mix in blender. Put sugar or sugar substitute in first. If dry milk is put in first, it sticks in the bottom.

2/3 cup sugar or equivalent sugar substitute
1/3 cup boiling water
3 tablespoons margarine or butter
1 cup of dry milk or powdered non-dairy cream.

Equals 1 can of sweetened condensed milk.

Midge Hole Carlson
My Sister-in-law
Vermillion, South Dakota

Grandma's Watermelon Pickles

Trim the green off the watermelon rinds and cut in pieces about 1 1/2 inches in length. Boil in slightly salted water until tender. Drain thoroughly. Make syrup as follows:

3 pounds sugar
3 pints vinegar
1 1/2 ounces of stick cinnamon

Boil sugar, spices and vinegar and pour over rinds. For three days, drain the syrup off the rinds and reheat to boiling. Put in jars and seal with lids and rings.

Most of my memories of Grandma Orr's home are of the kitchen or dining room. The dining room was large with tall windows facing the yard and garden. There were sliding pocket doors leading into the sitting room where nobody really sat. At the end of the dining room was the door to the upstairs bedrooms. On cold mornings, we would hurry down the steps to the dining room and stand over the heating duct on the floor before sitting down to breakfast. We had strange things for breakfast like oatmeal, poached eggs and prunes served in small sauce dishes.

It wasn't until lunch or dinner that we got to have my favorite—watermelon pickles! I couldn't believe how good they were. How could the sweet, crisp pickles come from a watermelon? Grandma canned them in small, green fruit jars. She often served them when we visited.

My father's sister, Edis, included this recipe in her tribute to her mother—*Jennie's Cookbook*. She commented that the recipe was sent to Grandma Orr from a lady in her community club. The lady prefaced the recipe copy with the comment: "Sorry, I didn't get this to you before, but our son and wife came home on his furlough." The United States was at war—but ladies still made pickles!

Cyndi Orr Parrott
My Daughter
Omaha, Nebraska

Coincidences are God's way of remaining anonymous.

—Doris Lessing

Hot Dill Pickles

(Makes about 12 quarts)

1 market basket of cucumbers
Garlic
Dill
Pickling (not iodized) salt
Vinegar
Hot peppers, such as jalapeno or banana

Wash and brush cucumbers and refrigerate overnight, or place in ice water overnight. This makes crisp pickles.

Make a brine of 2/3 to 3/4 cup salt, 1 quart vinegar and 3 quarts of water. Boil for 15 minutes.

Pack cucumbers in clean, sterile jars. To each jar add 1 clove garlic, one hot pepper, a head of fresh dill and 1/8 teaspoon powdered alum. Cover with the hot brine and seal.

Let stand for three weeks before eating.

This is an old Polish recipe. My Texas sons look forward to our visits, hoping I'll bring a jar or two of these pickles.

Gladys Woods
Lincoln, Nebraska

Mrs. MacFarlane's Dill Pickles

2 cups water
1 cup vinegar
2 level tablespoons of pickling salt

Boil all together and pour over dill and cucumbers packed in jars while hot.

I found this recipe in the recipe box of my mother, Lillie Rasmussen. I remember Mom making them often.

Joan Martin
A Rosenquist Cousin
Concord, California

Clarice: The MacFarlanes lived about a mile from the Carlson homestead where I grew up. They had a wonderful garden full of vegetables even when we didn't. Mrs. MacFarlane told me the story that she walked across the pasture in February to see the Carlson's new baby boy, Clarence, who was my father. That was 100 years ago. It's curious that the Dill Pickle recipe is still going!

More This 'n' That

Pioneer Recipe to Relieve Constipation

| 1 cup bran | 1 cup applesauce | 1/2 cup prune juice |

Mix all ingredients. Keep refrigerated. Dose: 2-3 tablespoons twice each day, as needed.
Just for fun, I want this recipe to be included. It probably works!

Twila Wilson
Lincoln, Nebraska

Stressed Elimination

1. Eat only pineapple with lettuce or celery 3 times a day for 3 consecutive days. Have a cup of hot Postum or cereal drink at the end of each day.
2. Begin the 4th day with juice of 2 oranges, 3 times a day for 2 days—a dozen oranges.
3. During these 5 days, bowels are kept open with large salt water enema, preferably at 4 P.M. with 1 teaspoon salt to 1/2 gallon of water.
4. 6th day—Breakfast, one thoroughly toasted shredded wheat biscuit dry with butter. Sip slowly 1 cup hot drink, Postum or hot tea (2/3 cup hot water and 1/3 cup milk.)
5. For lunch, meat broth and lettuce and tomato salad. No dressing except salt.
6. Dinner is several vegetables—creamed or buttered, (no flour dressing) buttermilk or half milk and half water. No bread.
7. After this week have bread once daily. Avoid tea, coffee, white sugar, white flour, lard, vinegar, mustard, pepper, canned meats, nuts, commercial ice cream, soda fountain drinks.
8. Until well, avoid vegetables with high carbohydrate content, fruits and sweets.

In my mother's handwritten recipe book I found this procedure for the constipation problem. I do not remember that my mother ever USED this routine, but, I found it strange to see it recorded. Farm families, like mine, had several reasons to have constipation. Most farms did not have indoor plumbing or central heating, which meant the only relief was found out behind the garage, summer, or winter. When you went to the "necessary house" or privy, you were at the mercy of the weather. Comfort on the hole cut in the bench of wood was not in the building plan! Many folks postponed their "trip" as long as possible, which may have caused the problem.

Clarice Carlson Orr

FUN
STUFF
FOR
KIDS

*Erma Bombeck
said her
kids wouldn't
eat anything
that hadn't
danced on TV.*

Grandma's House Was Not Worlds of Fun

It was fun to go to Grandma and Grandpa's. Grandpa was old, bald, had a handlebar mustache and a cane. Seated next to the radio, he'd catch my leg with the crook of his cane and tease me with pink wintergreens. Grandma didn't play; she did needlework. I heard the story that she played a concertina, until she lost her hearing. Momma had to talk Swedish right into her ear so she could hear.

Grandpa and Grandma lived in town; had electricity, a bathroom, sidewalks, and a concrete basement floor. It was fun to snoop around the house. I'd peek in their bedroom, wonder about their twin beds; go in the bathroom, turn on the faucets and dabble in the water.

Outside I'd play with more water, squirting my brother with the hose. We'd lug the rusty wagon to the sidewalk and pull each other to the corner. One Thanksgiving Day, I rollerskated on the smooth basement floor round and round the mountain of a furnace.

Grandma's entertainment center was a carom board. Keith and I dumped the caroms from the yellowed sugar sack and shot them around the board until our middle fingers were sore. All the books were dull, until I discovered Margaret Mead's, *Coming of Age in Samoa,* left there by Uncle Carl, a college professor.

Grandma's house wasn't Worlds of Fun or Disney World. But it was a place of fascination and mystique. And a place of security and contentment.

One of the best parts of growing up is the memories, although, I still have Grandpa and Grandma's carom board. Sometimes my grandkids drag it out and shoot caroms until their middle fingers are sore. Then, I pick up the caroms and put them back in the sugar sack.

Clarice Carlson Orr

Grandma Orr's Bubble Recipe

1 cup Dawn or Joy liquid detergent
1/3 cup white Karo syrup
1 gallon of water

That's all there is to it. Combine these ingredients, as in a plastic dishpan, without stirring to make bubbles. For a bubble machine, cut out the center of a plastic plate or draw a length of yarn through two soda straws and tie together to make a box shape. Warm humid days with no wind are the best bubble days.

For a large group, make up five gallons of bubble solution in a small child's wading pool. Have a child stand on the stool in the middle of a hula hoop that's in the bubble solution. When you raise the hula hoop the child will be encased in a bubble! It's good, clean fun for babies, kids, moms and dads, grandparents, and elders in wheelchairs…at family reunions, office backyard parties, church picnics, or at home when you're bored. It's perfect summertime entertainment.

Clarice Carlson Orr

Playing with Frozen Bread Dough

Children love to make and bake real bread and rolls. Purchase a loaf of frozen bread dough and let it thaw. Get out your rolling pin, a small plastic knife and fork, or any other utensils, and let the children do as they wish. If the dough doesn't get too grubby, you can bake it, as you would rolls.

Clarice Carlson Orr

Play Dough

1 1/2 cups salt
3 cups flour
3 cups water (add a few drops of food coloring)
6 teaspoons cream of tartar
    (keeps it from getting sour)
3 tablespoons cooking oil

Mix all the ingredients together in a large skillet. Cook over low heat, stirring constantly until mixture comes together into a ball and cleans the pan—like when mixing pie dough. Cool and knead until it is pliable. Store in a plastic container in the refrigerator. This will keep 2 to 3 months. Let it warm to room temperature before using. The feel is the experience!

Clarice Carlson Orr

Play Doh

1 cup water   1 tablespoon oil
Food coloring   1 cup flour
1/2 cup salt
1 tablespoon powdered alum

Boil water, oil and food coloring. Mix flour, salt and powdered alum together. Add flour mixture to boiling water mixture. Remove from heat and stir. Use a sheet of foil and knead it like bread. Do not refrigerate. Store in an air-tight container.

Twila Wilson
Lincoln, Nebraska

Edible Peanut Butter Play Dough

2 tablespoons honey
4 tablespoons dry milk
2 tablespoons peanut butter

Mix well. Put out chocolate and butterscotch chips, sunflower seeds and peanuts for older kids to decorate their edible creations with.

Clarice Carlson Orr

Grandloving's Play Dough

1 cup boiling hot water
1 tablespoon cooking oil
1 cup flour
1/2 cup salt
2 tablespoons corn starch
One package unsweetened drink mix,
    such as Kool-Aid.

Mix all. Allow the dough to cool before deciding it's too sticky—and before allowing your grandchild to work with it. You need a flat surface, such as a large cookie tray or table top. Kitchen utensils such as a garlic press to make "hair," popsicle sticks, straws, forks, a potato masher, a rolling pin for the older child, cookie cutters, a spaghetti server, an egg cutter, etc. Turn your children loose and let them enjoy molding and playing with the soft dough.

Sue Johnson and Julie Carlson
Mother-in-law/Daughter-in-law
co-authors of *Grandloving: Making Memories
with Your Grandchildren*
–Available by calling 1-800 262-1546
Fairport, New York

Spaghetti Painting

What grandmother doesn't have spaghetti in her cupboard? Merely cook and rinse spaghetti. Then add to bowls of water mixed with food coloring. After the color has been absorbed, drain and let your little ones enjoy the feel and creative expression of "painting with spaghetti!" They'll draw with it, pinch it, swirl it, and even eat a bit. As it dries on a piece of heavy cardboard, the gluten in the spaghetti will act like glue and make your grandchild's creation stick!

Sue Johnson and Julie Carlson

Face Paint Fun

It doesn't have to be Halloween to enjoy the fun of face painting. Why not try a family circus in your backyard for starters?

Mix together:

    1 1/4 teaspoon of Grandma's cold cream
    1 1/4 teaspoon cornstarch
    1/2 teaspoon water
    1 drop food coloring

An egg carton makes a perfect "pallet" to hold the different colors, and use your finger to create designs on that adorable little face…just be sure you have your camera ready!

Sue Johnson and Julie Carlson

Perfect Paints

3 tablespoons sugar
1/2 cup cornstarch
2 cups cool water
Food coloring
Liquid dishwashing detergent,
    the kind used for washing dishes by hand
Medium size pan
Small covered jars for storing paints

Have your grandchild mix the sugar, cornstarch, and water in the pan. It will then be your job to heat the paint mixture on low on the stove, stirring until it is smooth. Pour the mixture into small jars. When it's cool enough to handle, let your grandchild add a little food coloring to each jar. Add one drop of detergent to each jar and stir well. These paints can be used for either fingerpainting or brush painting, and if covered will keep well.

Sue Johnson and Julie Carlson

Doggone Good Goodies

The four-legged "kids" in your house will enjoy eating these as much as you and your little ones will enjoy making them!

Stir together:

2 cups whole wheat flour
1 egg
1/2 cup liquid (chicken or beef broth)
1/2 teaspoon each garlic salt
   and garlic powder
1/2 teaspoon onion salt
2 tablespoon wheat germ or oatmeal

Now the fun begins—roll the dough into about twenty dog biscuits, letting your imagination dictate the shapes. Put biscuits on a single layer on a large dish and microwave on high for 10 minutes or until firm.

Sue Johnson and Julie Carlson

Dog Biscuits

2 jars (3 1/2-ounce) of baby food
   strained meat (any type)
1/4 cup nonfat dry milk
1/2 cup wheat germ

Mix together and drop by spoonful onto cookie sheet. Smash them. Bake at 350° for 12-15 minutes.

Making dog biscuits for your kid's or grandkid's dog is a fun activity to do together. You can even make them for the neighbor's dog if you don't have one of your own.

Connie Mertz
Omaha, Nebraska

Carp Bait (Doughballs)

1 cup whole wheat flour
3 cups Wheaties cereal
2 1/2 tablespoons salt
2 tablespoons sugar
1/2 teaspoon cinnamon
1/2 cup boiling water
Oatmeal

Mix all ingredients together, except the oatmeal. Add oatmeal to the mixture until it is fairly thick. Add very little additional water, only if necessary, and mix thoroughly. Refrigerate until needed.

When ready to fish take a small amount of dough and form a little ball around the hook. Cast into the pond and wait for the big one!

Grandma was quite the fisherwoman. I have memories of swimming at Grandma and Grandpa Biere's pond, fishing with Dad and Grandma, and heeding Uncle Al's warning to "watch out for the snapping turtles 'cuz they'll bite your big toe and hang on 'til it thunders!" Grandma fished for carp, despite the fact that many people regard carp as "trash fish." They sure didn't taste like trash when Grandma fixed them! She donned her fishing bonnet and grabbed her gear and sack lunch and walked east toward the pond. While her dog checked out the clumps of weeds, Grandma patiently waited for her line to tug. If there was a fish to be caught, Grandma was sure to catch it; and she continued this pursuit into her 80s!

We always suspected that part of Grandma's fishing secret was her carp bait—or doughballs, as she called them. When Grandma died a few years ago, I ended up with her handwritten recipe card containing the infamous doughball recipe that had been passed on to her by a friend, Henry Guenther. While I may never duplicate the recipe that I cherish most, it is a sweet reminder of Grandma's love and acceptance of God's gift of the earth.

Julie Haberman
Lincoln, Nebraska

I like a friend the better for having faults that one can talk about...
—William Hazlett

Coal Crystal Garden

1 piece of coal or briquets
6 tablespoons of salt
6 tablespoons of blueing,
    purchase in the laundry detergent aisle
1 tablespoon of ammonia
1 cup of water
Food coloring

Put the coal or pieces of coal into an aluminum foil pie pan. Pour the water over the coal. Sprinkle the salt over the coal, then the blueing, and then the ammonia. Decide what color you want the crystal garden and squeeze a few drops in various places on the coal. Set it in a place where it can remain undisturbed for several days. Add water to maintain growth—about once a week.

Twila Wilson
Lincoln, Nebraska

Elephant Stew

1 elephant   Dash salt
Dash pepper   1 rabbit (optional)

Dice the elephant into small pieces. This should take about 2 months. Add enough brown gravy to cover and season. Cook over kerosene stove about 4 weeks at 465 degrees. This will serve 3,800 people. If more are expected, 2 rabbits may be added, but only if necessary, because most people do not like to find hare in their stew.

Trent, my 10-year-old grandson, thinks this is funny, but he asked these questions. 1) How would you "catch" the elephant? 2) What do you do with the tusks, toe nails, and tail? And 3) Would you save the skin? Trent added, "Sounds like a lot of work!"

Twila Wilson
Lincoln, Nebraska

Homemade Glitter

5-6 drops of food coloring   1/2 cup salt

Stir ingredients well. Cook in microwave for 1-2 minutes. Spread the glitter mixture onto waxed paper and let it dry. Store in airtight container. Substitute sugar for salt and use for decorating cookies and cakes.

Clarice Carlson Orr

Top Eleven Reasons to Give Books for Gifts

11. Books are cheaper than most toys.
10. Books don't break.
 9. Books don't need batteries.
 8. You don't need a box to wrap it.
 7. It's cheaper to mail a book.
 6. Books are always the right size for a child.
 5. Books can be chosen to fit a child's interests.
 4. Books don't wear out and can be recycled.
 3. Books build imaginations.
 2. Books don't cause tooth decay.

And the number one reason to give books as gifts is:

 1. BOOKS ENCOURAGE READING, THE MOST IMPORTANT
    CONCEPT FOR LIFE.

—Clarice Carlson Orr
from *The Joy of Grandparenting:
Grandparents Make a Difference*

RECIPES

225

CAKES AND PIES

COOKIES AND BARS

DESSERTS

MAIN DISHES, MEATS, POULTRY, EGGS AND CHEESE

227

SOUPS

KIDS PLAY

CONTRIBUTORS

ABOUT THE AUTHOR

Clarice Carlson Orr has been talking and writing for more than 25 years about the values of appreciating grandparents and the culture of the extended family. Since its publication in 1995, her book, *The Joy of Grandparenting: Grandparents Make A Difference,* has enriched family life all across the country, especially the relationships of grandparents and their grandchildren.

The retired University of Nebraska editor received her bachelor's and master's degrees in Home Economics after she became a grandmother. She squeezes her talks and writing in between the recitals, concerts, sports, and other significant events of her ten grandchildren and four married children who live in Nebraska, Ohio, and California.

Growing up on a farm near Mitchell, South Dakota, Clarice savors the memories of the homemade breads, pies, and cakes along with roast beef and fried chicken dinners. She treasures the myths and legends that keep cropping up at family reunions, picnics, and holiday potlucks.

Clarice Carlson Orr lives in Lincoln, Nebraska. For more information about scheduling a talk or workshop, call 402-483-0652, or e-mail her at co41418@navix.net.